MORE
GUERRILLA
MARKETING
RESEARCH

MORE
GUERRILLA
MARKETING
RESEARCH

Asking the right people, the right
questions, the right way and effectively
using the answers to make more money

**Robert J. Kaden
Gerald Linda
and Jay Conrad Levinson**

**KOGAN
PAGE**

London and Philadelphia

First published in Great Britain and the United States in 2009 by Kogan Page Limited

120 Pentonville Road
London N1 9JN
United Kingdom
www.koganpage.com

525 South 4th Street, #241
Philadelphia PA 19147
USA

© Robert J Kaden, Gerald Linda and Jay Conrad Levinson, 2009

ISBN 978 0 7494 5547 7

British Library Cataloguing-in-Publication Data

A CIP record for this book is available from the British Library.

Library of Congress Cataloging-in-Publication Data

Kaden, Robert J.
  More guerrilla marketing research : asking the right people, the right questions, the right way, and effectively using the answers to make more money / Robert J. Kaden, Gerald Linda, Jay Conrad Levinson.
    p. cm.
Includes index.
  ISBN 978-0-7494-5547-7
  1. Marketing research. 2. Small business—Management. 3. Success in business. I. Linda, Gerald. II. Levinson, Jay Conrad. III. Title.
  HF5415.2.K245 2009
  658.8'3—dc22   2009017052

Typeset by Saxon Graphics Ltd
Printed and bound in India by Replika Press Pvt Ltd

Bob Kaden and Jay Conrad Levinson would like to dedicate this book to the 2005 Chicago White Sox, who brought us a world championship and the blissful peace that comes with the end to a lifetime of hoping.

And Gerry Linda dedicates this book to:

My family: Claudia, Jonathan and Jessica, who always said of me, sometimes teasingly and other times less so, 'You ask him a question and you get a pageant.'

My teachers at Boston Latin School, Northeastern University, and the University of Michigan, who kindled a lifelong love of learning, marketing and, yes, marketing research.

My colleagues at Tatham Laird & Kudner, Marsteller and Kapuler Research, where my skills were honed and polished.

And my clients at Kurtzman Slavin Linda and Gerald Linda & Associates, for whom it has been a privilege to serve.

Contents

About the authors   *xi*
Foreword   *xv*
Acknowledgements   *xvii*

Introduction   **1**

1.   **Marketing research – why should you care?**   **5**
What does listening to consumers really mean? 6;
Do customers really tell you the truth? 9; What if
consumers say one thing and do another? 11; Will I really
learn anything I don't already know? 12; Insights 14;
Does research work for all types of businesses? 15;
Digging deeper 17

2.   **Setting research goals and objectives**   **19**
Where are your greatest opportunities for making more
money? 21; Understanding the needs of your customers
and prospects 23; Turning research questions into research
goals and objectives 24; Refining research goals and
objectives 26; What actions might you take? 27;
Digging deeper 29

3.   **What Guerrillas can learn from large-company research**   **33**
Strategic vs tactical research 35; Which comes first – a
strategic or tactical study? 37; What kinds of studies do

large companies conduct? 39; Test market research 43;
Developing new products 44; Conclusion 45

4. **How to get started**   47
Understanding current and potential opportunities 47;
Knowing what questions to ask – revisited 49; Attitudes vs
behavior 50; Determining the best research approach from
the options available 52; Which comes first? 54;
Determining whether the product meets customer
expectations 55; Generating more business from current
customers 57; Taking customers away from the
competition 58; Increasing the size of the market 59

5. **How to set a research budget**   61
Determining a meaningful research budget 63; Coming to
grips with a budget 64; What business are you in? 66;
Digging deeper 67

6. **Using research professionals**   73
Should Guerrillas try DIY research? Maybe! 73; How to
judge credentials 73; Are research suppliers or consultants
really all that necessary? 76; Understanding supplier
pricing 77; Costing a project 77; Are research suppliers
worth what they charge? 87; Being a good client 88

7. **How much research should you do?**   91
A little *can* go a long way 91; Research can have a long
shelf life 92; How to maximize the return on research 93;
So how much research should you do? 95; How much
research, really? 97

8. **The research plan**   99
What is a research plan? 99; Developing your plan 100;
The overall goal 101; Specific objectives 102; Target market
respondents 104; A final word 108

9. **Secondary research**   109
What is secondary information? 109; The attractiveness of
secondary information 111; Common valuable sources of
secondary information 112; Which comes first – primary or
secondary research? 114

10. **Brainstorming and other ideation processes**   115
Conducting a brainstorming session 116; Other ideation
processes 117

11. **Focus groups and qualitative research** 121

What are they really? 121; Can focus groups alone provide
the basis for a marketing decision? 123; Focus groups and
brainstorming 127; Setting up focus groups 131; How to
be an effective focus group moderator 141; Group
exercises 155; Pre-group homework 157; Building from
one group to another 158; Recall respondents 158; Types of
qualitative research 159; "Qualiquant" 164; Creative
consumers 165; Digging deeper 167

12. **Research into emotions** 171

A little more history 173; Evoking emotions in
marketing 174; The researcher's dilemma 175; Where are
we today? 177; It's not all or nothing 178; Where to go
next 179; Digging deeper 180

13. **Surveys and quantitative research** 187

Types of surveys 189; Strategic study goals and
objectives 191; Determining your target respondents 192

14. **Types of surveys** 197

The internet 197; Telephone interviewing 201; Mail
surveys 204; In-person interviewing 207; Panels 208;
Digging deeper 210

15. **Writing questionnaires** 213

Types of questions 214; Questionnaires for telephone and
personal interviewing 215; 1. The cooperation phase 215;
2. The respondent qualification phase 217; 3. The main
body phase 220; 4. The demographic phase 246; 5. The
thank you phase 247

16. **Customer satisfaction research** 249

Approaches to assessing customer satisfaction 249; Why
customer satisfaction measures are important 250; How
often is enough? 251; The cost factor 252; Defining
customer satisfaction research 253; Measuring customer
satisfaction 254; Importance of performance variables 257;
Net promoter score 258; Digging deeper 259

17. **Sampling** 261

Sampling, error range and making predictions 263;
Determining sample size 266; Achieving good response
rates 269; Sampling guidelines 270; Sources of samples 272

18. **Organizing data** 275
Cross-tab plan 276; Banner points and stub 279;
Tab plan example 281

19. **Statistical techniques** 285
Significance tests 285; A word about determining sample
sizes 288; Regression analysis 290; TURF analysis 291;
Factor analysis 294; Cluster analysis 295; Other statistical
techniques 296; Keep your wits about you 297

20. **Telling the story: analyzing survey results** 299
The Zen of data 301; Using controls and comparisons to
analyze survey results 301; Beyond the first blush 305;
Going beyond cross-tabs 312; Writing the report 313

21. **Putting results into action** 317
Communicating results and actions 318; Champion the
process 320; Review the research three months later 320;
Periodically review the research 320; Land mines 321;
Try the bonus system 321; A culture for change 322;
A final word 324

22. **The future of marketing research** 325
The challenge 326; Predictions 328

Glossary of Terms 337
Index 343

About the authors

Robert J Kaden

Bob Kaden is the author of *Guerrilla Marketing Research* and President of The Kaden Company, a marketing research company.

He has been in market research his entire career, spending a number of years in the research departments at various Chicago advertising agencies and, in the early 1970s, becoming President of Goldring & Company. Goldring became one of Chicago's premier research suppliers, employing a staff of more than 40 market research professionals. He and his partners sold Goldring to MAI plc, a UK financial and market research conglomerate, in 1989. In 1992, he started The Kaden Company and continues today to serve his marketing research clients.

Bob has worked extensively in the retail, banking, credit card, food, consumer package goods, health care, educational, toy, technology and direct marketing industries. He has been involved in more than 4,000 focus-group and survey studies and has pioneered many unique quantitative and qualitative market research approaches.

Over the years, he has written numerous articles on market research and new product development approaches for a variety of business websites and professional journals. He speaks frequently to business and university audiences on a wide range of research topics, with particular attention on the Guerrilla approach to marketing research. His speaking engagements have taken him to many US cities, as well as London, Paris and Moscow, where he addressed audiences on the use of attitude research in the direct marketing industry as well as on the application of creative problem-solving principles to marketing research problems.

Bob Kaden has lived in the Chicago area all his life. He is married to Ellie, the father of Hilary, the father-in-law of Henry and the grandfather of Samantha. Kaden has an AA degree from Lincoln College in Lincoln, IL, and a BA in Communications from Columbia College in Chicago.

In addition to his professional activities Bob is a percussionist and plays regularly with The South of Disorder Band (Chicago's premier Jimmy Buffett cover band). His golf game is getting better.

For additional information contact: The Kaden Company, 6725 N LeRoy Avenue, Lincolnwood, IL 60712, Tel: 847–933–9400, e-mail: thekadencompany@sbcglobal.net

Gerald Linda

Gerry Linda re-established the marketing consulting firm, Gerald Linda & Associates, in 1994. The firm provides marketing strategy, planning and research services to a mix of large, sophisticated marketers as well as smaller, entrepreneurial companies. A second service is aiding advertising and public relations agencies with their new business and account planning efforts. And a third service area is assuming senior marketing leadership/executional roles on an interim basis.

Immediately prior, he was the number two executive and a Principal at a 'Top Fifty' research firm. In addition to corporate duties, his responsibilities included managing two client service groups, which fulfilled the marketing counsel and research needs for such clients as Miller Brewing Company, S C Johnson & Son, Inc. and BP/Amoco.

Between 1989 and 1993 Gerry was a co-founder and Director of Client and Marketing Services at Kurtzman/Slavin/Linda, Inc., an agency that practiced integrated, coordinated marketing communications including advertising, design, public relations, direct marketing, sales promotion and the research which under-girded their strategic creation.

From 1986 through 1989 Mr Linda was President of the first incarnation of Gerald Linda & Associates.

Between 1980 and 1985 Gerry worked at Marsteller and its successor companies (which was the 18th largest ad agency in the world at that time). He joined the Chicago office as its Research Director and quickly became Vice President and a member of the Operating Committee and the Strategy Review and Creative Review Boards. He was promoted to Regional Director of Marketing Planning and Research, which added offices in Pittsburgh, Denver and Los Angeles to his responsibilities.

Another promotion made him Corporate Senior Vice President reporting directly to the company President in New York. In this assignment he was Secretary to the Board of Directors and specialized in new business acquisition and in raising employee skill levels, and he carried out a wide variety of special projects including developing the corporation's business plan.

Mr Linda received a BS in Business Administration and an MBA at Northeastern University, Boston, and he received the Candidate in Philosophy degree from the University of Michigan for completing his doctoral course work. He is a frequent writer, whose thinking has appeared in dozens of trade and professional journals. And he has made over 100 presentations and speeches at association meetings and conferences. He also serves on the editorial review board for the *Journal of Current Issues in Research and Advertising*.

Gerry is married, has two children and lives in Glenview, IL, a suburb of Chicago.

For additional information contact: Gerald Linda & Associates, Suite 3000, 2100 Fir Street, Glenview, IL 60025, Tel: 847–729–3404, e-mail: glinda@gla-mktg.com, website: www.gla-mktg.com

Jay Conrad Levinson

Jay Conrad Levinson is the author of the best-selling marketing series in history, *Guerrilla Marketing*, plus 58 other business books. His books have sold more than 20 million copies worldwide. And his Guerrilla concepts have influenced marketing so much that his books appear in 62 languages and are required reading in MBA programs worldwide.

He was born in Detroit, raised in Chicago, and graduated from the University of Colorado. His studies in Psychology led him to advertising agencies, including a Directorship at Leo Burnett in London, where he served as Creative Director. Returning to the US, he joined J Walter Thompson as Senior VP and Creative Director. Jay taught, wrote, and created guerrilla marketing for 10 years while teaching in the extension division of the University of California in Berkeley.

A winner of prizes for creative excellence in every medium, he has been part of the creative teams that made household names of many of the most famous brands in history: The Marlboro Man, The Pillsbury Doughboy, Allstate's good hands, United's 'Friendly Skies', the Sears Diehard battery, Morris the Cat, Tony the Tiger, and the Jolly Green Giant.

In addition to his many books, CDs, and DVDs, Jay conducts guerrilla marketing training programs, hosts the very popular internet website, www.gmarketing.com, and formed The Guerrilla Marketing Association – a marketing support system for small business. In his presentations all over the world, he has seen 'Guerrilla Marketing' become the most powerful brand in the history of marketing publishing.

At its heart 'Guerrilla Marketing' provides a way for business owners to spend less, get more, and achieve substantial profits. The best Guerrilla to transform you into a Guerrilla marketer is 'The Father of Guerrilla Marketing' – Jay Conrad Levinson.

For additional information, see www.guerrillamarketingassociation.com.

Foreword

Although Aristotle had it wrong in saying that we have five senses, when in reality we have far more than five, he did manage to call attention to one of the miracles of life – our sensory selves. In animals, it's that sensory self that is the key to life and death, failure and success, joy and sorrow. The sensory part of a business is the research it does, that reaching out beyond ourselves to learn. That's why it is an endless process, one that must be engaged in continuously.

If you're to be a successful spouse, it's not as important to know everything about marriage as it is to know something about your partner. Similarly, if you're to be a success in business, your job is more about understanding your customers and prospects than about knowing everything about management. The truth is we all dwell in the environs of the future and research is the only way to learn how to live there.

The toughest part of research, as in writing and painting, is to know when to stop. Those who practice the art of research with the touch of a Rembrandt are masters at learning what is essential and not fuzzing their minds and messages with unnecessary details. Bob and Gerry, in this masterpiece of a book, tell you what you need to know, invite you to wade in a bit deeper, but never let you waste your time in the shallows or get in over your head.

What they've left out of this book doesn't deserve to be here in the first place, and what they've included should bask in the golden glow of a yellow hi-liter because it is that crucial to the success of your company. I don't want to tell you to toss all your other books on research away, but I am sorely tempted to because of the innate quality and in-depth insights of this one.

I have this feeling that when you've completed reading this book, you'll have your own feeling that your competitors are operating with blindfolds on.

Jay Conrad Levinson
Orlando, Florida

Acknowledgements

In completing *MORE Guerrilla Marketing Research*, I acknowledge and am humbled by the many thousands of professionals who saw fit to purchase *Guerrilla Marketing Research*. Without you, this second effort would not have reached the light of day.

To my co-author, Gerry Linda, thank you for your massive contribution and for enduring the frustrations of working with my opinionated self.

To Jay Conrad Levinson, my other co-author, mentor and friend, thank you for your inspiration and insight. Because of your willingness to embrace marketing research as a key to success, Guerrillas everywhere will find added profits.

Finally, to all the Guerrillas who toil day in and day out to outflank the competition and to have their voices resonate above the fray, thank you for realizing that marketing research is certainly, undoubtedly, finally and ultimately one key to your success.

Bob Kaden

I first met Bob Kaden in the mid-1980s, when he was President of Goldring Research and I was Research Director for Marsteller Advertising. We shared a common client, The Speigel Catalog, and sometimes worked together and at other times competed to lead them in the paths of research righteousness. So I can say with certitude that Bob Kaden is a research master, a doer, an energetic leader and long-time friend and business colleague.

When he suggested early in 2008 that we co-author a book, I was quite flattered. Like many, I felt "I had a book in me." And the chance to work with a friend, who had already published, would be a great way to get started.

Initially, Bob's first idea was to write an advanced book on marketing research for practitioners while my first interest was the future of marketing. Given how far apart these ideas were, it may come as a surprise that you're holding a copy of *MORE Guerrilla Marketing Research.*

While our initial ideas didn't quite mesh, the idea of working together was strong cement. And eventually, over breakfasts and lunches and meetings, we came to understand that the already successful *Guerrilla Marketing Research* was in need of an update and a broadening. We are delighted the good folks at Kogan Page agreed.

So I want to acknowledge Bob, whose *Guerrilla Marketing Research* provided the strong foundation on which this book rests.

I also want to thank Jay Conrad Levinson, whose steady hand and deep experience made our team effort a dream.

Gerry Linda

The soul and spirit, the energy and wisdom that make this book rich and satisfying, valuable and timeless, derive from one purebred Guerrilla, who goes by the name of Robert Kaden (though I never called him Robert) and his marketing guru, writing partner, Gerry Linda.

I remember the illumination that flashed through Bob's eyes four years ago when he first sensed the chemistry between guerrilla marketing and research. Our first book, *Guerrilla Marketing Research,* proved him right. This second book builds on the success of the first, deepens its coverage of key topics, extends the guerrilla-research connection to new areas and looks to the future of research.

Acknowledgments are always deserved by a team of people and in this case, it's a two-man team. I am proud to be associated with them – both within these covers and everywhere outside them.

Jay Conrad Levinson

Introduction

Guerrilla marketers are the ziggers, when the rest of us are zagging. They rewrite the rules, find the overlooked niches, overturn staid thinking and find ways of thriving when others do not.

Many Guerrillas start as entrepreneurs, but many entrepreneurs have nary a clue about how to benefit from being a Guerrilla. Large well-known brands like Virgin, Jet Blue and even Walmart started as Guerrillas and, even as they grew into behemoths, maintained their Guerrilla roots.

Guerrillas hold a common belief that growth is tied to being more nimble and creative than the competition. Rather than being defined by sales, profits or employee count, they share iconoclastic tendencies that continue to serve them well at every stage of their growth. What many Guerrillas have lacked, though, is an understanding of marketing research and how it can be used to hasten their success.

In his many books, Jay Conrad Levinson writes about the way of the Guerrilla – how to think like one, act like one and be one. His landmark book *Guerrilla Marketing* finds him talking about the value of free market research, commonly called secondary research.

In *Guerrilla Marketing Research*, the notion of the free kind of secondary source research was left behind in favor of more complete discussion of primary research, the kind of research that is custom-designed for the particular needs of a company and often conducted by professional researchers. That book argued, eloquently we hope, about why and how primary research was an essential and economical tool for Guerrillas. It focused on how Guerrillas could use marketing research on their own – or at least, pay far less to research suppliers and consultants when they did need outside help.

In *MORE Guerrilla Marketing Research*, you will again be introduced to tried and true research techniques that will help you grow your business. And you will also benefit from expanded discussions for effectively planning research, conducting studies and using results. You will come to understand why consumer emotions and feelings are more important to your growth than ever before. And, you will learn what the future holds for the industry and how you can be among the first to benefit from embracing 21st century marketing research approaches.

Defining marketing research

Marketing research, or information about the marketplace, can follow two general paths. One is the customer attitude path, which seeks to determine the attitudes and perceptions of customers and prospects. By understanding what motivates customers and prospects, marketers can develop plans for increasing their likelihood of success. This is often referred to as the *why* of the marketplace:

- *Why* don't my customers spend more with me?
- *Why* can't I get new customers faster?
- *Why* isn't my advertising more effective?

The other path is the customer behavior path, which seeks to determine marketplace patterns. How much money is being spent in the product categories of interest? Is the market itself growing or diminishing? Which brands and products have the strongest shares? Which television or radio programs are watched and listened to, which magazines are read? This is referred to as the *what* of the marketplace.

In fact, a great deal of both *why* and *what* information is free and available through secondary sources. And, Chapter 9, on secondary research, details how you can tap into secondary sources to help you understand the marketplace and your position in it.

However, secondary research is rarely enough to answer all the *what* and *why* questions that are unique to your company or brand and important to understand if you hope to grow you company. Therefore, we steadfastly hold to the belief that by clearly understanding the benefits of conducting primary research, you and your company will be better served.

MORE Guerrilla Marketing Research is mainly a book about conducting primary research of the why variety. It includes qualitative studies such as focus groups and quantitative studies such as internet and telephone surveys. It delves deeply into how research should be planned, how the right targets should be chosen to be interviewed and how an effective questionnaire should be written.

It will give you guidance in determining the right number of respondents to interview and explain how to organize and analyze data. Critically, it discusses how research findings should be used in your company so that they generate greater profits.

When you finish this book, you will understand why doing both secondary and primary research the right way is important to growing your business. And you will know how to get it done for far less money than you thought. We hope that will intrigue you enough to buy this book.

1

Marketing research – why should you care?

A survey conducted for Service Merchandise, the onetime catalog showroom company, included a question that asked Service Merchandise customers whether purchasing from a catalog showroom was an excellent, good, fair, or poor way to shop. About 25 per cent said it was an excellent way to shop. The remaining 75 per cent, the vast majority, said it was only a good, fair, or poor way to shop. And, of these, almost one in five said it was a poor way to shop.

This was startling. How could Service Merchandise's own customers have such a low regard for shopping the Service Merchandise way?

During the presentation of survey results, company management were asked what they felt were the benefits to the customer of shopping at their catalog showrooms. Their blank stares indicated they weren't sure. Well, it was abundantly clear that customers weren't sure either.

Two other questions were raised. Did Service Merchandise exist to serve its customers on their terms or on its terms, and what was the Service Merchandise reason for being? Service Merchandise never really could answer those questions. It existed for about 10 years after that, mostly doing business the same way it always had. Not surprisingly, fewer and fewer customers walked into its stores over those years.

When customers did visit, they were confronted with a slow and cumbersome shopping experience that research continued to show they hated. Service Merchandise tried running frequent sales and promotions to attract customer traffic. It put emphasis on its profitable jewelry business, basically abandoning its electronics and technology business to the many new competitors that were popping up. New company management teams came and went. As the losses mounted, it tried to stay in business by closing unprofitable stores. Finally, Service Merchandise went into liquidation.

Service Merchandise was a US icon. It was the first mass merchandise discount store. The original business concept was brilliant, inspired. It allowed customers to purchase at deep discounts, and all they had to do was look in a catalog to find what they wanted, fill out an order form, and wait 10 or 15 minutes while their merchandise was picked from a vast warehouse behind the showroom and put on a conveyor belt. They just had to wait for their number to be called – if there happened to be someone available calling numbers.

Of course, many times customers waited only to find that half their order was out of stock. This wasn't so bad, at first anyway, because this was the only game in town. And they saved a lot of money for their patience. When the "big boxes" arrived, consumers fled for a better experience.

Then there is the case of the venerable and one-time pioneering Spiegel catalog, which during the late 1970s and 1980s had strong marketing management, a vibrant research voice, a knack for listening intently to consumers and potent advertising, which reflected all this learning. It's no fluke that Spiegel enjoyed its greatest success during the years marketing research was integral to making decisions.

What Service Merchandise ultimately forgot, what Spiegel forgot, what K-Mart forgot (and has not learnt to this day), what Oldsmobile forgot, and what many others forget is that, when customers become dissatisfied, you had better pay attention. When what you are doing or what you are selling is no longer an important benefit to your customers, your days are numbered.

WHAT DOES LISTENING TO CONSUMERS REALLY MEAN?

Nothing will ever replace entrepreneurial inspiration – the energy, joy, and exhausted delight that come from knowing with certainty that one day your vision will become a profitable reality. Ah yes, those heady days when you just know your product or service will make you millions.

There are legions of companies that have sprung up from the fertile minds of entrepreneurs: Leonard Lavin and Alberto-Culver; Harland Sanders and KFC; Bill Gates and Microsoft; Robert Noyce and Gordon Moore and Intel; Walt Disney and Mickey Mouse; George Halas and the Chicago Bears. And on and on. Did these geniuses listen to the customer? Probably not – at first anyway.

Marketing research is not intended to be a substitute for inspiration, although it can often foster breakthrough thinking. It is intended as a connection with your customers or prospects that, if used fully, will get you where you want to go faster and more profitably than you can without it.

At the very heart of market research is the keen belief that listening to the opinions of customers is important. It's really so simple: when asked the right questions, customers will tell you what to do to make your business more profitable, and by listening to them you will do the smart thing far more often than if you just decide to go it alone.

Remember when Coca-Cola introduced New Coke – and failed miserably? Here is what Sergio Zyman, who was Coke's chief marketing officer at the time, had to say about listening to the consumer (*Worth Magazine*, January 2005):

> We orchestrated a huge launch [of New Coke], received abundant media coverage… were delighted with ourselves… until the sales figures started rolling in. Within weeks, we realized that we had blundered. Sales tanked, and the media turned against us. Seventy-seven days after New Coke was born, we made the second-hardest decision in company history. We pulled the plug. What went wrong? The answer was embarrassingly simple. We did not know enough about our consumers. We did not even know what motivated them to buy Coke in the first place. We fell into the trap of imagining that innovation – abandoning our existing product for a new one – would cure our ills.
>
> After the debacle, we reached out to consumers and found that they wanted more than taste when they made their purchase. Drinking Coke enabled them to tap into the Coca-Cola experience, to be part of Coke's history and to feel the continuity and stability of the brand. Instead of innovating, we should have renovated. Instead of making a product and hoping people would buy it, we should have asked customers what they wanted and given it to them. As soon as we started listening to them, consumers responded, increasing our sales from 9 billion to 15 billion cases a year.

In the case of New Coke, listening to the consumer might have prevented an expensive disaster. Yet, as with so many businesses, large or small, there is often too much entrepreneurial ego or downright stubbornness to listen to the customer. Particularly for small businesses, consideration is rarely given to the importance of research and listening to the customer. And if it is considered, it is likely to be written off as being unaffordable.

An entrepreneur once asked, "Where would I ever get money for research? I don't even have enough money for all the boxes I should order to pack my products." He walked off without knowing that his new shampoo was no different from dozens of competitors and that a little research would probably have convinced him to look for something else to sell.

During the height of the popularity of health clubs in the US, a potential Guerrilla had the idea of developing health clubs/training facilities for young children through the age of high school athletes. This would give kids a safe place to go, would be fun, and enhance their athletic opportunities. Or so he thought.

Some focus groups were conducted in the Midwest and parents hated the idea. They said it was going to be an additional, significant monthly expense; that they'd have to drive their kids, pick them up later and probably waste time waiting for them. They also said they would likely have trouble fitting another activity into an already hectic schedule.

The research recommendation was against proceeding.

The entrepreneur was livid. "The groups hadn't been properly conducted," he argued. "The idea wasn't well enough explained," he complained, and so on. At his insistence, additional focus groups were held in California, where the interest in exercise and fitness is greater than in the Midwest.

Now not only were the same objections found, but a new one emerged. Parents simply didn't want their kids inside when the weather in California is so beautiful.

The lesson from these two cases is that in fact one of the best uses of marketing research is to kill a bad idea. Do you want to invest your life's savings and run up bills to the limit of your credit cards on an idea that has a low probability of success?

One struggling restaurant owner said, "My customers are getting older, and I'm not attracting a young crowd. It worries me. In a couple of years many will die off. Then what?" It was suggested he do a couple of focus groups with younger people in the neighborhood, who hadn't visited the restaurant recently.

His response was, "What will they tell me? That I should lower my prices or change my menu?"

Well, perhaps that is what they'd say. We don't really know because he was too stubborn to look at the situation objectively. Maybe they would have said that the restaurant décor was too old-fashioned or that the lighting was dim and depressing. They might have said that they remembered the food wasn't very good when they visited the restaurant years ago. Maybe they would have said something simple, like they wished the menu would offer other than the elaborate six-course dinners it featured, because they always left the restaurant feeling uncomfortably stuffed.

Whatever they might have said, the restaurant owner would have been more informed and certainly clearer about his problem.

Listening to the customer starts with listening to yourself. It means suspending your ego and setting your stubbornness aside. Ask yourself these questions the next time you're thinking of going it alone:

1. If I'm wrong, how much will it cost me?
2. How long can I afford to be wrong before I run out of money?
3. Even if I'm right 50 per cent of the time, is that good enough to grow my business the way I want?
4. Would input from customers, who have no stake in whether I succeed or fail, help me make better decisions?
5. Have I asked customers/prospects what they need and want from me and my business so that they'll purchase more often from me?
6. Do I know what else I can provide my customers so they'll pay me more – and be happier about it?
7. Do my customers and prospects even know the benefits of buying from me?
8. Can I accept the possibility that my customers might be smarter than I am in understanding their own needs and thus help me to grow my business?
9. Do I know what my competitors are doing better than me that might eventually cause me to lose even my best customers?
10. Do I know exactly why prospects go to a competitor rather than me and if I do, should I care?
11. Do I think the feelings and emotions that my customers have about me can cause me to lose business?
12. Do I care if my prospects have stronger feelings toward my competitors that make it difficult for me to ever capture them as my customers?
13. Do I feel that I can't afford market research so there's no point in considering it as an option?
14. Do I feel market research is just an expense and won't give me a good ROI anyway?

If you feel these questions are irrelevant to the growth of your business, marketing research really isn't for you. Simply skip the rest of this book and spend a few hours on something else more useful than improving your business. If, though, some of them give you a nagging feeling that you're missing opportunities for growth, your mind is open and you would do well to read on.

DO CUSTOMERS REALLY TELL YOU THE TRUTH?

It never really made sense to us, but we have encountered many business types who don't use research because they think customers will lie to them. Or that customers and prospects will be unjustly critical. In our combined 60+ years in market research conducting thousands of focus groups and surveys, we have never run into a respondent in a properly recruited focus group or analyzed data from a survey where it was evident that customers or prospects were lying or were overly critical just out of spite.

No, customers don't lie. They don't really know how to lie about your business because they haven't a clue what you want to hear. Mostly, they don't care enough about your business to tell you anything other than the truth – other than what comes to their minds at the moment you ask them a question.

A bigger problem is that you often get customers or prospects who don't think very deeply about the issues that you are researching. Therefore, the real challenge in talking with customers is in getting them to give you enough depth of thought so that their answers mean some-thing that allows you to take actions that result in greater sales. It is never an issue of lying. It is always the issue of getting to the real truth!

Note the following give and take from an actual focus group for a home improvement retailer:

Moderator question: What is the most important thing that will cause you to come into our stores more often?
Consumer answer: Lower your prices.
MQ: Besides lowering prices, what would be important?
CA: Probably faster checkout. There are usually long lines when I go to any of your stores.
MQ: Anything else?
CA: Well, it would be nice if the employees knew more about the prod-ucts. Usually, they can't answer my questions. I think I know more about the products than the people working at your stores.

Look back at the line of questioning. The moderator asked the initial question in a totally objective manner. Stopping there, without further moderator probing, the indicated action would have been to lower prices. We can tell you that there is not a marketing problem in the world to which customers won't first respond, "I'll buy more from you if you cut the prices." And it's always a red herring. It's not a lie. It's a knee-jerk customer response – and, while it's a legitimate response, it can't be taken at face value.

It is always your job as the researcher to dig below the surface – to probe customers again and again to uncover the below-the-surface factors that will motivate them to buy more. Think of an onion with its many layers. It's the same with customers. They don't lie. They give you what's top-of-mind, and you have to be smart enough to know what to accept and act upon and what to discard.

In this example, chances are that this customer might be likely to buy more from the home improvement retailer if he knew he could get in and out of the store faster. He might also be inclined to visit the store more often if employees were more knowledgeable.

Customers don't tell us what we do or don't want to hear. They simply respond to our questions. The key to an insightful research study, then, lies in asking the right people, the right questions, in the right manner. Chapter 11 on focus groups goes into detail on how to probe customer motivations effectively.

Certainly there are times when lowering prices is, in fact, the right answer, or perhaps the only answer. The street is lined, however, with failed marketing programs and obscure products for which marketers took customers and prospects literally and simply lowered prices to compete. Almost always, though, it is more an issue of providing better value than providing better prices. Our advice usually is you don't have to be a good marketer to cut the price.

As you use research, you will begin to understand those factors that will make a big difference. Sometimes when you've tried all the rest, when you've probed deeply and there is nothing left to make you competitive, price becomes your only point of leverage. However, following a price strategy can be perilous, as has become evident in the airline industry.

The inability of major US airlines to differentiate themselves on aspects of value has brought them to the brink. Not a single carrier has been able to convince flyers that paying a little more to fly them is worth it. As a result, they continue to compete on price alone and seem to be in a never-ending financial spiral – downward.

Stupefyingly, they have mutually cooperated in commoditizing their business. Someday one of them might figure out how to add enough value to justify raising prices.

WHAT IF CONSUMERS SAY ONE THING AND DO ANOTHER?

It is a true and valid argument that what consumers say and do can be quite different. A survey may indicate consumers would buy your products more often if you came out with additional varieties. However, in doing so, you only discover that they get confused by all the choices and walk past your product display.

Focus groups can provide strong evidence that lowering your prices is the only road to consumer loyalty, but when you follow such advice, your best customers switch to a competitor because they feel your lower prices indicated lower quality or a lower level of service.

As researchers, we're getting smarter about this. We realize that consumer attitudes might not fill in the whole picture and that the complete picture can only be viewed when we look at what consumers say and then relate it to how they behave. Recall in the Introduction we spoke about the importance of investigating both the *what/behavior* path as well as the *why/attitude* path.

In the past few years there has been a global explosion of consumer behavior information available to companies. Massive databases exist that allow marketers access to credit card spending patterns, for example, and how consumer purchase habits and demographic data vary by zip code. Marketers who sell their products via the internet or through catalogs capture purchase data about customers that is not available when conducting surveys or focus groups – information that should be considered when conducting attitude research.

It is only prudent and wise to stress the importance of combining attitude data with actual behavior information – when such an effort is indicated. Greater insight and learning will usually take place when it's possible to match both what consumers say they will do and what they actually do.

The collection of consumer attitude information, when combined with actual consumer behavior data, is discussed throughout the book and points to how Guerrillas can take routinely captured customer information and use it more effectively to grow their businesses.

WILL I REALLY LEARN ANYTHING I DON'T ALREADY KNOW?

In countless research presentations we've heard clients say, "You aren't telling me anything I don't already know." We've always found this a defensive and self-defeating attitude. It smacks of someone who is unsure or lacks discipline to follow his or her own convictions. If it's something you already know, why aren't you doing something about it?

If research tells you what you think you know, but haven't acted upon – great! Act upon it. If it confirms what you've already been doing – great. Continue doing it, and learn how to do it better. Here's why.

Sometimes research will confirm your pet theory about customers, the market, the competition, or your product's advantages and disadvantages. If this is the case, have you wasted your money? Absolutely not! Turning a theory into a fact is a highly useful outcome. It allows you to move forward with confidence. And you're likely to spot a nuance in the data that will help you move ahead better. The point is simple. Customers and prospects are the ultimate judges of your success. If you listen to them closely, you'll hear many ideas for growing your business. While you can always decide not to follow their advice, failure to listen is a much bigger mistake.

What do you need to know?

Guerrillas, or any business for that matter, would benefit from gaining as much information about the marketplace as time and resources allow. The list of relevant questions is endlessly long and will vary by your industry and marketing situation or problem. In order to put you on the right track there are certain background questions that are relevant and will help you determine where marketing research might fit in. Here are some:

- What is your sales history, and those of your category and your key competitors? If trends in the marketplace are up and yours are down, what does this suggest about you? And, if you are ahead of curve, how might you do even better?
- Do category sales differ by stock-keeping unit (SKU), by channel, by geography, by segment, by season? If so, what does this indicate about allocating your marketing dollars more effectively? Are there any social, macro-economic or governmental influences that must be taken into account? If so, how would riding the waves of change be beneficial to your business?
- How has your marketing and advertising budget changed in recent years? How does it compare to the competition? Does knowing that you are either over-spending or under-spending your competition help you in using your funds more effectively?
- Do you know how customers and prospects think of you and your key competitors? Would such knowledge guide you in the types of marketing efforts that would have the greatest impact?
- What benefits or features does the consumer perceive your company brand, product or service to offer versus competition? If you know how you're perceived, would it help you develop more effective marketing programs?
- Have you considered the emotions and feelings that customers and prospects have toward you? Would knowing, for example, that customers feel you're a company that is sensitive and considerate rather than aloof and inconsiderate lead you in a more profitable direction?

All these questions deserve attention and at some point in the growth of your business should be answered. If you are planning to be in business for any period of time, it's important to realize that lack of data does not mean that you lack the need for answers.

We would say that when concrete research is not available on a timely basis or not affordable, careful thinking, informed speculation and intuition based on experience and conducting free secondary source research will have to suffice. We have found, however, that an over-reliance on intuition is often disguised laziness.

The scope of marketing research is shown in Figure 1.1. It includes everything there is to know about your product/service's strengths and weaknesses and perceptions about your brand, including its personality. It covers everything there is to know about competitors and their brands, and it encompasses everything there is to know about customers' needs, wants, perceptions, beliefs and experiences with the brands and the category. Interestingly, marketing strategy is found at the intersection of all three.

INSIGHTS

We'll say it in this first chapter and we'll say it again and again. Good research, properly analyzed, should provide insights into the marketplace in a way that allows you to grow your business. And, just to be clear, an insight to us is the moment you go "Aha!", the moment the research suggests a great opportunity.

Here are some examples of insightful thinking that flow from research findings:

● The market for toothpaste has been flat for years so any new sales must come at the expense of competitors. Therefore, if you're marketing toothpaste, this might suggest going after the smaller brands rather than attempting to take business away from Crest or Colgate, which could outspend any competitor in order to hold share.

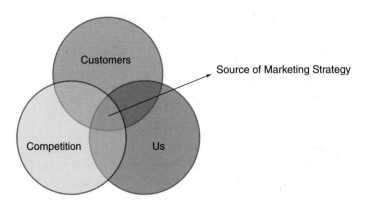

Figure 1.1 The scope of marketing research

- The run-up in the price of gasoline in the US has changed the public perception about use of their automobiles. Therefore, many businesses, e.g., dry cleaners, might have an opportunity to grow by starting a pick-up and drop-off service.
- Women using hair spray are older and fading away... literally. Therefore, being in the hair spray business today suggests the need to convince younger women that the use of hair spray is a contemporary way to hold hair in place. If that seems like too big a task, other ideas might be to develop other hair care items or other items that require aerosolized release or items that can be distributed through the same channels as hair spray.
- Cable channel food programs have made general tastes in food more sophisticated. Therefore, for someone in the canned food business, more sophisticated flavors would do well today where they haven't in the past. Similarly, opportunities for ethnic food restaurants might now exist in smaller towns.
- Consumers do not understand that fleas are ever present in the environment. There is an opportunity for makers of flea control products to educate consumers that flea treatment requires year round attention rather than just in warm weather.
- Farmers do not understand that newer pyrethroid insecticides work differently than traditional chemical insecticides. They have been applying them improperly and not obtaining good results. Pyrethroid manufacturers must re-educate an entire generation of farmers.

DOES RESEARCH WORK FOR ALL TYPES OF BUSINESSES?

Research works as long as you have customers, prospects, and competitors. Research works to help you get more of your customers' attention, time, energy and money. Research works if you want to convert prospects to customers more quickly.

Research works everywhere, for any business, and for any product or service for which people can give you opinions. It even works if you ask your own employees for ideas, which is a very inexpensive tool that Guerrillas woefully ignore when looking for ways to grow their business.

Research will help any business determine the potential for making more money, whether that business happens to be selling gaskets to other manufacturers or cereal to children. To make this point even more clear, look at this listing of some of our clients:

- a manufacturer selling switching equipment to phone companies;
- a cemetery selling grave sites;

- a company selling wallpaper over the internet;
- a catalog selling office furniture;
- a company selling pantyhose to women who weigh more than 250 pounds;
- a company trying to convince smokers to quit;
- a tobacco company trying to convince men who chew to change brands;
- a mail order music club trying to convince members to buy DVDs;
- a technology company trying to convince web developers to use its software;
- a snack company interested in creating a new popcorn flavor;
- a museum generating visitation and donations;
- a charity needing to increase donations;
- a publisher of encyclopedias selling its yearly updates;
- a publisher of art selling its limited-edition prints;
- a health insurer trying to get policy holders to participate in its wellness program;
- a consulting company selling services to CEOs of Fortune 500 companies;
- a digital photo company selling usage rights to designers and art directors;
- a gambling casino trying to improve its reputation with "heavy rollers";
- a company selling janitorial supplies to building owners;
- a company selling cutting tools to industry;
- a company that cleans the exteriors of skyscrapers;
- a company that sells slot machines to casinos;
- a company that sells car washes to consumers;
- a company that sells the digital maps used in GPS systems.

Research also works for companies that aren't so unusual: department stores, cable TV, supermarkets, beer, fast food restaurants, cars, mobile phones, industrial chemicals, pharmaceuticals, insurance, financial planning, banking, food, hospitals, TV stations, furniture stores, and so forth.

In the early summer of 2008 Greenfield On-Line/Ciao research estimated that the size of the US market for market research was $8.295 billion (population 320,144,000) and growing at 2.1 per cent/year. The comparable figures for Europe (population 804,232,000) were $10.451 billion and 2.4 per cent; and for Asia (population 3,861,320,000) $3.270 billion and 7.4 per cent.

You get the idea: everyone can benefit from marketing research. The marketing research industry is very large because it offers value to its many users. And to reiterate, Guerrillas are no exception!

DIGGING DEEPER

Defining your target audience

Sophisticated marketers spend a lot of time defining their target audiences. The thinking is that there are two very broad approaches to strategy. One is to use a sharper nail and the other is to use a bigger hammer. Few have the luxury of being able to outspend their competitors by wielding a bigger hammer, so most prefer the sharper nail. This we define as meaning a tightly defined strategy.

Here's a list of the types of customer and prospect information that big companies and large ad agencies generate when seeking to develop tightly defined strategies:

- attitudes, beliefs;
- perceptions;
- lifestyles, psychographics;
- personality traits;
- frequency of purchase;
- frequency of use;
- volume of purchase;
- rate of use;
- occasion(s) of use;
- brand loyalty (your share of total purchases);
- previous experience with the brand: current users (heavy, medium, light), former users, users of competitor products (which one(s));
- previous category experience: currently in the category, formerly in the category, those who never used a product in this category, etc.;
- price sensitivity, price level;
- buying situation/occasion;
- channel(s) used for purchase;
- demographics: age, gender, personal income, education, home ownership, occupation, geographic areas;
- firmographics: titles, function and profile of key decision makers, company size, industrial classification code, industry, sales, number of years in business, and so forth.

Common research myths

Finally, as a fitting end to this first chapter, we'd like share a list of research myths put together by Jon Arnold of the Toronto-based J Arnold & Associates:

- Marketing research is complex – all smoke and mirrors. Cannot trust what you do not understand.

- Research is highly technical – our management will never be able to relate to it.
- Do not see any ROI – not tied to any measures of value or tangible outcomes that drive our business, like increasing sales, reducing costs, or improving margins.
- Our industry is very complex – research people don't understand our business and could not possibly help us.
- Takes too long to do – not helpful for our fast changing business.
- No one in our industry does any, and we're doing just fine. Just don't see the point.
- Research only confirms what we already know – we know what our customers want.
- Only important for sales/marketing – it's not a management tool.
- We tried doing research in-house – it wasn't very helpful and no one read the report.
- We used a research supplier once – did not work out, haven't bothered since.

Arnold says, "None of these should turn you away from marketing research, especially if you understand the full range of applications to your business." We couldn't agree more and trust the remainder of *MORE Guerrilla Marketing Research* will dispel these myths.

2

Setting research goals and objectives

Don't take it lightly. Establishing clear and concise research goals and objectives is critical to the success of any research project and doing so is not as easy as it might appear. In fact, the more time you spend setting research objectives, the more likely your research results will lead to profitable actions.

Always begin by asking yourself, "What is the most important question I want answered, what is the second most important, third most, etc.?" And the answers to these questions, when provided by customers/prospects, should impact a marketing decision you need to make; otherwise they are the wrong questions.

Without clear questions about what to research (it should be clear here that we are not talking about wording on questionnaires), it's impossible to determine whether the answers you get will be meaningful. Without clear questions, you will get answers that are likely to suggest actions you are unwilling or unable to take and/or information that is irrelevant.

Think about a company that sells wallpaper by phone or on the internet and follow this conversation:

Company marketing director: Something must be wrong with my catalog because a lot of people who look through it don't buy.
Researcher: What people?
CMD: A lot of people request a catalog from the company and then don't buy when it's mailed to them.
Researcher: What makes you think it has anything to do with your catalog?

CMD: Well, they asked for one, didn't they? Why would they ask for one if they weren't interested in buying?

Researcher: Maybe they were just shopping around and still might buy in the future. Maybe they love the catalog. Maybe the reasons they didn't buy have more to do with things other than the catalog.

CMD: What do you suggest?

Researcher: I would suggest studying why people do and don't buy and the role of the catalog in the buying process.

If the marketing director's initial statement ("Something must be wrong with my catalog because a lot of people who look through it don't buy") was accepted on face value, the research would be very narrow in its scope. Further, the results might suggest the need for a great many expensive changes to the catalog which, if followed, might make the catalog better, but still not influence the number of people who buy from it.

By studying the larger question ("What is the role of the catalog in the buying process?") a much greater opportunity exists for learning how to convert catalog requesters to buyers and whether changes to the catalog would be a major or minor influence in this conversion.

Here's another example from the president of a company selling gifts:

President: I want research to convince my biggest customer (a large retailer) to carry more of my Christmas gift line.

Researcher: What if the research shows people don't like your line?

President: Well, I know the products in my line sell better than my competitor's lines. So somebody must like my stuff.

Researcher: What products in your line sell better?

President: The products we put in designer boxes really sell well.

Researcher: Maybe it has more to do with the design of your boxes than with the products themselves. Maybe we should be testing your package designs against your competitor's package designs. It might be a combination of your product, package attractiveness and price that leads to the good sales result. Maybe we should be looking into both these issues.

President: I know most people want a great gift box that they can just put under the tree without having to wrap it. But doesn't the product inside have something to do with it?

Researcher: I think we have three avenues to pursue. First, we should determine why people are buying the current gift boxed items. Then the strongest graphic designs for your gift boxes that communicate value should be tested. Finally, we should determine which products work best with your strongest boxes.

President: Right. That way we can convince them that our box designs are better and should get more display space, and that the products we put in our boxes are the most appropriate for the box design itself.

It's easy for research to provide answers to questions. It is hard to determine whether the questions are worth answering in the first place. When creating questions for research, it is usually prudent to get input from others. Follow these guidelines:

1. Write down ten marketing decisions you need to make.
2. Write down all the questions that you have for the research.
3. Rewrite the same questions, but use different wording. If rewriting gives you a different slant on them, create a new question list.
4. Read each question one at a time to an associate. Pose this question to your associate: "What will be learnt if we get answers to this question?"
5. If you find that your associate's response doesn't reinforce what you hope to learn from the question, your question is unclear. Reword it again.
6. Have the associate take your questions and conduct the same exercise with yet a third associate. Again, reword as necessary.

You will be amazed at how this simple process will make your research topics more focused and indicative of what you want to learn. And, as a result, your research will become even more effective and action-oriented.

WHERE ARE YOUR GREATEST OPPORTUNITIES FOR MAKING MORE MONEY?

There are many ways to make more money. They include:

- Attract new customers.
- Get current customers to spend more each time they buy.
- Get customers to buy more often.
- Improve product lines.
- Add product lines.
- Get customers to use the product in a new way.
- Raise prices.
- Negotiate lower prices from vendors, but keep current prices to customers.
- Reduce overhead.
- Motivate employees to sell more.
- Grow the markets for the products you sell (only recommended for industry leaders; otherwise all you'll be doing is feeding your competitors).
- Increase or change the number of channels by which you offer your products, either making it less expensive to distribute your products or making it easier for customers to obtain them.

When thinking about your research topics, think about implementing the results of the research. If you learnt that you have to add new products to grow your business, is this viable for you? If you have to spend money to grow the marketplace as a whole, can you make the investment?

Again, you should continually be asking yourself, "Once I get the answers to my research questions, will it be realistic for me to implement the research results?"

In going through this process an answer we often receive from clients is: "I don't know what I'd do until I see the results of the research." While this seems like a reasonable response, it will likely produce research results that might be interesting, but which are never acted upon. To us this is a cardinal sin: why waste the time, energy and money, if you don't intend to act upon the findings?

So, getting answers to interesting questions where taking action is out of the question is verboten! However, answering questions where actions can be taken, if indicated, is always worth the effort. So to reiterate, you should consider how the information will impact a decision you need to make, before you ask the question.

Take the research for the wallpaper company again. Say the results suggest that the real reason people don't buy when they get the catalog is because they are afraid to buy wallpaper sight unseen using only pictures and descriptions in a catalog or on the internet as their guide. Perhaps they want to actually see the color, match it to a specific room's décor, feel the texture, etc. What actions might the company take if this proves to be the major stumbling block?

Maybe they should open retail stores so that customers can see their products before they buy – an unlikely solution. Maybe they should offer free returns if the customer doesn't like the wallpaper once they see it – a reasonable, but perhaps profit-sapping solution. Maybe they should more strongly educate potential buyers that their policy is to send them free samples of wallpaper prior to purchase, if the customer so requests – which would be easy and perhaps cost-effective. Maybe the company can't afford to do anything that is cost-effective that would address this problem.

While there is no apparent solution to this dilemma, it highlights why many research studies are not action-oriented. If you were Kraft or Procter & Gamble, that might not be such a problem. The cost of such research is often an insignificant part of their profits.

For a small company, however, the cost of research can divert funds that could be used for other important initiatives. Therefore, it is far more important that those new to research be able to conceptualize solutions or areas where action might be taken prior to engaging in research. Anticipating possible actions that you might take would make you far more likely to conduct research that could lead to a profitable outcome.

UNDERSTANDING THE NEEDS OF YOUR CUSTOMERS AND PROSPECTS

Customers and prospects buy products because they need them, e.g. an economy car to commute to work or a simple watch to tell time. They buy products because they want them, e.g. a BMW or a Rolex, because it makes a strong statement about their success. They buy products they wish for, e.g. a Porsche because it is a symbol of automobile perfection. They buy products they desire, e.g. a PT Cruiser because it takes them back to their childhood. And, importantly, they buy products because they have an emotional attachment to them, e.g. loyal Apple customers are fiercely involved with the brand, an emotional connection even they find hard to express.

Needs, wants, wishes, desires and emotions – they are all part and parcel of why people buy, whether a business is selling to consumers or selling to other businesses. And they are all critical to understanding both the rational and highly emotional associations that are key to keeping your current customers and attracting new ones.

Consider the case of a customer choosing a new dry cleaner because he wanted same-day service and the old cleaner couldn't provide it. This situation was beyond a simple need for clean clothes.

Or the patron, who wished every time he went into the restaurant closest to home that families with little kids, who are likely to whine, would be put in one dining room with the other room reserved for adult peace and quiet. Actually, one restaurateur did just that, and was rewarded with more than two dozen visits in the last year.

Few consumers really need, want or wish to spend several dollars a day on coffee, but they certainly desire their daily Starbucks fix.

With luxury products such as perfume, liquor, automobiles, and choice of an airline or hotel, it is essential to understand the wishes, desires and emotions that customers bring to the purchase situation rather than their largely fulfilled needs and wants. Even with products such as cereals, instant dinners, or computers, there may be many needs and wants still unfulfilled, but wishes, desires and emotions also play a pivotal role in the choices customers make.

For better or worse, we live in an ever-increasingly competitive and global economy. For most products and services, we have choices that extend far beyond the simple fulfillment of basic needs. We have moved to a point where uncovering and exploiting what might have been a significant need or want several years ago is now basic to just being competitive.

What once might have been differentiating is now a poker chip you ante up just to play the game. The issue is salience. As competition forces products to offer similar benefits simply as a cost of entry, it is important to dig further. To probe and explore new or additional benefits or features will differentiate you, causing customers to remain loyal and prospects to give you another look.

In an article entitled "How can we help you? the costly challenge of discovering consumers' unmet needs – and meeting them," published in *The Wall Street Journal* (New York, January 2005, Classroom edition), D Ball, S Ellison, and J Adamy said: "Companies are digging deeper into shoppers' homes ... to discover 'unmet needs' and then design new products to meet them ...."

P&G appears to have hit the jackpot with an unmet need it discovered among those consumers who wash their own cars. Consumers told P&G that half of the time they devoted to washing the car was actually spent drying the car, so that water spots won't form. For these consumers, P&G designed Mr. Clean AutoDry Carwash, a sponge along with a nozzle and a liquid-soap cartridge that attaches to a garden hose. A filter in the nozzle removes the minerals in water that cause the spots.

The AutoDry product is on track to generate more than $100 million in first-year sales.

Good research digs below the obvious. While it should tell you if you are meeting your customer's basic needs, that is often not enough. Good research should strip away the apparent in an effort to surface exploitable advantages. It should determine the unmet wants, wishes, and desires which, if addressed, will motivate customers and prospects to choose you rather than one of the many competitive options that they constantly face.

TURNING RESEARCH QUESTIONS INTO RESEARCH GOALS AND OBJECTIVES

In order to uncover unmet wants, needs and desires – emotional and rational – you have to ask the right questions. Those new to research often have so many questions they think they want answered that it's often impossible for research to address economically all at once. Therefore, it is imperative that research questions you feel are important are clearly and concisely translated into research objectives.

A client that sells Easter gifts in retail stores said:

> I think I can sell my line of gifts at higher prices, but I have to prove that people will spend more. My question is, "Can I do research to prove that the higher-priced line will sell?"

Given this question, we set about defining exact research objectives. The following overall goal was developed:

In planning for the coming Easter season, Acme is developing new ideas for its line of Easter gifts. The new gifts come in packages that are a strong departure from previous lines. The product line sells at $5 per gift. Additionally, Acme has conceptualized themed gifts at a higher $10 price point and wishes to determine how they would sell in comparison to its lower-priced line.

The following specific research objectives could now be identified:

- What unit and dollar share of business might Acme expect from its line of $5 and $10 Easter gifts as compared to its previous line and to lines of competitive Easter gifts?
- What price points generate the greatest interest? What is the price sensitivity to Acme gifts priced at $5 and $10 versus competitive gifts priced the same way?
- How are the Acme gifts priced at $5 and $10 perceived in comparison to competitive gifts in terms of being:
  - gifts of good value;
  - gifts that feature good toy / candy quality;
  - gifts that have good play value;
  - gifts that are colorful and pleasing to look at?
- How does the current Acme gift line featuring unique packaging compare to gifts packaged in the past? Does the new packaging have the same gift-giving potential as baskets or tins?

With these objectives agreed upon, it became easy to write a minimum number of questions that addressed them.

To reiterate, the art of digging from either one general question or a multitude of questions to obtain a clear research goal and objectives takes some work. Redefinition or stating the problem differently is a good technique for digging below the obvious. Just as you reworded your research questions to ensure you were addressing important issues, generating a precise research goal is also important.

The following is another approach for digging below the obvious to generate a more clearly defined goal:

1. Write down your research goal, for example "The overall goal of the research is to determine how to get customers to buy from me more often."
2. State the goal a second way, for example "The overall goal of the research is to determine whether better customer service will cause customers to buy from me more often."
3. State the goal yet a third way, for example "The overall goal of the research is to determine whether offering customers incentives would get them to buy from me more often."

Suppose #2 is determined to be the most important research goal. You would then create secondary research objectives that further elaborate on the overall goal. In this case, it might be to determine whether better customer service will cause customers to buy more often. Another secondary research objective might be:

> To determine how customers rate the customer service in the following areas: being knowledgeable; being friendly; providing answers quickly; being able to understand my problems; offering solutions that I hadn't considered; etc.

However, if #3 is thought to be your most important research goal, the secondary research objectives then might become:

> Determine the incentives that would cause customers to buy more often. For example, what incentives do other companies offer that cause customers to be loyal? Could a customer loyalty program that provides discounts for frequent purchases be effective? What levels of discount would be adequate? Could awarding points that could be redeemed for merchandise, travel, etc. be effective?

REFINING RESEARCH GOALS AND OBJECTIVES

The further you refine your research goal and objectives, the more likely the information that you collect will be richer and action-oriented.

Another effective technique for determining the precise research goal and secondary objectives is to conduct three to five in-depth interviews with some of your customers. You'll be amazed at the feedback your own customers will provide you if only you ask.

Conduct these interviews in person or over the phone, but in a very businesslike manner. This is not about being a friend to your customers and hoping they'll be nice to you in return. And this contact is not about sales. It is about being able to get their honest, objective feedback. And, because you don't want them to feel defensive or on the spot, you might try opening the conversation as follows:

> Hello, John. We're going to undertake some research among our customers and we're trying to formulate the objectives. Would you be willing to give me your objective feedback on some questions I'm thinking about? Good!

> 1. Sometimes customers come to us because the places they usually buy from are out of stock. If you were me, what would you say that would encourage them to buy more from me, not just when my competitor is out of stock?

2. If you knew that a customer was buying from me 50 per cent of the time, what would you suggest that would cause the customer to increase that buying to 75 per cent?
3. Sometimes I hear that our customer service is great and sometimes not so great. What is it about customer service in our industry that you like and don't like?

Certainly, these interviews can take a different tack, given your relationship with the customer and your research questions. The point is to try to keep it objective and not to be defensive. Listen to your customer and read between the lines. You'll find that your research objectives will sizzle with clarity.

So you see, customer feedback is important not only in evaluating your products and performance, but also in determining areas that should be evaluated in the first place.

WHAT ACTIONS MIGHT YOU TAKE?

Being clear on the actions that you might take is far more important for smaller companies than it is for larger ones. Large companies often conduct what is referred to as "exploratory research." This is research for which no particular problems need solving. Large companies often conduct exploratory research because they know that it is important to stay ahead of consumer thinking and to spot trends as they are beginning.

In conducting exploratory research, large companies hope to get an inkling of changes that might be taking place in the market or uncovering unmet consumer needs, wants, wishes, desires and emotional connections that they could be the first to exploit. As large companies can more easily afford to conduct research "fishing expeditions" than can Guerrillas, they are often happy to conclude that nothing significant is happening that would be cause for concern.

When planning a project, a research director at a large food company said:

> We don't really have any idea what we might learn from your focus groups, but if something is changing out there we have to know. Even if nothing major is happening, we always learn something about our products or advertising that can stand improvement. Our first line of defense is to periodically conduct exploratory focus groups.

For Guerrillas, conducting exploratory research without first thinking through how the research will be used is usually unwise – and costly. When looking at the results, internal arguments often surface as to what actions, if any, the research might be suggesting. Often, a feeling starts to pervade the company that research doesn't really lead to anything other than conjecture and supposition.

Therefore, before you engage in the research, define several actions that you might take if the research points more to doing A than doing B, or if it suggests that C is the best way to go even though you know that you can't afford to do C.

Defining your actions

At this point you will have clearly a defined research goal and have thought through your secondary objectives. Now you can begin to determine the actions that you'd likely take when the results come in. The following format can be useful for brainstorming potential actions:

1. State the overall goal that the research will address.
2. State the secondary objectives that you would like answered by the research.
3. Write down what you think the findings of the research could be as a result of your research goal and secondary objectives; that is, what you could learn:

   A. I might learn that _____
   B. I might learn that _____
   C. I might learn that _____

   Continue until all options are written down.

4. For each option write down three actions you would consider taking on the basis of your learning:

   For 3 A: Action #1 _____ Action #2 _____ Action #3 _____.
   For 3 B: Action #1 _____ Action #2 _____ Action #3 _____.
   etc.

   Continue until at least three actions for all findings are identified.

In completing this exercise, it is important to ask yourself whether you have the people, the resources, or the money to take the actions that you contemplate. If so, you have created action-oriented research scenarios. If not, you should rethink both your research objectives and action steps.

Elements of the above outline are illustrated again in Chapter 8, "The research plan," and should be used when developing a completed research plan.

In this chapter we have worked hard to stress the importance of setting good research objectives and have provided concrete tools to help you do so. Remember, "If you don't know where you are going, any path will take you there." Relatedly, there's a wonderful cartoon that shows a bunch of executives furiously rushing around in circles and bumping into one another. The caption: "Having lost sight of their goals, they redoubled their efforts."

DIGGING DEEPER

Investing in marketing research

Research is often implemented in support of sales goals. There is a school of thought that would have you believe that the only reason a Guerrilla should employ any form of marketing is to influence sales now. While we wouldn't argue that increased sales are not the ultimate goal, there is a legitimate question regarding how soon this can be accomplished. Remember, not everyone is a retailer who runs an ad on Sunday and sees sales on Monday.

For many, to increase sales it is first necessary to increase the level of awareness of your company and/or improve attitudes towards your products or services. Changing pre-existing attitudes or beliefs so that customers are more positive about purchasing from you may be a first step that in so doing will increase sales at a later point in time.

We understand Guerrillas are impatient and want sales results sooner rather than later. Frequently though, marketing communication programs cannot work overnight. Further, your goal may not be immediate sales, but rather to shift the timing of sales from one season to another or from one daypart to another or from one day of the week to another. Your sales goal might even be to reduce the number of customers at peak periods, or to attract one type of customer and not another.

Maybe you have to change social patterns of thinking such as encouraging people who have never voted to go to the booth at the next election, or to get a medical check-up, or to donate time or money.

Your goals might be to motivate your competitor's customers to switch to you. Or you might conclude that increasing the frequency of product use among your loyal customers is the best key to growth. Maybe increased sales will only come when you grow the entire marketplace and motivate consumers totally new to your product category to become users.

Marketing research can help achieve all of the preceding sales goals, but it's true that, when implementing findings from research conducted at one point in time, sales results might not be noticeable until months later. Frequently, the changes suggested by research require altering your course of action in major ways – and such changes often take time to penetrate the hearts and minds of your targets.

That's why many refer to "investing" in marketing research.

Examples of marketing communications actions

Earlier in this chapter we talked about the importance of anticipating the marketing actions that might be taken based on what was learnt in research. Let's examine a few examples of what we mean – just looking at actions that might be taken in the area of marketing communications.

Why marketing communications? The simple truth is that marketing communications – advertising, PR, packaging, sales promotion efforts, brochures, direct mail, website content and design, e-marketing, corporate identity programs, etc. – comprise the most common marketing actions that Guerrillas take. Here are some examples of the type of actions we mean:

- Inform customers and prospects about the benefits, features and attributes of your products and services versus the competition and seek to convince them there is more value in choosing you.
- Seek to change the importance customers and prospects place on various benefits and features – presumably those where you have a competitive advantage.
- Provide an emotional framework around your company or brands so that the consumer has more passion to choose your products or services over your competition.
- Convey new and important information to various types of people who are currently using or who could use your products or services.
- Cajole customers and prospects with soft arguments designed to make it easier to at least consider purchasing distasteful products, such as long-term health insurance or grave sites.
- Work to calm suppliers, attract prospective employees, inform thought leaders in the media, influence government or local community officials, or influence investors in purchasing company stock.
- Sometimes, too, advertising outside can also work inside to guide employee behavior.

In thinking about marketing communication goals, Guerrillas should always consider the many audiences and constituencies that can help them grow their business. And for each and every target, marketing research can play an important role in, first, determining how to communicate with them in the most compelling manner possible and, second, making sure that the communication is working as planned.

Exploratory research – a final word

As previously discussed, exploratory research is research that is conducted even though the marketer isn't sure it will result in any particular action. Such research is regarding as a fishing expedition, in that research objectives can be broad, vague, and less-well defined. Nevertheless, exploratory research allows marketers to keep up with ever-changing market conditions and may tip them off as to areas where a well-defined research project is needed.

We are not against exploratory research for small companies, if your budget allows. Conducting research that suggests actions that you might be unwilling or unable to take can, indeed, be helpful. Research outcomes that indicate an action that you are unable to take can open your eyes to the realities of the marketplace. Even if you can't do anything about them, they can force you to rethink your priorities and perhaps put limited resources to use where they will do the most good.

Further, exploratory research may save money by steering you away from areas where your resources would produce only a limited impact. It could be a waste, for example, to venture forward in areas where you are likely to have an undifferentiated offering or that might require large communications budgets, for example. In fact, perhaps as much as half the exploratory research studies we've conducted point to action steps where the client fails to act because the funds necessary to address the findings adequately are not affordable.

Exploratory research findings that prove arduous for you to implement may actually give you a head start in counteracting potential threats that will eventually come from a competitor with deeper pockets.

3

What Guerrillas can learn from large-company research

We have hard-won opinions about large-company research and the accompanying battle scars. On one hand, we hold great admiration for large-company researchers, who strive mightily to have their voices heard and to make a difference. At their best they are the voice of the consumer and they are listened to and respected for the clear direction that they provide their companies.

On the other hand, we are greatly frustrated by the second-class status that research departments sometimes occupy at many large companies. At their worst, they are the reluctant, silent keepers of information. They are unable to navigate the many levels of company management in order to communicate research findings to the people who are willing and able to take action. They are unable to sell the value of what they do and, alas, too meek to fight the corporate fight necessary to ensure that the research they conduct is used to its fullest.

As a very senior executive in one of the largest US research companies put it, "The background and personalities of many in research provide them with a higher level of concentration and intellectual analysis, but not necessarily the skill set to sit at the big table."

Certainly, this criticism could describe many departments in a large company, but it seems particularly attributable to the research function. In the well over 200 large companies that we have served, we are aware of just two researchers who became a CEO or COO, or even ascended to the Board of Directors. Usually such status goes to people who have toiled in finance, operations, or marketing and have been successful in getting the attention and trust of top management.

Here's an instructive tale. Once we were invited to attend a series of presentations by major company chief financial officers. We thought it would be a waste of time. As career marketers and researchers, why should we care about being an effective CFO or comptroller? Nevertheless, out of sheer curiosity we went.

The theme of all the speakers was basically the same and could apply to almost any staff function – and they really drove it home. Simply put, to get a meaningful seat at the table it's imperative for financial people to behave first as business people and secondly as purveyors of numbers. For the financial executive this means having less of an eye toward the numbers and more of an eye toward what the numbers mean for the business and toward what actions they suggest.

Substitute marketing researcher for financial executive and the advice remains exactly the same.

The CFOs and headhunters who spoke implored the audience to learn their trade well and then become generalists. This meant that once those in the audience achieved success in providing valid financial numbers, they must turn their attention to what the numbers suggest. A corporate recruiter was particularly forceful. He said:

> Companies hiring top financial positions assume a level of technical competence. What they are looking for are financial stars – executives who can take information and synthesize it, interpret it and then provide a strong voice that will help their company make important strategic decisions.

Marketing researchers, and even Guerrillas, should take note as the analogies are many – and indeed some are getting the message. John Lees, General Manager of Global Market Knowledge & Intelligence at Kimberly-Clark, notes: "Researchers have been too tangled up with technology and have not been getting the information used." Lees goes on to say, "The gateway to getting funding for projects (at Kimberly-Clark) is testing the logic of the questions being asked."

Danielle Jackson, Director of Marketing at Sonance and former Research Director at Kia Motors, says, "Researchers are focused too much on methodology and not enough on how data will be used. They've been too black and white in their approach and should be less about the data they generate and more and more about providing direction."

In this era of exploding information, where management is usually inundated with numbers, the researcher who can interpret, synthesize and provide creative direction for making important strategic decisions will become a superstar. Again we remind you, it is more important for Guerrillas with limited funds to conduct research only when they're convinced they are asking questions where the answers will lead to actions. Otherwise, the only people who'll make money are the researchers you hire.

Unfortunately, it's sad that the rate of failure of new products is almost the same today as it was five, 10, 20 and 40 years ago. In 2003 for example, 34,000 new products were introduced – and 90 per cent failed. In 2008, the failure rate is still about 80 per cent – exactly what it was in 1968! That's right, 80 per cent of all new products will fail to turn a profit!

Jack Trout at Trout & Partners states that the average US family turns to the same 150 items for as much as 85 per cent of its household needs – exhibiting a strong disdain for most of the new products that marketers throw at them.

The irony is that good research, effectively planned and communicated, can prevent much of this unnecessary waste of money and effort. This will only happen when management in large companies begin to listen more intently to research people like Lees and Jackson and when research people become more effective in getting them to listen. Hopefully, this is not an issue for you and your company.

In any event, large companies, or any company for that matter, have only two general categories of research to choose from. Their studies are either strategic or tactical in nature.

STRATEGIC VS TACTICAL RESEARCH

We have briefly mentioned the differences between strategic and tactical research already; now we'll expand that discussion. There are two kinds of research that large companies undertake: 1) strategic research, which helps to determine the most promising and profitable courses of action; and 2) tactical research, which helps to determine how best to achieve the courses of action deemed to be most promising.

According to another head of a large research company, strategic research, "tends to be owned by officers of the company in that it is focused on big issues." He goes on to say:

> The nature of strategic research is global and cross-sectional in character and the research provider is usually viewed as a senior consultant. The results of actions taken based on strategic research will not be known immediately and may even take years to discern.

As for we Guerrillas, we're far less inclined to view the implementation strategic research findings as taking "years to discern." Unlike some large corporations, Guerrillas tend to be focused, impatient and nimble. Once Guerrillas have the results from a strategic research study, there is no reason whatsoever that shifting strategic gears can't take place quickly with sales results close behind.

Strategic research studies seek to determine:

- Needs, wants, wishes, desires and emotions in the marketplace and how customers and prospects are being served by companies hoping to capture their loyalty.
- Likely demographic targets for the products or services being sold (older or younger customers, big or small families, higher- or lower-income families, etc.) and likely psychographic targets for the products and services (early adopters, reluctant followers, technology averse, etc.)
- Strengths and weakness of the companies or brands in the marketplace as measured by how they are perceived by the targets (e.g. company image or brand image).
- Gaps in the marketplace or the areas in which companies or brands fail to deliver what is desired by customers and prospects (e.g. the opportunities that exist for strengthening your hold on the market and/or for exploiting competitive weaknesses).
- New product business opportunities.

Strategic research is about creating a road map and deciding the best direction to drive.

On the other hand, tactical research is about determining the best roads for getting to the final destination once you know where you're driving. In the words of the aforementioned research executive:

> Tactical research is run at a manager level in the organization, studies a particular aspect of a problem, is driven by events temporal in nature, and the line of sight between research evidence and decision is very close and narrow.

So tactical research studies seek to reinforce your strategic direction by determining such things as:

- Whether the benefits delivered by your products or services are in keeping with your strategic direction.
- Improvements or changes that should be made to your products and services so that your strategic direction is strengthened.
- Improvements or changes that should be made to the manner in which you serve your customers so that your strategic direction is strengthened.
- Most convincing messages for communicating your strategic direction.
- Most compelling executions when advertising or promoting your products or services.
- Most effective website design, copy and features for capturing, holding the attention and motivating visitors to embrace your offerings.

- Strongest packaging for your products that reinforces your strategic direction.
- Strongest name for your products or services that reinforces your strategic direction.
- How well your communication efforts are being seen, heard, remembered, and acted upon.
- New ideas, products, or services are worth pursuing that will strengthen your strategic direction.

Tactical research is about ensuring that the important details essential to achieving your strategic direction are effectively executed.

WHICH COMES FIRST – A STRATEGIC OR TACTICAL STUDY?

We are often questioned by Guerrillas as to where to start the research process – with a strategic study or a tactical one? One way to answer the question is to look at what large companies do.

Large companies often conduct both strategic and tactical research studies at the same time. For them, there are always large road map issues to contemplate, and advertising, packaging, pricing, product, e-commerce or other smaller tactical issues to decide.

Thus, the cycle of research can become mutually beneficial. Studies designed to provide strategic direction often surface meaningful tactical changes, while tactical studies may suggest an alternative or modified strategic direction.

In our experience most large consumer-goods companies will budget for at least one large strategic study per year. And, often, one study might encompass several brands and product categories. Further, mega-companies like Kraft and Procter & Gamble may budget for dozens of strategic studies across their many business units.

Large banks, such as Bank of America or Citibank, retailers such as Home Depot, Staples, or Best Buy, or even energy companies such as Nicor or Exxon may conduct an overriding strategic study somewhat less often. Four years ago we wrote, "These companies are not as prone to new competition that suddenly pops up or to drastically changing trends." Looking back on that statement, we certainly were mistaken.

Consider now the drastic upheavals that have taken place for virtually every large corporation. Whether financial, housing, automotive, retail or energy, industries we previously characterized as stable are now prone to drastic disruptions. What a change in four short years.

Today 10 per cent of home owners in the US can't meet their mortgage obligations and hundreds of thousands of people have already or are about to lose their homes. Financial giants like Fannie Mae and Freddie Mac needed massive government intervention to stay alive. Bear Stearns and Lehman Bros have gone out of business and other banks and lending institutions are struggling to stay liquid. Sales and profits of virtually every retailer, particularly those connected with the housing industry like Home Depot and Lowe's, have suffered dramatically. And look at what damage the upheaval in the energy industry is causing in the automobile industry.

Four years ago we also wrote:

> Companies that are in a stable and slowly evolving marketplace are less likely to shift their strategic direction as quickly as companies in fast moving competitive environments. Nevertheless, they should always be questioning their strategies and exploring opportunities that can be addressed by less ambitious tactical research.

Today, we'd emphasize that companies, even stable industries, that have failed to stay current by researching their marketplace and understanding the strategic implications of the times are behind the curve. During difficult times, companies that stay in touch with customer attitudes and emotions, and seek to communicate an understanding of what customers are going through, will certainly be in a leadership position when times get better. The same holds true for Guerrillas.

For large companies, as we said, the research cycle is circular. Some will follow firm schedules for when large strategic studies are to be conducted throughout the year. Others will plan to conduct only smaller tactical studies, but find market conditions changing and conclude it's time to step back and question their overall strategies.

Still others don't plan at all. They simply conduct studies as issues arise. There may be a question about changing the advertising approach. R&D might decide it needs to test new products or to assess improvements to current products. Logos, packaging graphics, line-extension opportunities, website improvements and other e-commerce issues might take center stage and require either strategic or tactical research to be initiated.

Essentially, it is less important for these large companies to set strict priorities than it is for them to establish research as an important contributor to their decision making. Studies usually get done when they are needed in order to provide guidance on a pressing decision. That is usually priority enough.

Large companies recognize that marketing research measures the pulse of customer sentiment at a point in time, but that time is fleeting. They know that taking a research reading only when times are good and everything is orderly is as ill-conceived as talking to customers only when times are bad. They know that by staying regularly in touch with customer attitudes and behaviors, they'll be better able to control their business destiny.

In this regard, Guerrillas would do well following the large company approach. Whether you start the research process by conducting a large strategic study or a smaller tactical one is of far less concern than simply getting started in the first place.

WHAT KINDS OF STUDIES DO LARGE COMPANIES CONDUCT?

There are two basic types of market research studies: qualitative studies and quantitative studies.

Qualitative studies

Qualitative research uses small samples and in most such research participants influence what others think and say. As a consequence, results from qualitative studies may not be indicative of the opinions held by a larger population. Findings are not reliably projectable to customers or prospects as a whole.

Results from qualitative studies are best used to clarify objectives, to provide background information, or as thought starters, hypotheses producers, or indicators of what might work for customers or prospects at large. They are also employed to hear the language customers and others use to talk about your category. Often they can provide input regarding how to phrase questionnaires in quantitative studies.

Qualitative research studies consist of a small sampling of the population and include the following.

Focus groups

Generally a two-hour discussion revolving around questions and issues deemed important and consisting of a moderator and eight to 12 respondents. It's interesting that in the US the usual practice for the number of respondents in a focus group is to use the upper end of the range, while in Europe they rarely would use more than eight.

Mini focus groups

A one- to two-hour discussion consisting of a moderator and four to six respondents covering the same topics as a full focus group. Mini focus groups are a less expensive option to larger focus groups. They do place a greater demand on each participant to communicate.

Dyads and triads

Most likely a one-hour discussion consisting of a moderator and two or three respondents. Issues discussed tend to be more limited in nature than in focus or mini focus groups. A common dyad is a husband–wife pair. For many products, such as furniture and automobiles to name two, the genders tend to focus on different aspects of the purchase decision. So, for example, to understand how to market furniture you need to talk to both wife and husband. This can be done separately or together in a dyad.

To continue with the furniture example, women are more interested in emotionally tinged criteria like overall aesthetics, color, design, and the extent to which the furniture matches what's already in the house. Men tend to pay more attention to rational criteria like how comfortable it is, the size, and, yes, the price. Talking to both at the same time can be quite revealing.

In-depth personal interviews

Generally a 30- to 60-minute give and take between a moderator and one respondent. Personal interviews are used when the topic might be sensitive and difficult to discuss in a group setting and also when it is important to obtain respondent attitudes without the influence of other respondents. Sometimes called "one-on-ones," these are often used to learn exactly what is being communicated by advertising.

Observation studies

Usually consist of a researcher observing respondents as they go about tasks related to the marketer's products. These studies might include placing a video camera in a respondent's home or place of work, for example, to record his or her movements and actual behavior under normal conditions.

Researchers have learnt that respondents may say one thing in focus groups but sometimes behave differently. This is because they can be quite unaware of why they behave as they do or even as to the particulars of habitual activities like how they might sigh (negatively) when they fold towels, or scrunch up their face in concentration when reading a recipe. As a result, observation studies have become popular in recent years as another means of understanding the consumer.

Brainstorming and other idea-generation processes

Brainstorming and other idea-generation processes can take place in any configuration of the qualitative approaches discussed, but their aim is to generate new ideas, not to discuss customer or prospect issues and motivations. In Chapter 10 there is a discussion of brainstorming and ideation processes.

Quantitative studies

Results from quantitative studies are indicative of what is true for the population as a whole because they employ a sample of respondents that is large enough to offer statistically reliable estimates. While qualitative studies help determine the issues to study, quantitative studies determine which of those issues are important.

Quantitative studies consist of larger and projectable samplings of the population and include (but are not limited to) the following.

Segmentation studies

The backbone studies that help set the strategic direction for large companies. They determine the demographics and attitudes that customers and prospects have when making purchase decisions in the category being studied. They also measure attitudes or images held about the various companies, brands, or products that compete. You may have heard the word "benchmarking." It really refers to comparing how you do vs the competition in a study like these.

Segmentation studies are expensive and often include sophisticated statistical procedures for determining the various market segments that exist. They are extremely important in understanding which appeals will be most effective to various segments of the market and to winning them over. Segmentation studies are also referred to as image and attitude studies, psychographic/typographic studies, market structure studies, or simply background studies.

Communication studies

After the strategic direction for a company, brand, or product is set, developing communication goals is often the next step. That is, various approaches communicating the strategic direction are developed and explored. Communication studies determine which approach is most compelling and believable, and should become the communication "strategy" or communication "cornerstone" for motivating customers and prospects to buy. These are alternatively termed "concept tests."

Advertising execution studies

A clear communication strategy will serve as the guiding principle for developing various advertising approaches. Advertising execution studies determine which broadcast commercials (TV and radio) or print ads most strongly communicate the strategy and are likely to capture the customer's attention. Ad execution studies ensure that the message being communicated is, in fact, being communicated as intended.

There is an entire sub-industry devoted to this subject of copy-testing. Note that if you have one dollar to spend, it should go to the concept test rather than the execution test. Getting the strategy of what to say correct takes precedence over expressing the approved strategy the best way.

Advertising awareness and tracking studies

Advertising awareness studies are designed to measure brand awareness, advertising awareness, and recall of the advertising content that exist in the minds of customers and prospects. Most often, they also include measurement of attitudes or images held toward the various companies, brands, or products that compete in the marketplace. Ad tracking studies are usually undertaken yearly, although they often are done more frequently. It depends on how quickly your environment changes.

If the goal is to track changes that might have occurred in awareness or attitudes in a stable marketplace, a yearly study is enough. If it is to observe changes in awareness that might occur during the year, quarterly or even monthly tracking studies are undertaken.

McDonald's, the hamburger chain, engages in what is called "continuous tracking" with interviews taking place every day. Sometimes, too, these studies are done to assess the impact of new advertising copy or a change in how much is being spent on advertising, with one wave of research conducted before the campaign runs and another right after the ads stop.

In tracking studies a single wave of research is like a photograph, but multiple waves are like a movie that changes in response to your marketing activities, those of your competitors and the macro-environment.

Name studies

Large companies usually consider a number of names for a new product or service that they are introducing. Name studies determine which name is most compelling for generating trial of the brand, and for determining whether it is enhancing the strategic direction and the communication goals that the company has set.

Packaging studies

As with name studies, large companies will consider any number of packaging approaches for a product. They will consider various package sizes, configurations, and graphics. Packaging studies will determine which package alternative stands out and whether it supports the communication goals of the brand.

Price studies

Price studies help determine the optimum price that can be charged for products before demand suffers. They can also help determine if lower demand at a higher price could end up producing greater profits.

Screening studies

Large companies are often faced with a variety of options when it comes to improving current products or introducing new ones. They might be considering dozens of new line extensions or formulation changes for current products. They could have literally hundreds of new products or services under consideration, or a multitude of packaging improvements or product name changes. Screening studies determine the alternatives that hold the greatest promise.

Product testing

Product development is always being undertaken at large companies. A new product might be developed to address an unmet need or improvements developed for current products. Product testing will determine if introducing a new product is indicated or if improving a current product will result in a competitive advantage.

Customer satisfaction research

Most companies understand that satisfying customers is Job 1 because satisfied customers are usually the most profitable customers. They will buy even when items are not on sale, are generally more loyal, purchase repeatedly, tend to have higher usage rates, don't tie up customer service personnel, and say nice things about you to others. The best way to know whether customers are satisfied and what makes them so is to formally assess satisfaction via research. This topic is so important that we have devoted Chapter 16 to a longer discussion of customer satisfaction research.

TEST MARKET RESEARCH

The cost of marketing a new, widely used, consumer product can easily top $50 million. Changing the image of an existing company, brand, or product in the mind of consumers can be equally expensive. No matter how many market research studies might have been conducted indicating potential success, nothing can simulate the real conditions in the marketplace except for a live test.

Test markets are real-world tests of the actual product being manufactured (in pilot plants, because usually the biggest cost of a new product will be the capital investment required to make it), packaged, priced and sold through distribution and promoted to customers. However, these tests take place in a few small but geographically distinct markets so what occurs can be precisely controlled and measured. A test market not only tests product sales and acceptance, but also the marketing strategy and tactics that research helped to develop.

For example, McDonald's research on pizza indicated that it could produce a product people liked. However, when it test-marketed it in a limited number of restaurants and markets, it discovered that it did not generate the sales necessary to roll it out to the entire system.

The same discipline applies at many large companies such as Kraft or Procter & Gamble. They certainly have conducted research studies for lots of new products that suggested success was just around the corner. Test marketing often proved otherwise.

Many of the same types of research studies previously outlined will be conducted in test markets. Only now, given actual market conditions, the frequency with which customers actually purchase products can be far more accurately gauged, as can the many other elements that go together in making a product successful.

Test markets are quite expensive – real products, real ads, real media exposure, etc., but shutting down a poor performing item after a failed test market is a much better idea than spending $50 million, maybe building a new plant or adding a new production line and then shutting it down.

DEVELOPING NEW PRODUCTS

Large companies are continually using research to conceptualize new ideas. Teams of marketing, product development, and R&D people strive mightily to find the next multimillion-dollar blockbuster product.

New products are the life blood of large companies. It's a truism that, if they're not one step ahead of the competition in uncovering and exploiting unmet needs, wants, wishes, or desires in the marketplace, they'll fall behind a worthy competitor before they know it. That's why it's been said that 50 per cent of the profits of most companies come from products that didn't exist five years ago.

Take any of these recently introduced new products:

- Febreze Scentstories – a P&G-developed air freshener that looks like a CD player and automatically gives off a new and different scent every 30 minutes. This product addresses a consumer complaint that after 30 minutes they adjust to the scent and can't smell it anymore.
- Bud Light Lime – a product clearly targeted at Corona drinkers, who are in the habit of squeezing a lime wedge into the bottle to give the beer a lime taste.
- Apple iPhones – the success of the iPhone line has not only launched a whole new approach to mobile telephony, but has spawned many imitators.
- The Ultrasonic Dog Barking Deterrent – Hammacher Schlemmer has introduced a product that emits a harmless ultrasonic tone that only dogs can hear, which startles them into silence.

Some of these products can be easily duplicated, but the very fact that a company is the first to introduce a new product provides it with a strong head start and the enviable reputation of being the market leader.

CONCLUSION

There are many other types of market research studies that large companies undertake. Sophisticated studies such as market share predictive modeling, conjoint analysis, and discrete choice analysis are but a few that large companies will often use. Some of these are briefly discussed in Chapter 19 on statistical techniques.

Guerrillas would be best served by sticking to the more basic research approaches that have been listed and that are discussed throughout this book. The more advanced techniques are better saved for a time when the research essentials have been mastered.

Real research vs the "quick and dirty" kind

Finally, we want to point to an area where Guerrillas can take an important lesson from large companies.

We've found that there are two common and obvious reasons that marketing research doesn't play a more prominent role for Guerrillas: time and money. For the most part, Guerrillas simply don't think to budget funds for marketing research, or plan the time necessary to conduct good research even if they do have funds.

If research is considered at all, Guerrillas are often happy to conduct research that we refer to as the "quick and dirty" kind. You know, the after the fact, when things are going bad, when you need the answers yesterday, when nothing you're doing seems to work kind of research.

What's interesting is that no one ever asks for a quick and dirty profit and loss statement, or a quick and dirty manufacturing process, or a quick and dirty insurance program. It seems that marketing research is singled out for this honor.

One thing about big companies that would serve Guerrillas well is their avoidance of the quick and dirty. Marketing and marketing research people at big companies are simply reluctant to put their jobs on the line by basing important decisions on less than proper research. They not only want to ensure that they're making the right decisions; they also want to be able to show proof that they didn't shortcut the process.

For marketing research to be "real research," it should be conducted early on – before major decisions are made regarding the marketing direction for current products or before new products and services are introduced. Usually, real research takes more time than the quick and dirty kind, and that is simply the price to pay for getting valid information.

If you're not giving yourself the luxury of a little time, if you want to bet your bottom line for the next year or so on the heat 'em up quick kind of research, if your concern is with thinking fast rather than thinking smart, quick and dirty research will do the trick.

You should know that if the internet is a good way to collect the information you need, the speed with which the internet can be used to produce useful primary research often makes the time argument seem pointless.

The money part, though, is big. It's hard to spend money on research when there is no clear guarantee of a profitable payback. Interesting isn't it though, that spending money to support short-term promotions, circulating additional catalogs or flyers, running a bunch of banner ads, adding to the sales force or tossing a new product or service into the market seems so easy to justify – even when faced with just as iffy a payback.

How should Guerrillas equate spending money and taking time for research when the payback often appears elusive? The answer relates to the size of your company, its financial condition, its growth in the previous few years, your ambition, your ego and your willingness to bet the ranch on your entrepreneurial instincts. These are complex issues and we'll have more to say on this in later chapters.

The fact remains that Guerrillas frequently feel the perceived lack of time and money are reasonable excuses for not undertaking real research – or in forgoing it altogether. They've always been issues for Guerrillas and, perhaps, they always will be.

4

How to get started

UNDERSTANDING CURRENT AND POTENTIAL OPPORTUNITIES

Let's be clear: marketing research is the servant of marketing – broadly defined to also include sales, customer service, product development and even human resources. It is employed to help make better decisions. The connection is intimate and all research must flow from the needs of the function it serves.

For example, take a look at the classic product–market matrix in Figure 4.1. It is a fundamental marketing planning tool that looks at any business in terms of its products and its markets. Part of its power derives from its simplicity. Each quadrant indicates important marketing tasks that might be required and labels them *retention, acquisition, penetration* and *diversification*.

For example, if we are attempting to sell new products to current customers, this is termed a "customer penetration strategy." Here you are essentially trying to increase your share of everything your current customer buys from you so that your sales volume increases.

What is useful is that there are important research corollaries that flow directly from the product–market matrix, because once a Guerrilla is in business for more than a couple of years, he or she will learn that he or she has to be active in all four quadrants. Given this matrix as a planning tool, here is the kind of research might be needed.

1. Understanding how to keep current customers and deter them from leaving you.
2. Understanding how to attract more customers like those who currently buy.

	EXISTING CUSTOMER	**NEW CUSTOMER**
EXISTING PRODUCT/ SERVICE	***Retention:*** prevent customer turnover or attrition, increase share of *category* purchases, increase rate of purchase, increase volume of *category* purchases	***Acquisition:*** attract new customers, enter new geography, open new stores, add channels, etc.
NEW PRODUCT/ SERVICE	***Penetration:*** sell more to current customers, increase share of *all* purchases, increase volume of *all* purchases	***Diversification:*** enter new businesses, sell new things to new markets

Figure 4.1   Product–market matrix

3. Understanding what will make customers who purchase the kinds of products or services you sell spend more with you than they do with your competitors.
4. Understanding what will make customers who purchase the kinds of products or services you sell buy them more often from you than from your competitors.
5. Understanding what will make consumers who don't buy the category of goods you sell to begin buying them – and buy them from you rather than your competition.
6. Learning how best to launch a new product or service.

In addition, there are two more major opportunities that Guerrillas will want to explore that do not come from the matrix:

7. Determining if manufacturing your products less expensively will not negatively affect your sales and, therefore, increase your profits.
8. Determining if you can raise prices on your products or services and not negatively affect sales or profits.

Outside of purely academic curiosity, we can't think of any other reasons whatsoever why you'd want to spend money on research. If you aren't trying to launch new products, attract new customers, attract your competitors' customers, convince your customers to buy more from you, increase the size of the market itself, or increase profits by cutting costs or raising prices, you don't need market research.

There are thousands of questions that you can ask your customers – or your competitors' customers – but there is only one reason to ask them. And that reason is to give you the best direction to make the most money possible.

This, however, does not mean that there are only eight kinds of research studies. These eight domains of inquiry can be explored in an endless variety of studies limited only by your business situation and your imagination. The trick, of course, is in determining which of the above eight areas offers you the greatest potential and then asking the right questions to produce that advantage.

KNOWING WHAT QUESTIONS TO ASK – REVISITED

Often findings from research fail to result in clearly defined actions. In Chapter 2 we talked extensively about asking the right questions. Consider this, though. What if you've done your homework in penning the right question and the information generated did little more than point to other questions that you should have been asking?

In an effort to understand how to better serve existing customers or attract new customers, even the best planned research sometimes doesn't always provide answers to all your questions. While it would certainly generate answers that lead to some actions, it may also suggest new questions. In fact good research usually raises questions that have yet to be considered.

The operative word in research is "search." Coming up short in one search can pinpoint where to start the next.

That is to say, getting answers is simple. Asking the right questions in the first place can be difficult. Archimedes said, "Give me the right place to stand and I'll move the world." It's the same with research. Once you've uncovered the right questions and gotten the answers to them, clarity and profits will be close behind.

Much of the effort that large companies put into research is in learning the questions that they can rely upon to be predictive of the actions customers will take. For example, assume you conduct a well-intentioned study designed to determine what would happen if you lowered your prices. Say that the results of a study show that 90 per cent of customers surveyed said they would buy more if prices were lowered, but 30 per cent said they would buy more if customer service were improved.

Would you lower prices or improve customer service?

It's hard to know if you didn't ask customers how much they'd be spending with you. Here a second study might be conducted where you learn that the lower-price group would spend an average of $100 more in the next 12 months while the customer-service group would spend $1,000 more in the next 12 months. You'd probably be inclined to put your major effort behind improving customer service.

This doesn't mean you've asked the wrong questions in the first place. Even Socrates wasn't smart enough to anticipate every possible contingency before making his postulations. It does mean that additional research might be necessary before taking action.

Determining the right questions to ask is of seminal importance and sometimes doesn't happen in your first research go-around.

Let's assume that you conduct a series of one-on-one qualitative interviews for a catalog selling women's clothing. Look at this interchange from one of the interviews:

Moderator: Would you ever spend $500 on a dress from a catalog?
Respondent: No, I wouldn't. I'd first want to see, try it on and look at the quality and the stitching, so I'd probably go to Saks in the neighborhood if I was going to spend that kind of money.
Moderator: Have you ever purchased an expensive dress, say over $500, from a catalog without first seeing it?
Respondent: Well, yes. I bought a Calvin Klein dress.
Moderator: Why would you spend so much for a Calvin Klein dress?
Respondent: Because I've bought enough of the Calvin Klein brand in the past to know the quality of their products. They also fit my figure perfectly. If I'm familiar with the brand and how it fits me, now that I think of it, I guess I'd take a chance ordering expensive dresses from catalogs.

This is a case where the respondent's initial answer shouldn't be characterized as wrong, nor should we disbelieve the respondent's answer. Rather, it's a case of the respondent giving a quick response to the wrong question. Had the moderator taken the first response as the answer and not probed further, the catalog company might have been discouraged from upgrading its product line by carrying well-known high-priced brands.

The right question in this case would have been, "Please tell me what dress brands you have purchased from a catalog where you have spent over $500 and tell me why you did so." However, that doesn't make the first question wrong. Experienced researchers never take consumers' initial responses at face value. The real truth is usually buried, and sometimes it takes a number of incomplete or less relevant questions to get to the right question that reveals the hidden gems.

And so it goes. The more you learn about your customer motivations, the more insightful and meaningful are the questions that you can ask. Sometimes asking the right questions means getting answers to the wrong ones first.

ATTITUDES VS BEHAVIOR

One of the hardest lessons in research is to understand that customers don't often give you the whole answer. On one hand, they'll tell you their favorite place to shop for groceries is a certain nearby store but, on the other hand, they'll travel miles each week to shop at a different one. Or they may say they love a certain vitamin-rich breakfast cereal, but purchase a sugar-coated one three times more frequently.

What consumers think and say must constantly be tempered with how they behave and act. Research is about asking consumers how they feel about companies, products, and services, but it's also about reconciling their attitudes with how they actually behave. Sometimes you'll find that those with the highest opinions of one company behave by purchasing most frequently from a competitor. And, conversely, those with the lowest opinions of another company may give them the lion's share of their business.

Critics of market research have a compelling argument when they say that customers don't know what they want and, therefore, can't be much help in predicting distant future trends. We agree with that argument primarily because the way much research is practiced focuses more on what is happening in the present. It measures customer attitudes as they currently exist.

That doesn't mean, though, that creative research approaches aren't available for better anticipating future trends. As you read Chapter 11 on focus groups, you'll get some ideas for conducting research that is better at uncovering large changes in the marketplace and better at anticipating trends.

There is great value, however, in understanding the present and research does a good job of describing present attitudes and behaviors. In doing so, it provides a strong road map for planning marketing strategies. We strongly believe that in the absence of information to the contrary, the best prediction we can make about the immediate future is that it will be a lot like the present. For Guerrillas this can become a major advantage in carving out a more successful and profitable business.

As researchers, we are getting better at knowing when customer attitudes alone might be incomplete or misleading and when it's prudent to temper the attitudes being heard by looking at actual behavior. The research steps necessary for reconciling attitudes and behavior aren't that complex and are discussed later in this book.

Our experience is that the majority of what Guerrillas need to know to improve their business will be provided by sticking to basic research approaches and by uncovering important attitudes, perceptions, beliefs and behaviors as they currently exist. Doing so will certainly increase your odds of success.

DETERMINING THE BEST RESEARCH APPROACH FROM THE OPTIONS AVAILABLE

The essence of marketing research is, indeed, about asking the right questions of the right people, the right way. We'll address "the right way" to ask questions in a questionnaire in Chapter 15, but for now, let's take an initial look at the various approaches for collecting answers.

There are only so many ways to collect research information. There are focus groups and other qualitative approaches. Quantitatively, there are phone (and even mobile phone), mail, internet, shopping-center mall intercept, panel survey research methods and, on rare occasions, personal interviewing in homes or places of business or observation and/or coding of behavior. On occasions, too, these methods can be combined.

Choosing which of these approaches, or methodologies, is most desirable is the first hurdle in conducting effective research, and Chapters 11 and 13 detail the various qualitative and quantitative methods and how to choose the one most appropriate for your situation. Here, though, we want to discuss a number of factors that must be considered before deciding on the right methodology.

Is it easy to determine the right questions to ask?

Often the right line of questioning isn't obvious and it is necessary to conduct some preliminary qualitative research before moving on to the major portion of the research effort.

Should the research be projectable, or is getting a feel for issues enough?

Results from focus groups provide a "feel," but they are not projectable and should not be used to represent the opinions shared by everyone. Focus group research will help frame the issues more effectively and can be a very prudent first step. There are even some instances where the results from focus groups are adequate and further research is unnecessary.

How easy or difficult is it to locate customers or prospects whose opinions are important?

For widely used products (toilet tissue, coffee, soft drinks, checking accounts, automobiles, computers, maintenance supplies, etc.), it is easy and inexpensive to locate target customers in order to interview them.

For narrowly used products, interviewing is more costly because of the difficulty in locating qualified respondents.

Examples here would be men who color their hair, home owners who have a separate movie theater room, diabetics who use insulin, heavy users of a product or light users. Or perhaps the research should be tightly focused to users of a particular brand, or users of the product within the past 10 days, or Fortune 500 executives, etc.

How easy or difficult is it to obtain respondent cooperation?

Just because you want to talk to certain targets doesn't mean they want to talk to you. In such instances, incentives may be required to obtain cooperation, which obviously add to the costs of research.

Senior executives and physicians, for example, are reluctant to spend time being interviewed and require large incentives, e.g., in the US a physician will demand as much as $250 for 20 minutes or so of his or her time.

Focus group respondents are always compensated, but telephone interviewees are rarely incentivized. Simply put, the use of incentives to motivate consumers to answer research questions is extremely important and often one key to generating valid research.

How is information best collected?

Will the questionnaire be long and/or is it necessary to show exhibits or pictures in order to generate meaningful information? Because it's difficult to keep respondents on the phone for more than 20 minutes, conducting the study by mail might be the best approach if you have 40 minutes' worth of questions.

Which methodology will produce a valid and reliable sample?

It is a constant research challenge to produce a valid sample of target respondents. If the research calls for collecting data from 300 customers, the question becomes how to best locate, gain cooperation from and interview a representative, random selection of those respondents.

How quickly must the research be completed?

Certain methodologies take much longer to complete (e.g. mail studies). Other methodologies, while faster, might not address all the research objectives. Timing frequently dictates the best approach.

What is the research budget?

Certain approaches are far more expensive than others. While the most expensive methodology might be the right one, it may be unaffordable and so compromise is necessary. Getting to a budget that is affordable and still provides the necessary information is usually an important issue.

These are some of the issues a researcher must consider when determining the right research design and methodology. While they may seem complex and overwhelming, they often require little more than a working knowledge of research. After completing this book, revisit this section. You should then be able to deal with each and every area with dispatch.

WHICH COMES FIRST?

As we discussed in Chapter 3, a study that provides the strategic direction a company, brand, or product should follow would best precede any other kind of research. Again, "strategic" research determines the overall direction to follow or "what to do" and, practically speaking, often also refers to research that requires a significant level of financial commitment.

Another way to think of what strategic means is research that addresses long-range issues and concerns. Remember, without knowing your destination, any road will get you there. At some point, whether as an initial effort or later one, Guerrillas should conduct the strategic research necessary to understand how they can compete most effectively.

But often, a smaller tactical study is the most appropriate initial research effort for Guerrillas. And to reiterate, "tactical" refers to research that addresses a short-term problem or "how to do it" and is generally less expensive to conduct than "strategic research."

Maybe there is a variety of new product ideas or services being considered. Perhaps customer traffic is down or less money is being spent per order. There might be a question regarding the effectiveness of the advertising and what it's communicating. Whatever the situation, these and others kinds of tactical research studies that are limited and narrow in scope might be the best first step for a Guerrilla when beginning to understand the value of research.

What is interesting about tactical research is that results invariably lead to insights that were unanticipated. Focus groups intended to shed light on the clarity of advertising might raise issues as to the company's overall marketing approach. For example, a customer in a focus group might say, "The advertising tells me that the products in their stores are the lowest price. That's okay, but the reason I really go to them is their great service. I'd even spend a little more with them if they reminded me about their great service."

In this example, if the advertising were intended to communicate a low-price message it would be seen as successful. However, now the more strategic issue of stressing customer service rather than price has been raised.

What's important to remember is not to jump to conclusions about broad, far-reaching company direction from small studies that are limited in scope.

DETERMINING WHETHER THE PRODUCT MEETS CUSTOMER EXPECTATIONS

A very good research priority is determining the extent to which the products you sell or the services you offer meet customers' needs and expectations. The market is littered with thousands of products that have come and gone because competitive products deliver better benefits or more abundant features, or the same benefits and features at a lower price than one-time leaders. Making sure you are at least competitive in this regard is a great first step for research.

Service Merchandise went out of business after discounters like Walmart and Target proved that they could deliver the same products more cheaply and more conveniently. Air Wick lost a huge share of the air-freshener market when Glade introduced more design-friendly dispensers. Sperry-Rand went into free fall while watching minicomputers steal the market from bulky, cumbersome, and costly mainframes. And DEC disappeared when PCs replaced minis. And now Dell is fighting for market share because competitors have developed an effective direct-to-consumer channel that has taken away Dell's unique advantage.

Understanding changing times will serve you well. The lifeblood of companies like Apple, P&G and Kellogg, DuPont and Siemens are new products that address needs, wants and desires that customers didn't know they had. There are continually conducting research and creating and testing new product ideas in the hope that they discover a benefit that, for whatever reason, captures customers' imagination.

Failing to keep up with the needs, wants, wishes, desires and emotions of the marketplace is the best way to lose customers as well as minimize the opportunity to attract new ones. By not continually searching for products and services, including the ones that customers don't even know they want until presented with them, you will only find yourself playing catch-up with a more aggressive competitor. Whatever you might sell, research ensures that you stay current and relevant to the market.

Tracking customer satisfaction

Assuming that you have a good fix on where your company is headed and you know that what you sell is relevant, you can turn your attention to how well you are doing the job.

One definition of marketing is understanding and then satisfying the wants and needs of customers at a profit to the firm. Continually measuring customer satisfaction, therefore, is critical. And the reason it has to be specifically researched is that repeat sales to the same customer, as very nice as that is, may not indicate satisfaction. Some customers continue to patronize you or buy your brand because they have not identified a better or more convenient option. As soon as one emerges, whoosh, they're gone.

Understanding whether you are satisfying customers is so important for Guerrillas, we've devoted Chapter 16 entirely to the subject.

Is your message being heard?

There was a company called Micro-Switch. It sold large, expensive switching equipment to telephone companies. Its customers were very skilled, highly technical purchasing agents. Every year, Micro-Switch spent about \$2.5 million advertising in technical journals. Year after year, its advertising message stressed its wide product line. One year, it raised the issue of whether anyone read its ads or even knew about the many products it sold.

Several market research studies determined that most purchasing agents couldn't recall seeing the company's advertising. Those who did, said they knew that Micro-Switch had a wide product line, but they didn't know much else about the company. They were unaware of how the company serviced the products it sold or the technical expertise its salespeople brought to customers planning to purchase switching equipment. Further, they said it was important that these areas were addressed before they'd ever call the company in for consultation.

This is a case of a company spending millions from its advertising budget on messages that not only weren't being heard, but which also failed to communicate in a relevant way. The cost of the research was \$30,000.

We're continually amazed that companies will routinely spend hundreds of thousands or millions of dollars on advertising and not spend a small fraction of that to determine whether what they are saying is being heard or whether it communicates an important message.

In considering your research priorities, think about what you spend on advertising, direct mail, sales promotion, public relations, telemarketing or other special events, and ask yourself whether the money is being well spent. If you don't know the answer, research can help.

GENERATING MORE BUSINESS FROM CURRENT CUSTOMERS

Again, when setting research priorities, it's wise to allocate funds early to study current customers. Assuming, then, that you are doing a good job with your customers, your next opportunity for growth is to sell more to those customers.

The relationships current customers have with a company make them more predisposed to listen when the company has something to say. It's far easier to encourage current customers to purchase additional products in the product line, purchase the same products more often, try new products, or take greater advantage of services you offer than it is to find totally new customers. And you "know where they live" so it is easier to communicate with them than with any other segment.

How you generate more business from current customers is, of course, dependent on what you sell. However, assuming you have the potential to sell them more, determining which customer segments have the greatest potential for additional sales efforts becomes important.

If you have a catalog or internet business, a current customer might be one who has purchased from you in the past 30, 60, or 90 days or even beyond. If you are selling automobiles, home décor, or other less frequently purchased products, you might be inclined to define a current customer as having purchased in the past one, two or three years.

There is no pat definition or time period for defining a current customer. It must be done using common sense and an analysis of your current customer database – presuming, of course, that there is a customer database you can access that captures such information. However you define current customers, you must realistically determine the period of time after which it is safe to assume that there is potential for selling to the customer again.

Take a company such as Cabela's, which has a fishing, hunting, and outdoor-products catalog. Cabela's might define a current customer as having made at least one purchase from its catalog or website within the past 30 days. Research and live testing might also prove that it receives the best return on its marketing expenditures if it appeals more strongly to past-30-day buyers. The company might also know that appealing to the past-60- or past-90-day buyers produces profitable returns, although less so. And appealing to buyers beyond 90 days is unprofitable.

Therefore, Cabela's could define past-30-day buyers as current best customers, 31- to 90-day buyers as current good customers, and buyers beyond 90 days as inactive customers. In setting market research priorities, Cabela's might determine that understanding what it has to do to sell more to its best and good customers would likely generate the most immediate return – even though their number may be smaller than the total number of inactive customers.

For inactive customers, it would be important for Cabela's to understand attitudes toward the company and issues that must be addressed so that the relationship can be reinvigorated. And for prospects, or those who have never purchased at all, understanding the hurdles to an initial purchase might dictate that Cabela's takes yet a totally different approach.

Each time you identify a customer or prospect target, you allow for the likelihood that attitudes and perceptions will differ from one segment to the next and that the marketing actions indicated for one segment will be different from those indicated for another. And remember, it can be a waste of money to study a variety of segments at the same time when you are unable to take different actions.

TAKING CUSTOMERS AWAY FROM THE COMPETITION

In determining your list of research priorities, studying what it takes to attract customers from competitors should come after you have shored up your relationship with current customers. That isn't to suggest that attracting competitors' customers is unimportant. Rather, there is no point in spending advertising or promotion budgets or sales-force efforts to lure your competitors' customers only to quickly lose them. Once you have done your homework and determined that your products or services address the needs of your current customers, you can begin to think about research to attract new ones.

In seeking to attract your competitors' customers, the same kinds of research studies that you'd use when studying your own customers apply. Here, though, your target respondents will include your competitors' customers and so will provide intelligence regarding your competitors' strengths and weaknesses. Such research will become a road map to the kinds of strategies that would be effective for determining which competitors are the most vulnerable and the messages that would be most compelling in convincing a competitor's customers to switch to you.

INCREASING THE SIZE OF THE MARKET

A warning

For almost every business there are a significant number of people who have never made a purchase in the category. Sometimes this group is the largest proportion of the population and because of their sheer number it's very tempting to want to bring them into the marketplace. There is an old expression here that is worth repeating: "Don't try to feed the skinny dog; the skinny dog is skinny for a reason."

In the scheme of things, though, attracting new users to your market and to you is the hardest task an individual marketer faces. The hurdles necessary to convince prospects that buying what you sell is in their interest are often substantial. For example, consumers who haven't purchased packaged low-calorie foods or have failed to buy exercise equipment for use in their home, are usually much tougher and more expensive to sell to than consumers who have purchased those products in the past.

And even if you jump hurdle number one by convincing consumers to buy products you sell, you face hurdle number two – convincing them that you are the best option from which to buy. Remember that spending your marketing dollars converting new consumers to your category also builds the category for your competitors. For example, consumers won't necessarily buy your exercise equipment just because you've convinced them exercise equipment is what they need.

We would caution, therefore, that one of last places to expend your marketing efforts, and spend money on marketing research, would be in trying to attract new consumers to your market.

We do realize that sometimes a product or service is so new and different that an existing market doesn't exist. Or maybe your market share is so robust that the only way to grow your business is to expand the marketplace. In such instances, understanding the reasons consumers have not moved into your product category or what it would take to attract customers to your new product or service, and you, is indeed the way to proceed.

Don't be surprised, though, if you conduct research among the uninitiated and find that they have little to say, don't care about you or your products, or don't even have a relevant point of view to discuss your issues. This in and of itself is an important finding and will show you the hurdles you will have to overcome to succeed with such a difficult target.

5

How to set a research budget

Budgeting for research is not a precise science. Here are a number of guidelines that could be considered in setting your research budget.

1. Allocating a percentage for research out of the overall marketing budget

If a company spends $50 million on marketing programs, anywhere from 0.5 per cent ($250,000) to 5 per cent ($2,500,000) might be allocated to research. In the case of companies such as Kraft or P&G, where there are many different brands, the research is generally allotted per brand using the above percentage ranges.

2. Allocating a percentage of the total marketing communications budget

Sometimes the advertising budget or the marketing communications budget alone is used in allocating research funds. The same percentages sited above (0.5 to 5 per cent) are used to allocate research dollars.

In fact, occasionally ad agencies are required by contract to spend a percentage of the advertising dollars spent with them on researching their client's advertising messages. Many feel it is the responsibility of their agencies to prove that the creative work resonates with the customer.

Guerrillas who spend a significant amount of money on marketing communications through an ad or marketing agency might try to insist their agency allocate a percentage of their fee to marketing research.

By the way, trade magazines typically allocate what they term "promotional allowances" to clients who buy space. One of the "free" goods they offer is research among the magazine's readership.

3. Allocating a percentage of sales

Some companies, particularly industrial or B2B companies that don't have substantial marketing or advertising budgets, often allocate research as a percentage of sales. Anywhere from 0.5 to 1 per cent is typical.

4. Assessing needs

A popular method to determine the research allocation is to list the projects that should be undertaken in the coming year and assign dollar figures to each project. An initial list is usually reviewed by those who will use the research results. This could be any number of people in the company, or perhaps the company's vendors might lend their expertise. From this collaborative review, projects are added that are believed necessary or eliminated where felt unnecessary.

5. Ad hoc

In large companies, the bane of a researcher's existence is the need to convince the holder of the budget to allocate funds on an ad hoc basis each and every time a research issue surfaces. In such instances there may be a research budget that is allocated, but the researcher is constantly forced to justify the use of the funds. However, this isn't completely bad, as it forces the researcher to consider whether the research is really needed and whether the cost will produce actionable results.

The problem with ad hoc research is that it doesn't provide a strong strategic focus regarding the forward-thinking issues that need to be addressed to grow the company or brand. When conducting ad hoc research, issues tend to be tactical in nature and responsive to immediate problems and, therefore, not impact strategic decision making.

6. Some combination of the above

Often, a firm research budget is agreed upon that will accommodate a number of strategic and tactical studies for the coming year. Additionally, there is an ad hoc "slush fund" that is available when unexpected issues arise throughout the year and research is indicated.

7. No research budget at all

This is akin to ad hoc budgeting, with many companies not allocating a research budget at all. In such cases, the budget might be in the hands of the president, director of marketing, or brand, product or advertising management. Research is then undertaken only when management feels the need is particularly strong. Unfortunately, not having a research budget is indicative of management's attitude toward the value of research.

Whichever budgeting process is used, it is important that a degree of flexibility should exist. No one can predict with complete certainty whether every research project that might be planned in a fourth quarter budgeting process will be necessary the following June.

Likewise, issues may surface throughout the year that cannot be anticipated and become a priority. What is ultimately important in research budgeting is that a commitment be made to improve decision making by spending research dollars. It is then incumbent upon the company to decide which budgeting process is the best to follow to that end.

DETERMINING A MEANINGFUL RESEARCH BUDGET

For small companies and entrepreneurs, research is one of the last things they think they can afford. Mostly, research is viewed as a highly discretionary expense, one that is difficult to justify because research costs aren't easily attributable to immediate paybacks.

The owner of a small manufacturing company once said, "If I spend $50,000 on research, will I get $100,000 back?" The response: "If you don't spend the money on research, how will you know that you won't ultimately waste $500,000 advertising your product using the wrong message? Or how will you know you missed the opportunity to earn back $500,000?"

Another said, "I could hire two salespeople for the cost of the research. If I do that, I know how much in sales and profit I can expect." The response was: "Maybe you should hire one salesperson and spend the money you would have paid the second to learn about your customers and why they aren't buying more from you. In this way you can increase the effectiveness of the salespeople you now have. It just might be that, if your salespeople were better informed, their selling efforts would increase dramatically. Right now hiring more salespeople may be like shoveling sand against the tide."

Trusting that marketing research will provide a meaningful return on investment is always an issue for Guerrillas. As researchers we strongly believe that well-planned studies will lead to smarter decisions which, in turn, will increase sales and profits that would not have happened otherwise. This makes it all the more critical that great care be taken in planning the research and anticipating the kind of actions that will be taken when the research is completed.

It is also important to realize that research might suggest action should not be taken. When considering a new venture or change of course, there are always costs associated with the risk. Often, research will indicate that an idea is not worth pursuing or that the money necessary to do the job effectively might be beyond company means. In such cases, the payback from the research is the prevention of costly mistakes.

In essence, then, a meaningful research budget is whatever it takes to get the job done – to get the information needed for making wiser decisions. Sometimes it can be as little as several thousand dollars and rarely have we found that an initial research plunge needed to be more than $25,000.

Another important budgeting factor is whether you conduct the research yourself, thus saving the costs associated with using research suppliers or consultants. This is a decision that should be made only after you have a better understanding of the research process, which will result when you complete this book.

COMING TO GRIPS WITH A BUDGET

There are three scenarios that are usually in play when determining research budgets:

1. "First project look–see" budget.
2. "It feels about right" budget.
3. "Let's do it right" budget.

1. The "first project look–see"

This approach is applicable for companies that have never spent money on research. They might determine that a problem persists after attempting to solve it in any number of ways. Or an issue might cry for fresh thinking and a different perspective, and research is looked to for solutions.

"Let's toss some money at it and maybe we'll learn something" is the thinking that typifies the first project look–see. The fact is that first-time research users often come to the research on a wing and a prayer. This is not necessarily bad. Getting to any point where research is given an opportunity is a big step forward.

Focus groups are clearly the most popular research approach for first-time users. It is almost always compelling and revelatory to hear customers and prospects talk about you and your issues. One multistate homebuilder with 20 years of experience said after observing his first focus group: "I have never learnt more about my business than I did in the past two hours." Frequently first-timers feel that getting new customers is their biggest problem and the one that they want to research.

For first timers, as previously noted, the quickest way for them to increase their business is to do a better job among current customers.

However, first-time users also tend not to look beyond the results of the first project. Although they may feel it necessary to take an unbiased look at a particularly nagging problem, they do not always generalize to the use of research as a way of life. Mostly, they are seeking a simple, one thing to do, silver bullet answer that is a sure fire approach to growing their business. They are often disappointed when the research points to many areas that need attention.

If you are a first project look–see company, though, you should plan on spending in the vicinity of $15,000 to $20,000 with an outside research company on that first project. And, if you think you can do the same project without outside help, cut that figure in half.

2. "It feels about right"

Perhaps you are trying to set a 12-month research budget. You can look at company sales and take an industry percentage (anywhere from 0.5 to 1 per cent of sales) to determine a research budget. You can allocate a percentage of your marketing or advertising budget. Or you can do almost any other kind of number crunching to come up with a figure.

Most often new research users trying to set a research budget tend to do so on a "feels right" basis. Most likely there will have been some success with a first project look–see, and research is now viewed as a potentially valuable ongoing tool. The company will regard research more as a series of projects than as an occasional here-and-there project – as a tool to bring a more disciplined approach to decision making.

Committing to any kind of yearly research budget is a big step. And arriving at a specific figure will probably require a series of compromises.

Because the money must initially come from somewhere, it becomes a give-and-take process. Perhaps less is budgeted for salary increases, new equipment or R&D. Maybe it is determined that the money should come straight from the bottom line.

In deciding how to budget for research, follow this line of thought:

One of the best reasons to conduct market research is that it is a form of low-cost business insurance. You can insure your company against making a big mistake – even an enterprise threatening mistake – by the judicious research study. You may cancel a bad idea or delay a new product you're hot on that needs to be reworked. Remember that at least eight out of 10 new products fail and you are not likely to beat the odds if you don't do some research.

Whatever rationale is ultimately followed, consider that a yearly research budget of $100,000 could generate four to seven meaningful studies. If you think you can conduct those studies without outside help, cut that figure by 40 to 50 per cent or double the amount of research you can carry out.

3. "Let's do it right"

Setting a research budget on the basis of company goals is usually the best way to go. If you choose this route, use a professional researcher in the budgeting process. Explore what you are trying to accomplish in the next 12 months and focus on the areas where research can help you achieve your goals. Consider both strategic and tactical issues. Make a wish list of projects that you'd like to do.

By retaining a research professional in this process, you'll probably be happy to learn that one large strategic research study will support a broadly defined research goal and wide range of secondary objectives and be less costly than a series of smaller studies. You also might find it to be less expensive to delay smaller tactical studies until you can combine several into one.

And, again, as with any budgeting process, you'll no doubt have to make compromises. If you choose the "do it right" approach though, you'll realize that research is essential to the way you conduct your business. And, as a result, you will find that the money you budgeted for research, whatever the amount, can be spent better than you imagined.

Of course, it depends on the size of your company and your resources, but doing research the right way may produce a research budget reaching beyond six figures.

WHAT BUSINESS ARE YOU IN?

Your research budget will obviously be impacted by the nature and size of your business.

Business-to-business marketers have a more limited customer and prospect base to study than do consumer packaged-goods companies, but they are harder to reach. Local or regional companies also have a smaller customer base to consider than do national companies.

Irrespective of your industry, however, there is a price tag associated with each potential target that you might research. Here are some likely targets that any business could study:

- Studying current customers could necessitate including targets such as those who:
  - are your best or most profitable customers compared to those who are your worst or most unprofitable;

- may have purchased once in the recent past, but not a second time;
- were heavy purchasers in the recent past, but stopped buying;
- currently purchase from you, but also purchase a substantial amount from your competitors;
- first came to your company as a result of various sales efforts (e.g. salesperson solicitation, direct mail/internet solicitation, telemarketing solicitation, referral, etc.).
- Studying your competitors' customers would include targets that might:
  - have purchased from you a year ago or more, but are no longer active customers;
  - be highly satisfied or dissatisfied with your competitors;
  - have purchased from more than one of your competitors, but have not considered purchasing from you.
- Studying non-buyers in your product category could include those who:
  - have purchased in your product category, but have done so long ago;
  - have never purchased in your product category, but whom you determine to have a higher probability of buying vs those who have a lower probability of ever buying.

While the nature and size of your business will impact how much you can afford to invest, by themselves they will not dictate where you place your research priorities. That's why you're a Guerrilla. What you will find, though, is that from year to year, as your learning increases, you'll want to dig deeper. Research targets that today don't seem to offer much payback become the ones that will offer the best potential for growth tomorrow.

DIGGING DEEPER

Calculating the return on marketing research

One of the hottest topics in all of marketing is calculating an ROI for marketing expenditures. The concept is quite straightforward. CEOs, Boards and Guerrillas want to know what return they'll receive on the marketing dollars they allocate. If a return can be calculated on a new capital project, why not for marketing expenditures in total and by an individual activity such as research?

ROI means, of course, return on investment or profits derived from an investment divided by that investment and expressed as a percentage. For example, if a large company earns $1 million in profits and spends $10 million on marketing efforts, the marketing ROI would be 10 per cent. If a Guerrilla earns $100,000 from his products and spends $1 million on marketing, the return is the same 10 per cent.

As a generalization, the amount spent on marketing is usually not that difficult to calculate. And an overall return is not that hard to calculate either – after the year is ended. The issue with overall marketing or marketing research ROI comes in calculating it in advance; that is, calculating whether making the expenditure is likely to generate more profit than not making the expenditure – or by making a different expenditure.

And for Guerrillas with limited financial resources, estimating the payback from marketing communication expenditures or for developing a new website or for making an expenditure on marketing research is far more important than it is for a large company.

For some aspects of marketing, ROI is relatively easy to calculate. For example, with direct marketing the costs of such elements as list acquisition, catalog or mail-package design and printing and postage can be exactly calculated – as can be the resulting revenue generated. Often, too, e-marketing returns can be closely calculated as can such ancillary marketing efforts as couponing, rebates, individual trade show appearances or customer appreciation programs.

The problem is that all marketing activities are collectively intertwined to produce the revenue results. Therefore, measuring the individual contribution of such elements as advertising or public relations programs, incentive programs for sales people and marketing research can become difficult.

Making a list and checking it twice

One way to estimate a return on investment in marketing research is to list all the research you might undertake, given a particular budget. Say your sales are $5 million and you spend $75,000 on research, or 1.5 per cent of your sales. Practically speaking, this might buy you four studies:

1. A focus group study among your customers and prospects to determine the many reasons customers buy from you and prospects buy from your competitors.
2. A survey among customers where they rank order of the reasons why they are purchasing from you less often than in the past.
3. A determination of which of four alternative marketing communication approaches is the strongest.
4. A customer satisfaction study that shows areas of strength and weakness regarding your customer service reps.

Would this be worth $75,000? Would it point to weaknesses or vulnerabilities that you have in the way customers and prospects perceive you? Would it lead to a new communications direction that would motivate prospects to try you? Would it point to areas where your customer service reps are weak and likely costing you incremental business?

Most likely it would. And, if you bit the bullet and spent the $75,000, you'd probably wonder how you ever ran your business without the knowledge the studies generated.

Calculate a break-even

Another very practical method is to calculate the break-even amount of incremental sales that would have to result in order to pay for the research.

Say you are an industrial manufacturer of forklifts and are planning to launch a new forklift. Your goal is to develop a new model that would attract customers who buy forklifts from your competitors.

You determine that the maximum prospects might pay for your new fork lift is $20,000 and that the cost to manufacture and market each unit would be $15,000. You are considering conducting focus groups to give the design team guidance in determining the features prospects want in a new forklift and marketing communications messages that would attract attention. The plan is to conduct six focus groups in order to represent the type of prospects you wish to attract; the research will cost $35,000.

Here, the ROI on the research is easily determined. If the profit margin per machine is $5,000, you'd have to sell seven more machines as a result of doing the research than you would without the research. Does this sound reasonable? Do you think what you'll learn will enable just seven more units to be sold? If your answer is "Yes," do the research.

Below is the formula for marketing research break-even in units. Try applying it the next time you are faced with a decision of whether or not to conduct marketing research.

Break-even in units = (cost of the marketing research) ÷ (margin/unit)

Break-even in units = (cost of the marketing research) ÷ (selling price/units − cost of goods sold/unit)

Break-even in units = $35,000 ÷ ($20,000 − $15,000)

Break-even in units = $35,000 ÷ $5,000 = 7

Are your hands sweaty?

At its purest, research is supposed to guide companies in making the best decisions possible. So when do you engage in research? John Lees of Kimberly-Clark put it this way:

> We're forced to make decisions with or without marketing research. We look at the decision we have to make and what it will cost us if we're wrong. If the value of making sure the decision is right is important, we'll do the research.

This is really a simple idea: if the cost of being wrong makes you very uncomfortable, then buy some research insurance. How much insurance? We suggest 5 to 10 per cent of the size of the potential loss.

Assume you are contemplating spending $350,000 to expand your restaurant. It might be worth spending somewhere between $17,500 and $35,000 to talk to current patrons to see if they'll likely visit more often, and to talk to those who live nearby but have not visited in a while to see if they'll pay a visit when you re-open. Of course, the research should be designed to explore many issues like hours of operation, décor and menu options, special promotions you might consider to drive traffic as well as prices that your menu could support for your neighborhood.

Have a little faith

Advertising is a key expense that usually is budgeted as a percentage of sales. However, many Guerrillas wisely increase their ad budgets when sales are soft. Sometime they don't know if ad budget increases will help, but they know losing consumer awareness is a great way to watch sales spiral down even more. In other words, they have faith that advertising will work.

Sales promotion budgets are often considered an expense whose return is difficult to measure. Guerrillas will go a long time without doing any research, but would not let a long time lapse without sale flyers and coupons. They have faith that when conducting frequent sales and promotions, the business will get a positive payback.

Adding operations staff in order to better serve customers is certainly considered an expense, but there is faith that better service will lead to increased sales.

For all these areas faith is often good enough. No return is calculated.

Try a test

Here's an idea …

Take a product or service you sell and give yourself at least a six month time period. Bite the bullet and let good research guide your marketing direction. Take another product and service and don't conduct any research. Make marketing decisions here as you normally would – based on gut, intuition, and your entrepreneurial instinct.

If you are company that sells only one product or service, but you do so in multiple markets or locations, let research guide direction for some locations and not others. In both these cases, compare the incremental sales and profits for the situations where research was used to guide your marketing decisions to where it wasn't. If your incremental growth is greater than the cost of the research and the growth in your non-research market, you'll have your answer.

Many Guerrillas have stand-alone businesses in one location. If this is the case, learn as much as you can afford about your current customers and follow the direction suggested by the research for the six month test period. Then compare sales for the period to the same six month period the year before.

We know the ultimate value of marketing research is to guide smart decision making. And we're sure you now realize that marketing research and smart decision making go hand in hand. Used together, we have no doubt that the ROI on your research investment will be one of the biggest surprises that you can imagine.

You're now five chapters in to *MORE Guerrilla Marketing Research*. By this time, we trust you feel research has a role in your business!

6

Using research professionals

SHOULD GUERRILLAS TRY DIY RESEARCH? MAYBE!

What we do know is that a good research professional is worth his or her weight in gold. However, if you have the time and interest to learn what it takes to do effective research, there is no reason you can't become a do-it-yourselfer and execute studies yourself at a fraction of the cost it would take to use a professional. At the least, you can determine those areas in which you don't feel qualified and then employing a research consultant on a limited basis would be prudent.

Assuming that you would hire a professional for at least some of your research or for the first few research projects until you learn enough to be comfortable flying solo, the remainder of this chapter will help you locate the best person or company and determine what to pay for aid. If you are intent on conducting your research yourself, this chapter will still help you achieve that goal as it lays out the key cost elements of common research projects so that you can identify areas where it's possible to save money on the projects you conduct.

HOW TO JUDGE CREDENTIALS

The American Marketing Association (www.marketingpower.com) is the primary association for professional marketing researchers in the US. The AMA lists more than 40,000 member companies and more than 750,000 individual members. There are over 1,100 market research suppliers listed as members. In looking at the Chicago business-to-business *Yellow Pages*, for example, there are more than 225 listings under the heading "Market research and analysis." So chances are good that there are plenty of research suppliers near you. And, if you really want to investigate the options beyond this, go to your favorite search engine, type in "market research companies," and start scanning the millions of listings.

In Western Europe, Asia, and Latin America, there are also many professional research organizations. In Europe, for example, you can access www.esomar.org, www.aemri.org, or www.efamro.org and find thousands of professional marketing research companies and field services. If you want to conduct research in Asia, Latin America, or Eastern Europe, simply do an internet search and type in "marketing research organizations" preceded by your country of interest (e.g. "Asia marketing research organizations") and you'll find all the resources you need.

There is no shortage of market research suppliers or individual research consultants available to assist you in your research effort. The trick comes in finding those resources best for you. To find them and pay them the least amount of money, follow these guidelines.

1. Find a smaller research supplier

Even a one-person research supplier or consultant would be good. Individuals, who work out of their homes, have little overhead to consider when pricing their services. It should be no surprise that the bigger the research company, the more overhead will go into the pricing of its projects.

2. Check credentials

Obviously, looking at a research supplier's website or reading its literature will tell you what services it offers, but it won't completely determine whether the company is right for you. It's not as much about the supplier you hire as it is about the person working on your studies. If the supplier looks like it's for you, call it, explain your situation and ask to speak to the person who would work on your business.

3. Meet the supplier personally

If a telephone conversation gives you a good feeling about the researcher, request a personal meeting. Prior to that meeting, ask for a résumé or biography of the person(s) you'd be working with as well as a client list with the names and phone numbers of references you can contact. You want to ensure the following.

The person you'd work with has at least 10 years of experience

While somewhat less might be okay, make sure that you are dealing with someone who has been around long enough to have seen a wide variety of problems. It is reasonable to expect a researcher at a large supplier to be involved in at least 50 projects per year. Having 10 years of experience will likely have exposed a person to whatever issues you might be facing. If you are considering a one-person shop, you definitely want a 10-plus-year veteran of the research business.

The person has some experience in your line of business and/or with your target audiences

If you are a retail business, you probably don't want someone whose career has focused on conducting research for food or beverage companies. If you are selling technology-related products, you would be prudent to find someone who has a technical education and/or research experience with technology companies. It would be quite beneficial, but not essential, to find a researcher who has worked for one of your competitors. Whether consciously or not the researcher will use that wealth of experience to make your project better.

Hire someone with user-side experience

If you are considering a one-person supplier or consultant, make sure he or she has previous experience in the research department of a large company or advertising agency research department. Both backgrounds will provide in-depth knowledge in translating your marketing problems to marketing research objectives and ultimately to effective market research methodologies. Hiring a researcher who only has had supplier-side experience should be done cautiously. Many have a limited perspective in translating an overarching marketing strategy to specific market research goal and specific objectives. So make sure that the supplier you hire has served clients in both consulting and project execution capacities.

The person should have worked with a range of clients

The person should have worked for more than one company, more than one size of company and in more than one industry. If you find someone who knows only the Apple, Kraft, General Motors, P&G, or Microsoft way of doing research, you are likely to get very-big-company research solutions to your problem. Further, if a researcher has worked only in very large companies, his or her perspective might be limited. Large-company researchers are certainly smart people, but someone from Kraft or P&G will likely approach your project with a big budget mentality. The perfect combination would be a person who has worked in research for small-, medium- and large-sized companies.

The person is an all-around researcher

Some researchers know only how to conduct focus groups and couldn't analyze a data set to save their lives. Others have experience only in certain kinds of research (e.g. product testing, advertising testing, sensory research), giving them a limited perspective. Most importantly, you don't want an individual who is likely to fit only the methodologies he or she knows into your problem.

Hiring a professor

If you can find a teacher or professor of marketing research at a nearby college or university, you might have stumbled on to something. We're not talking here about a professor of marketing, but rather about a professor of marketing research.

It usually takes some practical experience to be a good teacher of research. Practitioners who gravitate to teaching often have rich and varied backgrounds that include a great deal of relevant experience. And some professors charge less for their time than research professionals, because it represents incremental income. Just make sure you follow the guidelines above when you consider hiring a professor as your research supplier. The last thing you want is an egghead who will wow you with academic jargon and recommend impractical textbook approaches.

ARE RESEARCH SUPPLIERS OR CONSULTANTS REALLY ALL THAT NECESSARY?

You can become an acceptably competent researcher, if you have the time and interest, just as you can become capable of writing a bit of copy, producing a cable TV commercial, taking the straightforward photographs of products for ads, or using computer software to keep the books for your company. The trick is not to move too fast or waste money by getting in over your head.

Over a reasonable period of time you can learn to conduct an effective focus group, write a productive questionnaire, deal with field services that collect data, engage firms to process your data, and become good at interpreting results. However, you'll probably make a lot of mistakes, and waste a lot of time and money if you try it all at once.

If you have found someone you trust and think that person can help you, learn how to get his or her services at the most affordable price.

UNDERSTANDING SUPPLIER PRICING

When buying research, it is important to know something about the process. In general, there are two types of research companies. There are full-service research suppliers that primarily provide problem definition, help in developing your research goal and objectives, project execution and control, and analytical and reporting services. And there are field-service suppliers whose primary function is to provide data-collection services to full-service suppliers or directly to end-users.

Full-service suppliers provide project specifications to the field-service suppliers. This includes the type of study being conducted, the anticipated length of the questionnaire to be completed, the profile and number of respondents to be interviewed, and the manner in which data are to be collected.

Field-service suppliers, in turn, price their work to the full-service suppliers or end-users. The full-service suppliers make a large percentage of their profits by marking up field-service costs. If you become the direct client of the field-service supplier, you will save this mark-up. You should also know that field-service suppliers realize that they are often facing a competitor's bid. Therefore, most will negotiate price – at least somewhat.

There are a number of research suppliers that are full-service and have their own data-collection field-service arm. These tend to be very large companies, e.g. The Gallup Organization, Synovate, National Family Opinion, J D Powers and Associates, and The Roper Company. These are highly reputable research organizations that tend to service Fortune 1000 companies.

While certainly capable of both planning and executing research studies, these large companies have far higher overhead costs than smaller full-service research companies without a field-service arm. Having a high overhead means added costs, which must be passed on in the pricing of their projects. For Guerrillas, using these companies can be cost-effective for certain types of projects, which we discuss in Chapter 13, but as a steady diet, their higher costs are unnecessary.

COSTING A PROJECT

When full-service research suppliers price their projects, 50 per cent or more of the cost of the project usually goes to the consultant's field-service suppliers, not to the consultant's bank account. In the case of focus groups or other qualitative research projects the consultant will incur out-of-pocket costs to field services for:

- renting a facility where the focus groups will be conducted;
- recruiting costs for the field service to screen the right respondents and make sure that they show up at the right time;
- monetary incentives to respondents for participating;
- miscellaneous costs such as respondent and client food, videotaping/creating DVDs, or other material costs necessary to complete the project.

In the case of a survey, the consultant will pay field services for:

- List acquisition costs for phone numbers, mailing addresses, etc.
- The professional interviewers they provide for screening likely respondents and administering the questionnaire to the desired number of respondents.
- Line charges associated with phone studies and perhaps programming costs if the interviews are placed on automated platforms, mall charges associated with collecting data via interviewing consumers in shopping centers, printing and postage charges associated with conducting a study by mail, or programming and site maintenance costs associated with internet research as well as costs to send electronic invitations to participate, and/or setting up and hosting a questionnaire link.
- Depending on the methodology, separate data entry fees may be required, as might data maintenance fees for multiple-wave studies.
- Monetary incentives that might be required to ensure respondent cooperation in the research.
- If there are open-ended questions, charges for editing and coding responses so they can be quantitatively analyzed.
- Charges for having the questionnaires data-processed.
- Charges for statistical procedures that might be necessary when analyzing the data.

If you choose to work directly with field services, you should be ready to tell them exactly what you want them to do. Rarely, if ever, would you use a field service for professional advice on how to conduct or analyze a study. Field-service personnel don't generally have experience in designing or analyzing research data. They are, first and foremost, suppliers of respondents and are best used when told exactly what should be accomplished.

In the US, because there are only voluntary trade groups such as AMA and CASRO, and no formal accreditation agency, if you wanted to become a full-service researcher supplier, you would find it very easy to do because all you would have to do is put out a sign that says, "I'm a research supplier," and find a client who believes you. To price a study, then, all you need do is determine what you want your field services to do and how much you have to pay them to provide you with the number of interviews you need for your research. With that information in hand, plus a few other smaller out-of-pocket costs, you would simply decide how much more you want to charge your client for the project.

In the UK, Spain and France, researcher suppliers can provide proof they follow high quality standards by subjecting themselves to the scrutiny of EFAMRO – Market Research Quality Standard, which was established 1999. When conducting research in these countries, it would be wise to ask a supplier you might use if they have the passed the EFAMRO quality tests. And quite recently an international ISO standard has been issued as well (ISO 20252). You can look for progressive companies around the world starting to say they adhere to this standard.

Do all research suppliers price their projects the same way?

No. And to get the most for your research expenditure, it is necessary to understand supplier pricing. Only by knowing the elements that go into a study can you determine whether or not you are getting good value.

Essentially, marketing research can be purchased from a supplier in two ways. First, it can be purchased as a fixed-cost project. Fixed-cost projects are all-inclusive. That is, the supplier will quote you one cost, which will include fees for helping you define your research objectives, developing a questionnaire for a survey or Discussion Guide for conducting focus groups, collecting data, analyzing results, reporting, and making recommendations.

A fixed-cost quote will also include the supplier's out-of-pocket costs to their field services. These include costs for field services that conduct the actual interviewing for your project, for the data processing that will array the data so that they can be analyzed, for a statistician if special statistical procedures are necessary, and for any other costs associated with completing the project (copy and printing services, preparing necessary exhibits, and so forth).

Fixed-price costing is the most popular approach for full-service research suppliers. Because it is virtually impossible for a research buyer to know how much mark-up and profit are in a fixed-price bid, the only way to know if you are paying more than you should is to get competitive bids. If you get a lower bid from a second company, you might be satisfied that you have been given a good price. In reality, though, all it means is that the second company is more competitive on its pricing. It doesn't necessarily mean that you are getting the best possible price, as a third supplier could be even less expensive.

Second, market research can be purchased at an hourly rate plus out-of-pocket expense costs. Here, the supplier will give you hourly rates for the various services. Some suppliers charge the same hourly rate no matter what the task. Others will charge one rate for their time involved in problem definition and research objective setting, another rate for questionnaire development, another for quality control, and yet another for analyzing the data and developing recommendations. They will then provide you with an estimate of the hours and costs necessary for their services plus the out-of-pocket costs that they would pay their field services and other suppliers.

Given this approach to costing, you know exactly what you are paying in out-of-pocket costs and professional services. This makes it much easier to judge whether one company charges more for its services than another. And while some suppliers are certainly worth more than others, you'll at least have a level playing field when making a decision.

As we pointed out, the vast majority of research suppliers would prefer to work on a fixed-cost basis. Usually, fixed-cost pricing will produce greater revenue than hourly pricing. In fact, some research suppliers refuse to quote hourly rates for their services because it exposes their mark-up structure. If you run into a company like this, we'd suggest that you stay away from them altogether.

Focus group costs

How much will a moderator make on a focus group project?

Let's start with fixed-cost pricing and look at a focus group project.

A typical focus group might consist of four two-hour focus group sessions. The average out-of-pocket costs a supplier will pay a field service if they are conducting a "run of the mill" focus group study will be roughly as shown in Table 6.1.

Table 6.1 Example of out-of-pocket focus group costs

Costs	$
1. Focus group room rental – 4 groups @ $450/group	1,800
2. Recruiting respondents – 10 recruits/group at $100 per recruit for a total of 40 recruits	4,000
3. Respondent incentives – 40 respondents @ $75/respondent	3,000
4. Food, taping and refreshments	300
Total out-of-pocket costs	**9,100**

Let's say the average fee a focus group moderator will charge is $2,500 per group, which includes project design/planning/management, development of a screening questionnaire, preparation of a Discussion Guide, moderation, analysis, report preparation and recommendations. That comes to $10,000 for a four-group study. The fee quoted to the client, without travel, would be:

Moderator fee	$10,000
Out-of-pocket costs	$9,100
Total fixed-price quote	$19,100

This $19,100 cost is subject to a number of upward or downward swings. Some moderators charge far more than $2,500 per group. Many have a moderator fee that can be upward of $4,000, particularly for moderators from a large city such as New York, Chicago or London. Of course, some will charge less than $2,500 depending on their workload, their relationship with the client, their likelihood of leveraging the study into additional studies, or their level of experience.

Further, some moderators may be inclined to take a mark-up, in the 20 per cent range, on the fees charged by their field services. This would add another $1,800 or so to the above fixed-price quote.

Moderators will also make additional money on the respondent incentives they've budgeted. In this example, Table 6.1 shows that $3,000 was budgeted for incentives for 40 respondents. Rarely will the moderator have to pay out the whole $3,000 as it is unlikely that all 40 respondents will show up. If only eight show for each group, it means that only $2,400 in incentives will be paid out. Be aware, though, that it is the rare moderator who will rebate that $600 savings to the client.

Also, field-service costs can vary considerably given the type of respondents to be interviewed. Recruiting and incentive costs for respondents such as company officers, business professionals, purchasing agents, doctors or dentists, lawyers, and financial planners are far more costly than are costs for regular consumers. Recruiting other hard-to-locate consumer targets such as buyers of particular brands, users of products that are rarely purchased, or extremely high-income consumers can also be quite costly.

Saving money on focus group studies

If asked, many moderators will work on an hourly basis and are more than happy to have you pay their field services directly or show you the written cost estimates they receive from the field services. In order to save money on your focus group projects here are a number of suggestions.

1. Get competitive costs. Find at least two acceptable moderators and ask for fixed-price competitive quotes.
2. Ask a third moderator what would be charged by working on an hourly basis. Have the moderator give you the actual written estimate from at least two focus group field services. Compare the fixed and hourly bids and be prepared for a pleasant surprise.
3. Have both the fixed-cost and hourly moderators quote costs for both a full report and a brief summary. You can often obtain most of what you need from a summary report, especially if you view (or review) the focus groups yourself and take good notes. If the purpose of your focus group project is to help you write a more effective questionnaire for a follow-up survey, a full report should not be necessary. The moderator should lower fees by about $500 per group if he or she doesn't have to write a report.
4. Ask the moderator to give you tiered pricing. Many moderators might be willing to accept less per group after the first two groups. Particularly in larger focus group studies where six or eight groups are necessary, there could be a substantial saving on the moderator's fee with tiered pricing.
5. By all means, ask the moderator to rebate the budgeted but unused respondent incentives.
6. Determine whether you can conduct your focus groups in smaller, less expensive markets. In the US, try to stay out of the very large markets such as New York City, Chicago, Boston, Los Angeles, or San Francisco, where field-service costs tend to be 10 to 20 per cent higher. Even large markets such as Atlanta, Milwaukee, Tampa, Nashville, San Antonio, and Sacramento, are often more cost-effective than the major markets cited above. And smaller markets such as Des Moines, Knoxville, Jacksonville, or Fort Wayne, are even less expensive.

   The same holds true for almost any country around the world. Conducting focus groups in London or Paris, for example, would be more expensive than finding a focus group facility in Bath or Lyon. The point is that the larger the market, the more expensive it will be to conduct focus groups. Therefore, you will save money by avoiding large metropolitan areas if smaller areas are adequate for your objectives.
7. Determine whether video recording is necessary. Many moderators will suggest videotaping or DVD recording of focus groups. You should first determine if having a pictorial record of respondents would be valuable for you. Sometimes showing the video to people not attending the groups or to give emphasis in a sales or planning meeting is a good idea, and the extra expense is then warranted – especially because body language matters in interpreting what is

said and because often samples or exhibits are used in the sessions and need to be seen to understand the responses.

Increasingly, though, this is not a major source of savings as competitive facilities are offering such recordings for free (or have the expense bundled into other aspects of their pricing like room rentals).

Also consider whether FocusVision or ActiveGroup services are needed. These are services that stream the sessions in real time to a secure internet site so they can be remotely viewed from anywhere. They also record and store the sessions online for later viewing. The cost is around $1,500 per day.

8. Watch your food and refreshment costs. It always amazes clients when they're charged $50 by a focus group facility for the $15 pizza munched on while watching the group. Many facilities will take ridiculous mark-ups on the food they provide you or your respondents. Others are happy to bill only the costs that they incur. Be clear on what you are paying for food and refreshments.

How much will a supplier make on a telephone survey?

The fixed-cost quote that you will receive from a supplier conducting a telephone survey is calculated much like a focus group project. To reiterate, it will consist of three elements:

1. How much the full-service supplier will pay in out-of-pocket costs to its field service and other suppliers.
2. How much you are charged for the supplier's personnel who will work on your project.
3. How high the profit mark-up will be on 1 and 2.

Here is an example. Assume you had a telephone survey that you wanted to complete with 300 respondents who had eaten at a fast-food restaurant in the past week. Table 6.2 gives an example that is typical of how a full-service research supplier will arrive at your cost quote.

There are a number of major factors in this quote that affect the final cost:

● How well the supplier has negotiated the out-of-pocket cost with the telephone interviewing services. The $35 cost per completed interview could be high or low. Obviously, this one cost is a major component of your final price, and there is always the question of whether the consultant has negotiated a strongly competitive price with a quality telephone interviewing service.

Table 6.2 Example of telephone survey pricing

Cost component	
a. Out-of-pocket cost:	
Telephone interviewing field service (300 20-minute interviews @ $35 per completed interview)	$10,500
Purchase of random sample of phone numbers	$900
Data processing	$1,000
Statistical analysis (3 regression analyses)	$900
Courier delivery	$100
Printing report	$75
Internal cost allocation for phone, fax, etc.	$50
Supplies/other miscellaneous costs	$50
Total out-of-pocket cost	$13,575
b. Internal labor:	
Project planning (10 hours @ $150/hour)	$1,500
Questionnaire development (10 hours @ $200/hour)	$2,000
Field service project management (5 hours at $100/hour)	$500
Report and recommendations (25 hours at $250 per hour)	$6,250
Total internal labor	$10,250
Total out-of-pocket plus labor cost (a + b)	$23,825
Project mark-up (at 50%)	$11,912
Total	$35,737
Cost quoted to client	$35,700
Cost per interview ($35,700 divided by 300 interviews)	$119

- The estimate of labor hours and the hourly rates for each function. Research suppliers don't know with absolute certainty if they will spend more hours on a project than estimated. In a fixed-cost quote, their return will diminish from a project that becomes a problem and necessitates additional time that can't be charged to you. This is time that could be spent on other projects for other clients. Because of this, research suppliers tend to overestimate the actual hours needed to complete a project. If they are more efficient than they planned, they will enjoy an unusually high profit on the study.
- How their staff are priced. Hourly staff rates for the tasks necessary to complete a project can vary wildly from supplier to supplier.

Some suppliers will have junior staff members work on your project and charge you lower rates. Others will assign senior staff to the project and charge you accordingly. Then, too, some may charge senior staff rates, but assign junior people to your project.

- The mark-up. Larger full-service research companies have greater overhead and must mark up their projects more than smaller companies. The labor rates for larger companies also tend to be higher. While a 50 per cent mark-up is typical for both large and small suppliers, some will mark up 60 per cent, while others may mark up only 40 or 30 per cent. When business is slow, mark-ups tend to go down since suppliers are forced to get projects in the door to cover their fixed overhead and salaries. When business is strong, mark-ups may increase, as the loss of some projects might be a worthwhile risk. Increasing the mark-up to unsuspecting clients in particularly busy times will certainly result in extraordinary full-service supplier profits.

Saving money on your survey

While all this might be interesting, you might be wondering what it means for you. It is very difficult to purchase quality research less expensively if you don't have this background. When you know what you're dealing with, there is no question that you can get a better deal. Follow one or more of the approaches described below the next time you get a cost quote for a survey.

1. Always get two or three fixed-cost estimates from full-service suppliers that you have screened and feel comfortable using. The trick is to make sure that all the suppliers are giving you costs for exactly the same project specifications. Although suppliers hate this, it may necessitate taking the specifications of the project you work out with one supplier and giving those exact specifications to other suppliers.

   If you do this, tell the second supplier that you worked out the methodology with one of their competitors, but that you want them to provide competitive costs nevertheless. They will understand and appreciate your honesty. They might even tend to lower their mark-up because they know they are in a competitive situation. Also tell them that, if they don't agree with the methodology you give them, they should feel free to suggest alternative approaches, in addition. This way you can still compare apples to apples, plus you can look at some oranges as well.

2. Ask yet another supplier to quote for the project, but to separate the out-of-pocket costs from the labor costs. You might find that getting project quotes in this manner will come close to the fixed-price

quotes that you received. This is because the supplier simply adds the normal mark-up into the two costs. However, when costing this way, many suppliers tend to charge less for their labor or take less of a mark-up on their out-of-pocket costs.

3. Compare data gathering methodologies. For many studies there are alternate methods for gathering the data, e.g. telephone vs the internet vs mail. If there are no questioning requirements (e.g. you can't show pictures on the phone, you can't safely ask unaided awareness question via mail) or timing issues (e.g. phone and internet are quite fast, mail is slow) that might preclude or favor a particular form of data gathering, ask your supplier to bid using various methods.

4. Offer to pay 75 per cent of the cost of the project up front, and ask for a discount. Research suppliers, especially the smaller ones, tend to have cash flow issues. When you approve your project, it is normal for the research supplier to invoice you for 50 per cent of the contracted cost with 30 days to pay. The remaining 50 per cent is billed when you receive the final report and are satisfied. Until your money is received, it might be necessary for your supplier to front a significant portion of your project's expenses.

   Also, research suppliers may worry about a client's payment history or even their ability to pay. You might consider telling the supplier that you will write a check the day the invoice is received in return for a discount on a project. By showing concern and good faith in this area, you're likely to find research suppliers (particularly the smaller ones) willing to cut you a better deal.

5. Find a one-person research supplier you trust. Assuming that the person is not swamped with projects, there is no question that costs will be lower than any quotes you receive from a larger research supplier.

6. Defer the project. If you feel that the costs you receive are beyond your budget but you can afford to wait for the research results, ask the supplier if the research might be conducted less expensively when the supplier has more time – say in a month or two.

7. Consider more than one project. Think seriously about conducting more than one research study, whether at the same time or with the second several months later. If your supplier is aware that the first project will lead to a second, and you are ready to commit to more than one project, you are likely to get lower costs on both. This is particularly true if you commit to a significant research budget for the next 12 months. Like other suppliers and consultants, research suppliers are more interested in long-term relationships than in the money they make from your one project. Most are willing to take a lower mark-up when costing several projects than when they are costing only one.

8. Refer the supplier to another client. Give the supplier a lead that turns into another client and watch what happens with your final invoice.

9. Get the 10 per cent back. Research suppliers usually quote their studies plus or minus 10 per cent, for example $19,100 +/–10 per cent or $35,700 +/–10 percent. Ethical research suppliers would never take the 10 per cent contingency without informing you when they run into unusually high expenses. If during the course of your project unanticipated costs arise, the research supplier should inform you of the problem. You can then decide if you want to make additional expenditures or compromise elsewhere.

   You should know that it is highly unusual for a supplier to give you back the minus part of the contingency if he or she does better on your project than was estimated. At the end of your project, especially if you are happy and plan to use the supplier again, state that, and ask the supplier's opinion as to how the project turned out. Mention the 10 per cent contingency and inquire about the possibility of lowering the final invoice by some percentage.

10. Offer to pay the research supplier's out-of-pocket expenses directly. Any financial burden that you will assume might be a reason for the research supplier to lower the fees.

ARE RESEARCH SUPPLIERS WORTH WHAT THEY CHARGE?

Unequivocally, *yes*. And, unequivocally, *no*.

If you use a larger research vendor – any supplier with more than five employees – it is likely a junior person will work on your business and the larger the research supplier, the greater the likelihood. That means that the person who sold you the project and in whom you have placed all your trust may not be paying as much attention to how your project is executed as you think. This might not be bad if that person is at least available when his or her expertise is critical. Of course, you can never be sure this will happen.

Large, full-service research suppliers have powerful and convincing project principals and often weak and inexperienced project executors. If an inexperienced project executor is the person writing your questionnaire, analyzing your data and writing your recommendations, you are not getting your money's worth. If so, is the research worth as much as you are being charged?

The answer here would obviously be no.

If you haven't guessed, we believe that the best research option for Guerrillas is smaller research suppliers. These are usually companies in which the person executing your project is the person helping you plan the project. Often this means dealing with the company owner or a partner. In such instances, your questionnaire is being written by someone who has written hundreds or thousands of questionnaires and has analyzed data for hundreds or thousands of studies.

There is simply no substitute for this kind of hands-on experience. Are these research consultants worth what they charge? Unequivocally, yes! (And our contact information is available in the "About the authors" section of this book.)

Getting what you're paying for

You get far more for your research investment when dealing with a small supplier and a highly experienced researcher. You are a very important client to a small supplier. The success of your research effort and the resulting growth of your business will provide additional opportunities that are far more meaningful to a smaller supplier than to a larger one.

Large research suppliers are far more concerned with the Kraft, P&G, Siemens, or Coca-Colas of the world, companies whose yearly research budgets are in the millions. In 2006 for example, Unilever research expenditures were reported to be $600 million. For a large research supplier, capturing just 5 per cent of that figure means an astounding $30 million in revenue.

To put that $30 million in perspective, using CASRO data (The Council of American Survey Research Organizations), we estimate that the total marketing research expenditures on primary research in the US in 2005 (e.g. only surveys and focus groups) was in excess of $4.4 billion. CASRO reported that only 14 per cent of its research members had revenue in excess of $30 million. It seems clear that large suppliers are certainly better at focusing their attention on big companies than they are on Guerrillas.

For many large research suppliers, but certainly not all, a small research client is often more aggravation than opportunity. By all means, when you find a large supplier that has better capabilities to complete your project, use them. Just make sure you have experienced people working on your project.

BEING A GOOD CLIENT

You have completed your due diligence. You've found a research supplier that you trust, designed your study, negotiated a good price, and given the go-ahead to begin the project. All that effort will be minimized if you aren't a good client. To get the most bang from your budget and from your supplier, follow the easy *dos* and *don'ts* shown in Table 6.3.

It's a two-way street. The best research suppliers have a keen interest in making your project as insightful as possible. The best clients show respect for that effort.

Table 6.3   Being a good client

DO	DON'T
Pay attention to the research schedule	Be hard to reach, be unresponsive or show little regard to the agreed-upon timelines
Make sure others are involved in the project	Seemingly give responsibilities to others who must always check with you before a decision can be made
Stay aware of the progress of the study	Be a pest. The research company will inform you if there are issues that need your attention
Expect the results when promised	Push for faster results. It will only minimize the thinking time the supplier spends analyzing your data
Engage people from the research supplier in a personal meeting or presentation soon after results are available	Let the report sit around gathering dust
Use the research supplier in your decision-making process	Ignore the contribution of the supplier or consultant by not engaging him or her in how you use the research
Pay your invoices when they are expected	Worry the consultant about your ability to pay and make him or her bug you about overdue invoices

7

How much research should you do?

A LITTLE *CAN* GO A LONG WAY

There are many ways to begin your research process. An inexpensive customer satisfaction survey or a series of focus groups are common. How far you go after that is often a function of the benefits you get from the first study.

We've known clients who have taken advantage of what was learnt from a couple of focus groups over a six month period, making changes in how they approach customer service, what they say in their advertising and how their salespeople approach prospects. And we've seen how an expenditure as low as $15,000 for a survey can provide information that takes a year or more to fully digest and integrate. And we've also seen very expensive research whose findings were ignored or forgotten.

A quarter-million-dollar market structure study of the restaurant industry went completely ignored because the presenting company, in the client's Board Room, didn't gear its presentation of findings to the Chairman, President and other senior executives who were there. They began with an arcane discussion of statistical procedures, lost the audience in the first five minutes, and were directed to leave the room. The rest of the meeting was cancelled and no one was ever permitted to refer to that research again.

For another client we found that research had been conducted by several different departments and several different executives in those departments, but that no one had ever looked at it all together. The company understood its market no better than the fabled blind men understood what an elephant was. Recall they each grabbed a different part of the elephant and declared it to be like a snake (trunk), fan (ear), wall (side), spear (tusk), tree (leg) and rope (tail).

And we've commonly encountered newer employees in a company having no idea of what had been learnt in prior research.

In Chapter 4 we talked about getting started in research. We suggested that research into the best approaches to keeping current customers, motivating them to purchase more frequently, and attracting new customers away from your competition are all good options. The question of how much research to do, though, is usually a question of how much value you receive on your research effort – whether it's your first research effort or research has been part of your business over a period of time.

The need to maximize the return from your first research effort, and even the last one, is important enough to bear repetition. So we'll say it again: maximizing the returns from your research efforts is so important that if you fail, you're likely to leave money on the table.

RESEARCH CAN HAVE A LONG SHELF LIFE

The shelf life of most research studies doesn't expire for many months, or even years. What is learnt has an extended "use-by date." Granted, the speed with which technology is changing the marketplace can sometimes seem faster than a speeding bullet, but let's take a realistic look at that:

- Starbucks was founded in 1971. By 1992, there were 192 Starbuck stores.
- Costco was started over 30 years ago in 1976.
- Amazon has been around since 1994, but recently transformed itself from a bookseller into a sales platform for many products.
- Absolute introduced flavored vodkas in 1995.
- Google first hit our computer screens in 1998, but it took a while for it to figure out that its customer was not the one doing the search, but rather the company being searched for.
- The iPod was introduced in 2001.
- Blackberrys have been popular since 2002.
- Facebook was launched in 2004.

Today these businesses could probably all be classified as "mature." A mature market is defined as one where repeat sales are equal to or greater than sales to new customers. Mature also suggests a level of sophistication in operations. Marketing research that might be conducted today for these mature businesses will certainly be relevant for at least 12 months and perhaps a great deal longer.

Do you think these companies and others of their size revisit the findings from today's research a month later, much less a year later? Not generally!

Guerrillas can learn from large companies when it comes to the value of marketing research. In this case they can learn what not to do. Marketplaces don't change that quickly without major upheavals. And, just because large companies waste many research dollars by taking a "one and done" look at their studies doesn't mean Guerrillas should follow this poor example.

As we write this, the US and the rest of the world are experiencing an economic meltdown. Although consumers are cutting back on their spending, it doesn't fundamentally change how they perceive the products and services they purchase or the images that brands evoke. And while today's energy marketplace is dictating a renewed interest in fuel-efficient automobiles, significant changes will take years in coming to fruition.

Even these once in a generation financial disruptions don't render totally irrelevant the findings from your most recent research study. There is, however, a tougher business environment, which makes it harder to keep customers happy so that they stay with you. And this is why revisiting your past research and looking for new insights makes all the sense in the world.

So, again, don't make the mistake that many large businesses make. Don't have a meeting or two to scrutinize the results from your last important study and assume you've mined the research for all it's worth. Realize there is a process you can follow so that each research study can be used to its fullest.

HOW TO MAXIMIZE THE RETURN ON RESEARCH

Assuming you want the input of others, here's what we suggest (if you are on your own, complete steps 1 and 2, then skip to step 6 and continue):

1. You and the others should review the research individually and in a relaxed atmosphere. Sit back and take it in. Read it like a novel and don't jump to conclusions.
2. Scan the study again and jot down what you think it's telling you and what actions you might take. Give everyone a specific date to complete steps 1 and 2. We suggest no more than five business days.
3. Subsequently, if a research supplier conducted the research on your behalf, have them present the study to you and the others and let them speculate on the actions you should take. If you conducted the

research internally, have the person responsible for spearheading the effort make the presentation.

4. During the presentation, everyone should add to their list of potential actions as they occur.

5. Get together with the group the next day, or perhaps right after the presentation, and appoint a recorder. Have the recorder publically list everyone's potential action steps on an easel pad. Brainstorm or build on ideas as they are listed (see Chapter 10 on brainstorming techniques).

6. Alone or with the help of whomever you wish, decide which action steps could be taken in the next 12 months. Also list action steps that would take longer than 12 months to complete, but that you feel are important.

7. Write a brief (no more than three pages) action plan with dates for completion and assigned personnel for each action. Begin with the actions that you can immediately implement.

    Be disciplined. Mark your calendar on the dates you set for each action. First 30, then 60, then 180 days later. When the first date comes up, hopefully your team will have completed that first action. If not, get going.

8. Alter your action plan and schedule. Time always changes your perspective on research and how you view the results. As you occasionally re-read your study, some findings and recommendations will become more important and some will become less so. This is particularly true if market conditions, which are beyond your ability to control, are evident – such as a big run-up in the price of oil.

9. Continue to follow this process. Re-read your research every few months. That research is relevant as long as you are getting new insights and generating needed actions.

Every time you revisit a study you may get new insights. Actions you haven't yet taken become more or less important. You will visualize new actions and new priorities that you hadn't previously considered. Without a doubt, the biggest waste of your research expenditure(s) is to let reports gather dust after one reading. The more attention you give every study you complete, the more your business will improve. You can take that to the bank.

SO HOW MUCH RESEARCH SHOULD YOU DO?

As much as ego allows

Research reports are egoless. It's readers who suffer from the "not invented here" syndrome. If you are unwilling to be objective about what your research says, if you are unwilling to be wrong about your previous decisions, or if you are unwilling to test new approaches suggested by the research, you have not only wasted your money on your last study, you have also reached the point where you know how much more research you should do.

The answer is "No more."

More than your competition

Of course, it's hard to know the amount of research that your competitors are doing. However, after you conduct your first study, you'll get a pretty good idea. You'll likely learn things about your competitors' customers that hadn't occurred to you. It will become clear to you how and why your competitors advertise the way they do or approach their customers in a certain manner.

You will get insight into their marketing programs and better understand why they're doing a better or worse job in some areas than you. You'll get insight into their thinking regarding pricing or why their customer service or salespeople behave differently than your customer service and salespeople. Importantly, you will begin to understand why your prospects are prospects and not customers, i.e. why they are buying from your competitors and not you.

What you may see is that the competition has had intelligence that you're only now getting, explaining why they are stronger in the market than you – or perhaps why they are weaker. Importantly, too, you will become armed with new information and that will allow you to compete with them far more effectively.

You could also get lucky. You might learn that your competitors are overlooking the obvious or making the same mistakes as you. You could uncover needs in the market that neither you nor your competition are addressing. Perhaps you'll see an opportunity where a small shift in emphasis could produce a big advantage.

You will do well to assume your competition has the same problems as you and is probably doing research to address those problems. Without the same intelligence, you'll be at a distinct competitive disadvantage.

Focus on the largest competitor

Assuming that you have your house in order and are serving your current customers well, it is critically important to stay knowledgeable about your largest competitor. Big competitors should be doing everything possible to keep customers happy and loyal. However, size often brings complacence and they can overlook the obvious. It may prove easier for you as a Guerrilla to attack the weaknesses of a big competitor and entice customers to switch than it is to outmaneuver other smaller, hungrier competitors.

Big competitors usually set the standards for both attracting and losing customers. Their marketing power may be formidable, and customers flock in their direction as a result. However, if they are more focused on getting customers than keeping them, large companies are vulnerable to losing business to smaller and more nimble competitors.

Even if you have a limited research budget, spend a portion of that budget on learning what your largest competitor is doing right and wrong. If the competition is performing better than you and you can do something about it, do it. Find their weaknesses and exploit them, such as developing a new or improved product, offering a variation in benefits and/or features, or introducing a customer service approach that will delight and intrigue the big competitor's customers.

A word of warning here. If you choose to attack the leader, as Guerrillas, we're sure you realize that the attack should probably be from the flank. Leaders with deep pockets have both the capability and inclination to crush smaller competitors by outspending them mercilessly when they make a direct assault on their bread and butter products.

Focus on smaller competitors next

Once you have learnt how to attack your largest competitor, set your sights on your smaller ones. It is always valuable to understand what competitors your size or smaller do to get and keep their customers, and they certainly have the same problems in this regard as you do. Understanding the reasons customers choose one of your smaller or peer competitors rather than you will open your eyes and give you the ammunition to compete with them more strongly.

Take Starbucks, for example. If you want to open a coffee shop in your neighborhood, it's unlikely that you have any hope of competing directly with Starbucks. Here you'd be wise to study Joe's, Barbara's, or Pete's local coffee shop. Learn what keeps them afloat. Why do their customers keep coming back rather than going to a nearby Starbucks? Emulating or bettering their success could be the formula of success for you.

The principle is sound. Usually, markets are quite fragmented. While the big company may dominate, chances are it doesn't control more than 20 or 30 per cent of the market. Find the keys to defeating the many small companies that are also your competition. Their customers might be easier for you to capture than the big competitor's.

HOW MUCH RESEARCH, REALLY?

Surgeons cut. Carpenters hammer. To a researcher, every marketing problem can be solved with a research study.

In reality, there is no good answer to the question of how much research you should do. It's like trying to answer the question, "How healthy should I be?" Do you ever really get a totally clean bill of health from your doctor? Isn't there always something you could be doing to be healthier and to live longer?

It's the same with research. You can always be studying ways to grow your business. You're never really finished. Ultimately, the answer lies somewhere between your ability to use the research information that you generate and your available funds.

A client recently informed us that he wasn't going to allocate research for the coming year because a downturn in his industry was hurting sales, which, in turn, had made research unaffordable. He went on to say that he had received a great deal of value from his previous year's research expenditure.

We had two reactions to the client's decision. First, he was just being nice. If he had really realized great value from the money spent the previous year, he'd know he preserved business he would have lost without that research and that it would be appropriate for him to continue with revenue-producing research efforts.

Second, in a time of trouble it is always necessary to do things better and smarter. Research can help determine such directions and, in this regard, the client is being short-sighted. Even in shrinking markets, there are always opportunities. In fact, learning how to gain an advantage over struggling competitors during down periods in the market is perhaps one of the best times to conduct research. Ultimately, we did a poor job of helping this client understand the returns he obtained from the previous research.

When you run out of questions

Here's our "Top 10" list for knowing when to stop doing research. If you answer "yes" to all of them, buy yourself a new car, yacht, summer home, or whatever. You certainly don't need the money for research:

1. Will your business grow profitability on pure momentum?
2. Will your business grow without improvements?
3. Do you know everything that your competitors can possibly do to hinder your growth?
4. Are you convinced you can't lose customers or gain new ones?
5. Are you convinced there is nothing that can happen to cause your products to become obsolete?
6. Are you sure your business isn't subject to changing trends?
7. Are you sure you are the only one who can generate good ideas about how to improve your business?
8. Are you clairvoyant? Do you get tomorrow's stock market reports in today's newspaper?
9. Have you contracted for a sale of your business that will make you millions?
10. Have you spent at least between 0.5 and 1.5 per cent of sales on research already this year?

8

The research plan

WHAT IS A RESEARCH PLAN?

There is a difference between developing a research goal and objectives and potential action steps for one specific study, and developing a complete research plan. Research plans take into account all the information you might need during a specific period of time – usually 12 months – and how you will use that information.

Even for Guerrillas, who might have limited budgets and can't envision conducting more than a single study in the next year, going through this exercise can still be useful.

The purpose of developing a complete research plan is to provide a full perspective on all marketing problems you face where additional information would be useful in determining what to do. Whether you are contemplating two studies or 10 in the coming 12 months, developing a plan will force you to question where knowing the attitudes and/or behaviors of customers, prospects, employees or other targets might be helpful to the growth of your business.

A full research plan is your means of viewing the direction you hope to take your company and the information-gathering steps necessary to get you there quickly, intelligently and profitably.

In developing your plan we encourage you to stretch your thinking, even if you feel it's likely beyond your financial scope. In doing so, you'll be able to view the areas where research will have the greatest immediate effect on your bottom line. You can always cut back. The more complete the view, the easier it is to determine how information collected in one area of your business will impact the other areas.

DEVELOPING YOUR PLAN

First decide on a period of time – 6 months, 12 months, even 24 months. Now develop a working name for each study you'd like to undertake. For example:

- Study to determine why customers who purchased once did not purchase again.
- Study among my best customers to determine what it would take to raise their spending with me even more.
- Study among prospects who buy from competitors but have never bought from me.
- Study among employees to determine ideas they have for growing my business.
- Study among distributors to uncover perceptions about a new product launch.
- Study among the sales force to predict customer reactions to changes in policy.

Your research plan should consist of seven sections for each study you wish to undertake:

1. Overall study goal.
2. Specific study objectives.
3. Target market respondents from/about whom data will be gathered.
4. Potential learning.
5. Potential actions you'd take.
6. Research methodology.
7. Cost.

The order in which the projects should be carried out is based on two criteria: the importance or urgency of the marketing decision that needs to be made and any calendar determinants, e.g. research needs to be done before a trade show, or to support a loan you hope to get from a bank or from investors, or before a sales meeting to inform the sales force about changes in the marketplace and why new approaches are necessary.

While you might be tempted to do the least expensive or the easiest research first, consider strongly if that is your best bet. Although it might be a bit more expensive, we've found that doing the research that will have the biggest impact is where to place emphasis.

THE OVERALL GOAL

As we've discussed, the overall goal of each research project should reflect the larger picture. In developing your overall research goals, you may wish to refer back to the section in Chapter 2 on "Turning research questions into research goals and objectives."

The overall research goal is usually a one- or two-sentence statement that captures the essence of what you want to learn. Below are examples of overall goals from four different studies.

1. Air-conditioner study

The overall goal is to determine important criteria when consumers purchase window air-conditioners, additionally, to learn how my company and my competitors perform on those same criteria.

Stating the goal in this way focuses the study in two areas: 1) uncovering what is important when consumers purchase air-conditioners; 2) understanding your company's performance vs the competition.

2. Gift box study

The overall goal of this research is to determine what effect, if any, a reduction in the size of the gift boxes might have on the value perceptions consumers have when contemplating purchase of a gift.

In this case, the company wishes to use less expensive, smaller boxes when packaging its gift line, which, in turn, would increase its profits. The need to establish the relationship between box size and box value is precise and clear.

3. Hardware store study

The overall goal of this study is to determine which of three advertising approaches would most likely draw new customers to visit the hardware store for the first time, based on the ads' believability and ability to differentiate the store from competitors. The three approaches to be tested communicate: 1) best prices, 2) best customer service, and 3) biggest variety.

The goal here is lucid and concise: to generate new customers among those who have never been in the store before. It is also assumed that price, customer service, and variety are the strongest messages to drive new traffic. Importantly, the criteria on which the ads would be assessed are clearly established.

4. Dentist study

The overall goals of this study are to determine the factors taken into consideration when patients decide to change dentists and to specifically understand whether the criteria used to decide whether to change from a current dentist are the same as the criteria used in selecting a new dentist.

The goal here is somewhat general and exploratory in nature. It really is to better understand a decision-making process with regard to choosing a dentist. As such, it does not suggest that a particular course of action will be taken as a result of the study findings.

By writing an overall goal, you are forced into specifying an unambiguous purpose for your research. An associate of ours lamented about one of his clients, saying, "They always want to throw the kitchen sink into their studies. They want to learn everything there is to be learnt." What is rightly being suggested is that trying to focus on everything at once tends to make studies overly superficial in the very areas where more in-depth information would do the most good.

If you are not clear about your overall research goal, you are more likely to create a study that collects information for the sake of the information, not for taking action. This might not be a big problem if you have the research funds necessary to study everything. Usually, though, this is not a luxury that Guerrillas can afford.

SPECIFIC OBJECTIVES

Specific objectives flow from the overall goal, as also discussed in Chapter 2. They provide elaboration on the overall goal and set out important areas that should be included in your study.

Take the example from the air-conditioner study. Here, "The overall goal is to determine important criteria when consumers purchase window air-conditioners, additionally, to learn how my company and my competitors perform on those same criteria."

Specific objectives here would be:

1. Determine which of the following specific attributes are most important when purchasing a window air-conditioner:
   - ease of installation;
   - brand name;
   - price;
   - product warranty;
   - dealer knowledge;
   - friend or relative's recommendation;

- cost to operate;
- available at a nearby store.

2. Determine which of the following brands would most likely be purchased:
   - GE;
   - Frigidaire;
   - Kenmore;
   - Whirlpool;
   - Maytag.
3. Determine how the brands that would most likely be purchased rate on the attributes of importance.
4. Determine whether there are differences in how the brands are perceived by consumers who purchased window air-conditioners more than five years ago and intend to purchase a new one in the near future versus those purchasing in the past year.
5. Determine whether there are differences in perceptions based on the area of the country where consumers live.

Take the overall goal of the gift box study: "The overall goal of this research is to determine what effect, if any, a reduction in the size of the gift boxes might have on the value perceptions consumers have when contemplating purchase of a gift."

In this study the specific objectives are:

1. What is the overall purchase interest in the large boxed gifts versus the smaller boxed gifts? Does "intent to purchase" deteriorate because the gifts come packaged in smaller boxes?
2. In comparison to the larger boxed gifts, are two different sizes of smaller boxed gifts perceived as better, worse, or the same in terms of:
   - being a gift of good value;
   - being a gift of good quality;
   - being a gift that the giver would be proud to give;
   - being a gift that is pleasing to look at in the box;
   - being a gift that when gift-wrapped might be one that appears intriguing and be among the first to be opened?
3. Which of three graphic approaches for smaller boxed gifts is better at communicating value, quality, and the other attributes?
4. Would consumers who have not purchased boxed gifts be more or less likely to purchase if the box size were reduced?

Stating the specific objectives in this precise manner lays out all the factors by which the small and large boxes will be measured. In doing so, it provides a variety of data on which to base a final decision.

Assume that overall purchase intent, as stated in objective 1, does not produce decisive information as to a winning box. The additional information gathered for objectives 2, 3, and 4 could be used to break a tie. If purchase intent is equal, but the smaller boxes outperform the larger ones on the other issues, there is added information for making a decision. Further, if it is determined that the smaller boxes do not reduce the number of new buyers attracted to the gift products, the decision becomes even easier.

Now take a last example from the dentist study: "The overall goals of this study are to determine the factors taken into consideration when patients decide to change dentists and to specifically understand whether the criteria used to decide whether to change from a current dentist are the same as the criteria used in selecting a new dentist."

Specific objectives would be as follows:

1. What are all the considerations present when a patient first contemplates changing dentists?
2. Do those considerations change in any way while contemplating a change?
3. Do new considerations become important in the period leading up to a change?
4. Do patients express dissatisfaction to their dentist prior to changing? Why, or why not? If considerations are expressed, what is the reaction of the dentist?
5. Do patients interview one or more new dentists prior to changing? If so, what is said by the patient, and the potential dentist, regarding a change?
6. When the change is actually made, did the dentist being terminated make the change difficult or uncomfortable?

The specific objectives in this study are considered exploratory in nature. They do not assume certain factors or problems exist around which questioning must revolve. Rather, the research is intended to shed light on the process and to surface factors that might be important when changing dentists.

TARGET MARKET RESPONDENTS

Every market research study has target market respondents. These are the respondents whose opinions or behaviors are deemed to be most important. Target market respondents can have a multitude of characteristics, for example:

- particular demographic/firmographic characteristics (single or married, have large families or small families, college graduates or

have only a high school education, have incomes under or over a specified amount per year, work in certain industries, have specific titles, etc.);
- use particular products or brands;
- purchase only from you, only from your competitors, or from both of you, etc.;
- are customers who purchased from you once or who purchased many times;
- are customers who bought a great deal from you in the past but are no longer buying.

The range of possible customers and prospects you could target in a research study can be wide and varied. Therefore, in planning your research it is usually necessary to set priorities and to narrow the respondent target field.

Consider the following respondent targeting scenarios:

- If you are conducting a poll to determine which candidates will be voted for in an upcoming election, your target audience might be as general as registered voters, or it might be as specific as female registered voters, aged 18–35, who voted in the last election and say they intend voting in the coming election.
- If you want to grow sales quickly, you might want to interview customers who are also purchasing from a competitor. The target here would be very precise, and the objective would be to learn how to convince customers to give their additional expenditure to you instead of a competitor.
- If you are striving to convert prospects who have never purchased the kinds of products you sell, you might want to target respondents who have never purchased in the category, but have demographic characteristics that are similar to those of your current customers.
- If you are seeking to develop and sell new products or services, you might want to target respondents who are unusually imaginative and verbal and more likely to give you good ideas.
- If you want to sell more from your catalog, your target respondents might be people who requested your catalog but have not yet purchased from it.
- If you are considering enhancing your perceived quality by investing in achieving an ISO rating (International Organization for Standardization – a quality control/assurance standard-setting group) you might survey your current distributors.
- If you are launching an expensive, complicated software product, you might explore positioning options with IT directors in companies with sales in excess of $100 million.

There are a number of questions you should ask yourself in determining your target market:

- What targets offer you the best opportunity of increasing your business the fastest?
- What targets would be important for longer-term growth?
- What targets would be least costly to convince to buy more from you?
- What targets actually have the information you need to know?
- What targets would provide nice to know information but would be too costly to attract?
- If you knew the attitudes of one particular target, could you extrapolate to other targets without having to study them?
- Do you have the research budget available to cast a very wide net?

The study plan is a dynamic tool. It serves to focus your initial thinking, and it also serves as a discussion document. No doubt others in your company have opinions regarding important research goals, objectives and targets. Certainly your vendors, particularly your ad agency, sales promotion or PR agency could provide advice. Don't hesitate to pick the brains of the many advisors available to you.

The study plan helps everyone focus their thinking on those areas of information that will have the greatest immediate impact and which ones have longer-term implications. And it provides a clear view of how information gleaned from one study will help build the goal, objectives and potential actions that might be taken in another.

In essence, developing a study plan eliminates guessing. It provides a framework for everyone to agree on the important areas to study. It establishes the important role of research in helping to grow your business. And, as you will see in later chapters, it will prove critical in choosing the right methodology for conducting the research.

Use the following to develop your final study plan.

---

1. State your overall research goal(s):

_____

2. State your secondary research objectives:

A.

B.

C.

D.

3. Describe in as much detail as possible the target markets you wish to research:

Target #1:

Target #2:

Target #3:

etc.

4. State what you might learn as a result of generating information both from your primary research goal and secondary research objectives:

A. I might learn _____

B. I might learn _____

C. I might learn _____

Continue until all options are written down.

5. For each option, write down three actions you would consider taking on the basis of your learning:

For 4 A: Action #1 _____

                 Action #2 _____

                 Action #3 _____

For 4 B: Action #1 _____

                 Action #2 _____

                 Action #3 _____

etc.

Continue until at least three actions for all learning that might take place are identified.

6. Research methodology

For some Guerrillas, completing steps 1, 2, and 3 above may be all that is necessary to start the research process. If you are working with a research supplier or consultant, you can now provide them with your objectives and action statements and ask them to develop cost-effective research methodologies. A side benefit of going through this planning exercise is that you won't incur vendor or consultant costs for helping you develop action-oriented objectives.

If, though, you plan on conducting the research yourself, you should read Chapters 11 and 14, on executing focus groups and surveys, before completing this section. With information from those chapters in hand you'll be better prepared to complete your plan.

7. Cost

Finally, you come to the bottom line where you cost out each study. Some may be far more than you can afford and you may have to cut back on your objectives or compromise on the methodology. The low cost of others may come as a nice surprise. Whichever the case, you'll have a full view of the information that you feel is necessary to effectively grow your business.

A FINAL WORD

You may look back at this chapter and conclude that putting together a complete research plan requires quite a bit of time and effort. We would not argue. A good plan does require a great deal of consideration.

We would add though that putting at least some effort into this process will pay you back many times over. Whether you take days, weeks or months to complete your plan is of less concern than your willingness to try. By going no further than listing the various studies you wish to undertake and coming to grips with their goals, you'll be on the right track.

The information you need to move your company ahead will stare you right in the face.

We've encountered Guerrillas who start their research plan, outline several studies and then put the plan aside until one or more of those studies are complete. When they revisit the plan in light of the findings from those studies, they have a fresh and more insightful view of their future research needs. They find that the rest of the plan almost writes itself.

9

Secondary research

WHAT IS SECONDARY INFORMATION?

Secondary research is research conducted by someone else that is in the public domain. It is research that may prove useful to you and that you can access for free or for minimal expenditure.

For Guerrillas, secondary research is often a good place to begin the research process. It allows you to begin investigating your marketplace and access general information that might help you develop clear marketing goals and from those clear primary research objectives. Consider the following suggestions as to when secondary research is appropriate:

- When are you considering entering a market and are interested in learning what you can about the leaders in the market.
- When you are interested in general insights about the marketing and advertising approaches being taken by key competitors in the market.
- When trying to understand potential gaps in the market and where you might focus your attention in fulfilling consumer needs, wants, wishes, desires and emotions.
- When trying to get ideas regarding consumer motivations for purchasing particular products or services and thus understand the types of primary research that would be helpful to you in planning your marketing strategies.
- When looking for trends in the marketplace in order to better assess whether the market is growing or not and whether you could be a potential force by entering the market.

The above list is by no means complete and is only intended to give you an idea when secondary research would be beneficial. However, because secondary research is originally designed to meet needs other than your own, you have to consider a number of questions before deciding if it is appropriate information you can confidently apply to your business.

Keep the following in mind when determining the value of secondary research.

1. Was the information gathered from the right people?

If you need to talk to the male head of household about your product or service and you find a survey where the answers are from the female head of household, it's not likely to be useful. However, if you need information regarding the opinion of corporate CEOs and you find a survey on the right topic that was answered by CFOs, it might serve very well.

2. Were the right questions asked?

Obviously, a survey among male heads of household about their attitudes towards restaurants and dining out will not be much help if you run a local garage. On the other hand, if you are a city economic development director and want companies to locate in your community, general company information about planned capital expenditures might still be useful – even if you are primarily interested in plans about new plants or corporate headquarters' relocations.

3. Was the quality of the research up to your standards?

You probably won't be surprised to learn that just as with everything else, research quality can vary. Certainly surveys with large sample sizes provide more reliability than those with small samples. Companies with reputations for high quality may produce better work than less known organizations. Organizations that specialize in certain industries can produce more authoritative work than those studying an industry for the first time. You should also be sure the method(s) used to gather the information followed good sampling procedures and the sample was large enough to make reliable judgments.

4. Did the company conducting the research have an agenda?

Often companies that conduct primary research studies publish only self-serving information. For example, advertising and PR firms might try to convince potential clients that they are knowledgeable about a problem in the market and, therefore, should be considered an important vendor and one to hire. Or a company may have an axe to grind regarding their perceived quality and, therefore, might conduct research only among a biased target (e.g. satisfied customers).

5. Was the research quoted part of a newspaper, magazine or website article?

Newspapers, magazines, television networks and big company websites often quote numbers from research they conducted for an article, editorial piece or white paper – all of which may have a particular slant. While numbers don't lie, liars can use numbers anyway that they see fit. Be careful in relying on numbers when the source of those numbers might have a biased outlook. And always look skeptically at one single number that purports to explain something. Patterns of data are what matter, not a single number.

6. Is the research timely?

By the time you come upon it, many secondary source research studies have outlived their usefulness. An article about MP3 players published as recently as 2006 would fail to address the massive changes in the market since the introduction of the iPod Nano. Be careful you are not relying on information that's out of date.

In essence, when using secondary sources you must be vigilant about the companies providing the information as well as the method(s) used to gather the data. Further, the manner in which the questions were asked and the analyses applied to the data must be carefully considered before assessing the quality of the research and whether it is something on which you should hang your hat.

This all can be summarized: were the right people asked the right questions in the right way by credible sources? If you cannot favorably assess answers to these questions, then be very wary of using the data.

THE ATTRACTIVENESS OF SECONDARY INFORMATION

One advantage of secondary research is that it might be free. For example, the US Census of the Population, the US Census of Business and thousands of other reports are very authoritative and completely free (see www.us.gov or www.census.gov). Similarly, every state provides a wide array of free research as do most major cities. And many small cities publish free research from local Chambers of Commerce.

Another advantage is that, when not free, secondary research might still be available at a price much lower than you'd have to pay to conduct original research on the same subject. On www.marketresearch.com you'll find links to thousands of research reports for sale on every business topic you can imagine – no matter how narrowly defined. Published by many different organizations, these reports are usually three years or less old, amazingly comprehensive and sell for a few thousand dollars – many for less.

A third advantage is that secondary research may very well be immediately available. Much of it is online and readily downloadable. Even many of the reports on marketresearch.com can be downloaded and others are easily ordered for quick delivery.

So it is fair to say that gathering secondary research data will almost always be faster than conducting a primary research study and usually will be less expensive as well. Again though, the utility and quality of information must be carefully assessed.

COMMON VALUABLE SOURCES OF SECONDARY INFORMATION

This chapter is not intended to offer a comprehensive compendium of secondary sources. There are in fact several books devoted to just this topic. However, the list below will provide a good jumping-off point:

- *US government:* as was mentioned already, the US government, and federal governments in general, are a major source of secondary information and good places to begin to get an overview of an industry or to learn about the demographics of consumers. The government also publishes hundreds of special studies that might apply to your case. Even though these studies are conducted less than annually, they often are re-estimated in the off-years by government statisticians. So the data from the 2000 Census of the Population are still useful.

  Also useful are the required quarterly and annual 10K filings required of publicly owned companies. We are very fond of a book called *The Statistical Abstract of the United States,* which is published every year and contains thousands of the best tables from these federal data mines.
- *State governments:* the states replicate the kinds of studies done at the national level, but in terms of more local geography.
- *City governments:* same idea, only still smaller geography.
- *Horizontal business media:* in the US there are several horizontal business media whose daily, weekly or monthly output provides terrific

information on the macro-economy, industries and even specific companies. Examples, of course, include *The Wall Street Journal, The Financial Times, Investor's Daily, Barron's, Business Week, Forbes, Fortune,* and the business section of *The New York Times* to name a few. Not only is their regular output invaluable but, so too are the special issues and reports that they publish.

- *Trade associations:* trade associations are wonderful sources of secondary information – some of it is free, some is free to members and some is available for purchase even to non-members. Some trade associations, in fact, exist primarily as a means for companies to exchange data. In this fashion the size of an industry, its growth rate, and other important facts are quickly accessible. Particularly impressive is the information provided by the Advertising Research Foundation (www.thearf.org).

- *Trade publications:* no matter how small your industry there is probably at least one trade publication covering it – and most industries are covered by several magazines and websites. These publications are marvelous sources of information, not only in their monthly coverage and analyses, but especially in their annual or year-end publications. Many also conduct regular surveys among their readers and use the findings in an unbiased manner in their articles.

  Marketing and advertising information is particularly prevalent in publications such as *Advertising Age, Brand Week, Marketing News* and *DM (Direct Marketing) News,* all of which have websites.

  Another sometimes overlooked source within a trade publication is to talk directly to an editor or reporter. They can be reached on the phone and simply asked questions. (Strictly speaking, this latter idea is a form of primary research.)

- *www.marketresearch.com:* as mentioned, this is a gateway to thousands of published research reports that you can purchase, and is a great place to start. Even if you decide not to purchase, they'll usually let you download the table of contents, which by itself may give you some inkling of what's going on and what others at least think are important topics in your industry.

- *Stock/investment brokers:* if you have an account with a stock broker, you automatically have access to their very sophisticated analyses of business sectors and specific companies.

- *Company websites:* it almost goes without saying that one of the first places to look for information about your competition is on their websites. A trained eye can read between the lines of their public communications to discern their marketing strategy. Further, some company sites are quite large and many divisions and departments within the company contribute to the site. This sometimes leads to a lack of coordination and weak site management, which causes valuable and often confidential information to creep onto the site. This alone is a reason to visit competitor sites regularly. (A word to the wise – don't you make this same mistake.)

- *Blogs:* many large companies have bloggers who follow them and try to leak information about them. Apple and Microsoft, for example, are two companies that attract many bloggers with both positive and negative comments. Take advantage of this when you are researching a big guy.
- *The internet:* obviously, most of the information discussed above is available on the internet. We suggest using more than one search engine to fully explore a topic and we strongly suggest trying more than one set of key words to run your search.

  Think of information gathering as a kind of triangulation. This strategy will identify the best articles and sources because they will show up more than once. And it will also identify the most articles because the different engines employ different search algorithms and the variations in search terms will drive those engines in slightly different directions.

  And don't forget Wikipedia (http://wikipedia.org). Simply typing in a question you might have about your business will yield an amazing array of information and related links on your question.
- *The library:* your local library is still an excellent place to go to gather secondary information. Not only does it have an entire reference section for just this purpose, but it also has skilled professionals available to help you find what you are looking for. And most major cities also have a central business library with even more resources.

  What's more, most libraries have special search engines and data sources unavailable to you when conducting online research from office or home. (The largest city libraries may even allow linkages to their resources from your home or office computer, so remember to ask.)

WHICH COMES FIRST – PRIMARY OR SECONDARY RESEARCH?

This is not a trick question. You should always start your search for information using secondary data. As we said earlier, secondary sources of information are usually available quickly and certainly at a lower cost than primary research. So valuable is secondary research that, in fact, we recommend doing a major review of secondary sources of information relating to your business at least yearly.

Always remember, though, that research about your specific customers or prospects, their image and attitudes toward your particular products and services, and their attitudes toward your specific competitors almost always require custom-designed primary research.

10

Brainstorming and other ideation processes

At some point you have probably had experience with brainstorming – the group technique where anything goes, no ideas are barred, and nothing is too silly or stupid to express.

Brainstorming is often a precursor to research and is worth discussing at this point. Whether a company is looking for new products, new advertising approaches or ideas for generating additional business from current customers, brainstorming is a popular technique for generating a great many ideas and then putting them in a logical order for future action.

We have mixed feelings about brainstorming. On the one hand, brainstorming sessions are popular, easy to convene, and usually generate a lot of ideas. On the other hand, in our experience, the ideas generated tend to be superficial and not particularly unique.

There are several reasons that brainstorming sessions are often unproductive. Usually the length of time that they last, two to four hours, is inadequate. Just as ideas are taking shape, the session is over. Further, it takes a certain level of training and practice to fully understand the rules for an effective brainstorming session. The typical brainstorming group just doesn't invest much energy in learning the rules of creativity in order to optimize the session.

Nevertheless, many Guerrillas new to research might also be new to brainstorming. Just as conducting research for the first time will open your eyes, the act of convening a brainstorming team in your company or among your customers can do the same. If it does no more than serve as a forum for revisiting old ideas that still have merit, it will be time well spent, and you just might surface new ideas your employees and customers haven't suggested because they haven't had the forum for doing so.

CONDUCTING A BRAINSTORMING SESSION

Here are some simple rules to follow when conducting a brainstorming session:

1. Be clear in your objective. Go into a brainstorming session focused on one clear objective. For example, clear objectives would be:
    - generate ideas for new products not currently on the market;
    - generate ideas for improving current products;
    - generate ideas for improving customer service;
    - generate ideas for improving current advertising;
    - generate ideas for helping the sales force be more productive.
2. Consider branching objectives at another time. Invariably, generating ideas focused on one objective will turn up ideas not directly related to that particular objective. When this happens, there is a tendency to go off on a tangent and away from the original session objective. While this is not necessarily a big negative, we suggest trying to stay focused and to simply note down that an idea surfaced and should be investigated later. As you become more skilled in the various brainstorming techniques, you'll be better able to deal productively with tangents, thus allowing the session to be productive even when new, off-strategy opportunities surface.
3. Appoint a recorder. This is a person who stands at an easel and writes down the ideas that are expressed. The recorder usually refrains from writing down his or her own ideas. The recorder should be impartial to the ideas expressed while making sure that participants follow the rules of the session. For company brainstorming sessions, it is often best for the recorder to be the boss or the highest-ranking person in the room. This sends the message that the boss is not trying to sway the group one way or the other and is truly interested in ideas other than his or her own.
4. Agreement. Only people who want to be in a brainstorming session should attend. Shrinking violets or those with an axe to grind will inhibit the group. There must be explicit agreement that hidden agendas will be shelved and that judgment will be put aside.
5. Safe space. A brainstorming session will be unproductive if participants feel that the ideas they express might be used against them or in any way reflect on them negatively. The highest-ranking person should reassure everyone on this essential issue.
6. Suspend judgment and suspend "Yes, buts." In business, people "Yes, but" each other to death. In the normal course of business,

someone will come up with a thought or idea, and it is usual for others immediately to judge it. An idea will be expressed and someone will say, "Yes, but we tried that last year" or "Yes, but that will cost too much." "Yes, buts" will kill a brainstorming session. Therefore, it is essential for the recorder to listen carefully for "Yes, buts" and to remind participants not to judge ideas. Idea-bashing is the fastest way to an ineffective brainstorming session.

7. "What do I like about it?" Ideas will prosper and grow once a group moves from "Yes, but" thinking to "What do I like about it?" thinking. The sooner the group learns to express what they like about ideas, the better the ideas will become. When an idea is put forward, the recorder should ask the group to express their positives about the idea and how it can be made better.

8. Listen and write. The best ideas often surface when others are talking. Active listening is the act of paying rapt attention to ideas expressed by others and writing down ideas that come to your mind when others are talking. The recorder should continually encourage participants to listen to what is being said and to write down their ideas that pop to mind. We sometimes remind participants: "We were given two ears and one mouth for a reason." Active listening is hard when people are striving to be the first one to suggest an attractive idea.

9. Have fun. The very nature of new ideas is that they often sound funny, silly, or stupid when first expressed. Usually, ideas that are silly are the very ones that are new and should be nurtured. Learn to judge the effectiveness of a brainstorming session by the amount of fun and laughter present. More fun invariably equates to better ideas.

The above rules are basic to an effective brainstorming session – regardless of which specific brainstorming system you employ. There are a great many approaches to brainstorming and many websites available on the subject. Here's a site that details techniques to make brainstorming more productive: www.unc.edu/depts/wcweb/handouts/brainstorming.html. You can also visit any search engine and use the key words "brainstorming" or "brainstorming techniques" and log on to dozens of brainstorming-focused sites.

OTHER IDEATION PROCESSES

For a long time we've felt that traditional brainstorming can be helpful in generating a lot of ideas, *but* the quality of ideas and the extent of their "newness" is often lacking. The truth is that it's very difficult to be as creative and different as is needed in brainstorming. If it was easy, great ideas would just pop into our head on demand and we'd all be rich.

Further, if you were given a couple of hours, for example, and told your profits for the next year would be based on your ability to generate breakthrough ideas during those hours, you'd likely hedge your bet. So it is with brainstorming. As a result, what tends to be generated during a brainstorming session is commonly referred to as ideas of the "low hanging fruit" variety. Those are the ideas that quickly come to mind and are easily expressed, but not necessarily the ones that are the hit-it-out-of-the-ball-park ideas.

To reach beyond brainstorming ideas it's necessary to expand the ideation process. That means expanding the time frame devoted to generating ideas as well as the techniques that are used. It also means not assuming you've gotten all there is to get in one relatively brief session.

The Creative Education Foundation (CEF) was founded in 1954 by Alex Osborn of the famous BBDO (Batton, Barton, Durstine, and Osborn) advertising agency. Osborn also invented brainstorming. CEF "fosters a culture of courage that is open, dynamic and diverse. It is a community where a passion for creative thinking, learning and the sharing of ideas thrives."

Since the founding of CEF, there has been an ever-increasing body of knowledge on the creative process and what goes into generating breakthrough ideas. As such, CEF is a great place to go to learn about the creative process. Also, noted thinkers such as Edward de Bono, Roger von Oech and Michel Michalko have written widely on the subject. And the American Management Association publishes extensively in this area, and its *Trainer's Activity Book* is particularly useful when applying creative principles.

While it might be quite fascinating to spend years learning and studying the nature of creativity and creative processes, Guerrillas need not apply. With a minimal amount of understanding and a modicum of cheerleader mentality you can lead the people in your company to generating ideas you never imagined.

The work by the CEF and the many creativity-focused educators has surfaced a number of truisms about breakthrough thinking. What is most fascinating is the famous result of a creativity test. Children from age 5 to adults to age 45 were administered the test. The findings were that at age 45 fewer than 10 per cent of the population were scored as creative, while at age 5 over 50 per cent of children were creatively inclined.

Although happily changing, the fact that our education system has largely focused on what is commonly referred to as "vertical and logical thinking" is the likely culprit. Vertical thinking and problem solving are great when seeking to solve science, technology or medical problems, but terrible if you're an artist, musician, writer of fiction or trying to be a marketing genius – all of which require a higher degree of lateral and creative thinking.

Obviously, creativity is a valuable trait in scientists and doctors, too. Einstein famously said: "Imagination is more important than knowledge. For knowledge is limited to all we now know and understand, while imagination embraces the entire world, and all there ever will be to know and understand."

What has been learnt from the creative disciplines might be best captured by quoting Edward de Bono from his book, *Serious Creativity*. De Bono writes: "At its simplest level 'creative' means bringing into being something that was not there before. In a sense, 'creating a mess' is an example of creativity. The mess was not here before and was brought into being."

In business, it's strange and risky to create a mess. While a 5-year old isn't likely to have trouble creating a "mental mess" and making seemingly goofy "creative" connections, a 40-year old trying it in front of the Board of Directors probably won't get too far. The point is that if you are striving to generate new ideas, to be creative and different, you'd best learn and then follow some different rules.

However, this isn't a book about creativity, so at this point we'd only encourage you take the subject as far as you wish. There are many other techniques beyond brainstorming for generating new ideas – and a variety of companies that specialize in ideation processes.

Some of the processes you'll find include:

- more intensely focused brainstorming processes that last one or more days;
- processes that include workshops and interactive sessions with customers or prospects;
- processes that include developing graphic depictions or actual development of new products or prototypes;
- processes that include secondary source searches, homework assignments, and use of other stimulus material to generate ideas;
- processes that include training in creativity and how to look beyond the obvious when generating ideas;
- over-time processes that last for months, thus expanding the time frame for generating ideas.

Whatever the process, three features are common to all:

1. *Allowing time for incubation.* New ideas will surface when people are given time. Therefore, plan your brainstorming as an over-time process. Realize that point-in-time exercises are very limited in their ability to get below the surface.

2. *Stimulating observation.* Have your internal brainstorming team (or customers or distributors if they are involved in your process) keep diaries, shop with competitors, talk to friends, do anything that will activate involvement and stimulate their awareness of your ideation goals. Getting below the surface mandates that all the senses be involved. A good way to do this is by motivating even internal people to be more observant of their own behavior and the problems that result – and to write ideas down at the time they occur.

3. *Tapping into the unconscious mind.* There is a reason ideas come to us when we least expect them, e.g. in the shower, in dreams while we are asleep. It's because our minds process information on both conscious and unconscious levels. Therefore, the more involved your team is with your products and services, the more likely it is that their unconscious minds will "flash" on a new need, want, wish, desire or emotional connection. We like to call this "planned serendipity."

Whatever the process, it can work for you. All you have to do is allow over-time incubation, stimulate observation and provide an on-going opportunity for your people to express the ideas that surface.

In summary:

- Brainstorming or other ideation processes can be an effective tool for generating ideas and, thus, can motivate fresh thinking.
- Ideas coming out of brainstorming or other ideation processes almost always need a reality check. Whether they, in fact, address customer needs or wants that aren't already being addressed is generally the issue.
- Most ideas from brainstorming or other ideation processes need to be reworked from a customer perspective. Focus groups, for example, can provide such a perspective.
- Creativity can't be summoned on demand. Therefore, ideation processes that expand the typical brainstorming time frame are more likely to produce ideas that have greater potential.
- Ideation should be ongoing. When participants are regularly involved in generating new ideas, they are more attuned to the world and to unmet needs, wants, wishes, and desires that exist. They become aware of the little things that can make all the difference in discovering a breakthrough idea. Having a continual forum for expressing and building on ideas is extremely important.
- Rarely, if ever, is it wise to commit sizeable sums of money to developing ideas that come from brainstorming or ideation processes without first conducting a quantitative survey to determine the degree of consumer interest in the ideas that you are considering.

11

Focus groups and qualitative research

WHAT ARE THEY REALLY?

When most people think of market research, they probably think about focus groups. How many times in an election year have you heard: "Well, our focus groups told us that it's about the economy"? Or from a business friend: "We conducted focus groups, and people really liked the new flavor"? Or read in an article: "Focus groups indicated this was really a product that women would like more than men"?

While focus groups are universally known, they are equally well misunderstood. As we discussed in Chapter 3, focus groups are a qualitative tool. Formally, "qualitative" refers to research in which the sample size is too small to reliably make predictions about the universe from which the sample was drawn. Practically speaking though, the word "qualitative" suggests drawing tentative conclusions and refers to:

- Becoming aware of patterns of thinking, the criteria used in assessing things, and the relative importance of those criteria.
- Becoming aware of images and perceptions.
- Learning the range of likes and dislikes.
- Hearing suggestions and ideas.
- Hearing arguments for and against.
- Hearing stories good and bad.
- Discovering the language real people use when discussing your business, your marketplace and your pet issues.
- Uncovering patterns of behavior.

- Learning about the nature of decision processes and who is involved.
- Discovering notions, positive and negative.

When uncovering issues, no definitive value should be placed on whether one issue is more important than another. From qualitative research you cannot know for sure if an issue is true for one person or a million people. The reason is because of the small sample size and highly interactive nature of the group process.

In focus groups it's easy for one respondent to influence another. The focus group process is dynamic in nature and the interaction is intended to surface disparate and often conflicting opinions. Because we want participants to feel comfortable enough to tell the truth in front of one another, we accept the fact that opinions might sway one respondent to the view of another. So voting activities and use of questionnaires in a qualitative setting may be tainted by an unknown level of potential bias. Further, no two groups are alike even when respondents are recruited to have the same demographics or to use similar products or services.

For all these reasons we must be cautious when generalizing about issues.

Of course, it's important to know what issues exist, but this is often only a first step. Used most effectively, focus groups and other forms of qualitative research should be regarded as an hypothesis-generating process to be followed by quantitative survey research that seeks to validate those hypotheses. The two fit hand in glove.

How, then, should focus groups be used? They should be used:

1. To create a platform or context. Focus groups are a first step. They are exploratory in nature, with the main purpose of viewing the options around the issue, "getting a handle" on the factors that might be influential, and better understanding the conditions that exist in the minds of customers and prospects.
2. To clarify thinking and to set objectives. Focus groups seek to clarify thinking around the problem so that precise quantitative research objectives can be set. They allow you to gauge what you don't know and should seek to learn.
3. To determine the right questions. Focus groups help to determine what questions to ask and how to ask them in a quantitative questionnaire.
4. To provide an indication of where opportunities exist. Focus groups show what seems to be working or not working. They point to areas where improvements or changes might be indicated or where unmet functional and emotional needs, wants, wishes and desires might exist.

5. To examine possibilities. Focus groups allow us to ask "What if?" What if we did more or less of that – might our business increase? What new things could be tried that might work to give us a competitive advantage or to increase the odds for success?

There is agreement that the main value of focus groups lies in discovering what's going on. There is disagreement in the research community, however, regarding whether focus groups by themselves should ever be used for decision making.

CAN FOCUS GROUPS ALONE PROVIDE THE BASIS FOR A MARKETING DECISION?

There is no doubt that placing reliance on opinions and ideas expressed in focus groups is fraught with marketing and financial risk. So much so that some researchers believe that if you plan on making a major decision from focus groups alone, you should probably save your money and make an educated guess.

Others argue that qualitative research alone can be used to guide marketing decisions by an experienced, senior manager when the findings are consistent with other available information and the risk is acknowledged. Dipak Jain, Professor of Marketing and Dean of the Kellogg Graduate School of Management at Northwestern University, puts it this way: "Being approximately right is better than being 100 per cent wrong." In other words, he believes some research, even focus groups alone, is better than no research. We cannot settle this argument for you, but you should know it exists.

In fact, it is common for focus group reports to begin with a warning like the following:

> Focus group research is qualitative in nature. Results can best be thought of as hypotheses. The sample sizes are too small – even when findings from several groups are combined – and the group dynamic process is too volatile for results to provide confident predictions about true market conditions.

That does not mean, however, that we can't observe that the majority of respondents all felt the same way or that only one participant disagreed, or that men felt one way and women another, or that one advertising approach was strongly preferred over others. The limitation is that such findings can vary dramatically. For example, findings from focus groups conducted on a subject in one part of the country might be diametrically opposite those conducted in another part.

An argument against ever using just focus groups to aid decision making

Focus groups are the most intoxicating of all the marketing research techniques. They provide a direct, uninhibited, uncensored link between you and customers and prospects. There is an opportunity to observe first-hand what customers and prospects look like, to hear their tone of voice and to scrutinize their body language and facial expressions.

However, if you bet your company, job or marketing budget on what your groups say and it works out, don't be fooled into considering yourself smart. All you can do is consider yourself downright lucky.

The "Aha" syndrome

You're watching a focus group and the light bulb goes on. Or, just as bad, you're reading a brilliantly written focus group report and there seems complete clarity. You say to yourself, "Aha, that's it. That's what I should do."

Unfortunately, we've seen it many times. Sometimes it's so over-whelming that it ends up costing a company many thousands or even millions of dollars. Our advice is to treat such flashes of insight, such reactions from focus groups, like the plague.

Despite strong cautions to the contrary, a catalog client once decided to change its entire product mix because women in its focus groups said it didn't offer enough high-priced clothes. A home improvement ware-house eliminated its fast checkout lane for professional contractors when the contractors said they'd wait with everyone else if they could get a 10 per cent discount on their purchases. A snack food manufac-turer responded when it heard women say they wanted more healthy snacks and would pay more to get snacks with all-natural ingredients.

The results of these moves were unmitigated disasters.

It's critically important to remember that, in focus groups, what people might say and how they then might behave can be at polar opposites. Many marketers will forget this fact when they are faced with overwhelming consensus from a focus group study. So, take this as fair advice – if you are inclined toward committing meaningful sums of company money to drastically different but compelling ideas that emerge from focus groups, breathe deeply for five minutes and then lie down until the urge goes away.

As we said, focus groups should be used to develop insights and hypotheses. They can help better define problems or issues, to explore alternative solutions and to provide fodder for more effectively deliber-ating on "what could be." They are not a tool for determining signifi-cant changes to be made to your products or marketing programs or whether a new product or service that you feel will blow the socks of competition will really do so.

We've given the same speech to clients many, many times and somehow it never gets through. We urge:

> It doesn't matter if respondents in your focus group jump up and down and say they'll toss money at you because they are so excited about doing business with your company. And it doesn't matter if they sit there yawning, doodling or stone-faced because they are bored by the conversation.

What matters are the issues you uncover that might lead to greater success or to eminently preventable failure. Invariably, though, clients will start counting their profits if focus groups love their ideas, or be totally depressed if they don't.

So, what should you do if you get an "Aha" from your focus groups? Our advice is to feel good, assume you're on the right track and then proceed cautiously. If you don't get the response you want, simply assume you need to change your track before proceeding cautiously. In other words, don't plough blindly ahead with an idea that seems great and, conversely, don't kill an idea that could blossom with some intelligent tweaking.

We are often asked if doing focus groups is better than doing nothing at all. For example, if funds for research are limited, should an economical focus group study be conducted? The answer is, "Absolutely." In such instances, groups can provide a strong warning signal that what you think is a great new marketing, advertising or product idea could be a waste of time and money. Focus groups can, indeed, send a strong stop signal. In such cases, "disaster checks" provide value.

But that's it. Metaphorically speaking, focus groups should never be used on "bet your career" decisions. They are no more, and no less, than a tool for motivating your creative juices.

So, again, the next time you get a big "Aha" from a focus group, what you should do is conduct a projectable survey and learn with a high degree of certainty if your "Aha" will make you money.

An argument in favor of just using focus groups to aid decision making

The foundation of this argument is that findings from focus groups and other qualitative research are not a lesser form of life in comparison to quantitative survey findings; rather they are a different form of life. Indeed, the richness of qualitative insights often cannot be obtained in any other fashion. Let's take a look at some cases where a marketing decision was or could be made just based on qualitative input.

Sometimes qualitative research must address very complex subjects (e.g. attitudes about death or abortion or deep underlying motivations). In such cases a PhD in psychology, sociology or anthropology might be necessary in order to understand consumer emotions. Remember your Freud: motivations and the reasons for feelings may not even be known to respondents as they may be subconscious.

And, even if they are known to the respondent, who's to say the respondent is telling the truth? In such complex instances it takes a clinically trained professional, using a variety of projective tools and methods of probing, to uncover deep seated consumer motivations. In such cases, qualitative findings often stand alone.

As was mentioned earlier, qualitative results often resonate with what may be termed "the ring of truth." In a case involving a supplier of control room equipment to the nuclear power industry, we learnt that the influence of consulting engineers in specifying designs had declined and the role of internal engineers at the operating company had become more important.

This made immediate sense to the client, who felt advertising targeted at consulting engineers had been diminishing in effectiveness, but didn't know why. Here qualitative research was conducted and the findings were consistent with other information available to senior executives. A decision was made to reallocate hundreds of thousands of dollars to internal engineers. As a result, inquiries to the company greatly increased.

There's a quantitative concept called "regression towards the mean." It suggests that the bigger the sample, the more likely findings based on it will represent the population from which it is drawn. Think of it as adding additional cases.

If you have a sample of 10, it might or might not well represent a large population. As you increase the sample to 100 or 1,000, it becomes more and more accurate in representing the population. As you add to the sample, you are marching toward statistical accuracy. In egghead parlance that is "regressing toward the mean."

The same kind of thinking applies in qualitative research, too. If you conduct three groups, you will likely learn new things from each one. If you do six, you'll both learn new things and gain confidence that some of what you learnt earlier is generally true. And if you do 10 groups, you are regressing towards the mean in the sense that you probably will have learnt a lot of new things, and confirmed many of them.

So for a car wash client, two focus groups in each of six markets among current customers, competitors' customers and non-users of the category were enough to change its pricing policy and service mix. And for a manufacturer of BB guns, two groups in each of five markets lead to an effective new advertising campaign.

There is even a form of qualitative research that is based on just this notion called "going on a safari." The idea here is to stay out on the road doing sessions from place to place until you stop hearing something new. When that happens, you are done and know what you need to know.

Finally, there was the case where nine high school districts purchased artificial turf for their school's football teams. This was a capital expense on a product that would last for years. Three focus groups in three different cities were conducted with superintendents, principals and members of Boards of Education. The three groups included everyone in the universe so there was no need to do more.

For most of our discussion so far we have assumed that qualitative research either was employed as a first step or stood alone. Sometimes though, qualitative research follows quantitative efforts. This might be termed "a search for meaning." A manufacturer of big trucks (not pick-up vehicles) was examining its database of all truck registrations and noticed an anomalous finding. It seemed that its share of market among medium duty trucks, the kind used, say, by furniture stores to make deliveries, was declining in favor of imported trucks, and it couldn't figure out why.

A few focus groups among buyers of its medium duty trucks and buyers of the competitor vehicles revealed that the competitor trucks, being manufactured overseas, came fairly well-equipped, but there were no options. The manufacturer's trucks, on the other hand, had to be purchased by going through a detailed specification process with the salesman – type and size of engine, type of transmission, cabin features, carrying capacity, etc. For the customer like the furniture store, which was not in the shipping industry, buying the import was easy; it was right there on the lot. Buying the US truck was not only hard, requiring answers to questions about which it was unsure, but then it had to wait for it to be built.

So here's a case where focus groups led to a major strategy change to assemble some medium duty trucks to an average set of specs and keep a few on their dealers' lots.

In conclusion, using focus groups as the only research input to aid decision making can be successful, but you cannot do so without also acknowledging and understanding the risks.

FOCUS GROUPS AND BRAINSTORMING

In Chapter 10 we discussed brainstorming and ideation processes, but because conducting focus groups is often considered a good approach for generating new ideas, an additional few words here are appropriate.

We consider it a waste of money and time to conduct customer focus groups in order to generate ideas for growing your business. Whether you are hoping to generate concepts for new products or services or looking for fresh approaches to your marketing programs, focus groups simply fall short of producing truly breakthrough new and unique ideas.

The reasons for this are many, but boil down to the fact that recruiting customers or prospects to a typical two-hour focus group and assuming they can be "creative on demand" and generate brilliant new ideas that haven't been tried is unrealistic. Focus group attendees are expert on their own lives, but not on much else. They are very good at reacting, far less capable at generating.

So while we are not fans of using customers to generate new ideas, we do discuss how respondents can be made more productive in responding to new product ideas in the "Pre-group homework" and "Recall respondents" sections of this chapter.

Setting focus group objectives and the Discussion Guide

Below are the objectives of a typical focus group study, in this case for a wallpaper catalog of the Apex Company. They follow the line of thinking developed in Chapter 8 on research planning.

The overall goals are twofold: 1) to gain an understanding of attitudes consumers have toward purchasing from wallpaper catalogs received in the mail; and 2) to explore how to improve attitudes toward catalogs so consumers would be more likely to purchase from them.

Specific objectives regarding the catalogs included:

- Determining the elements that cause consumers to open and inspect the wallpaper catalogs that arrive in their homes.
- Determining the attitudes consumers have toward large 80-page catalogs versus smaller 40-page catalogs.
- Determining the strengths and weaknesses of a number of catalogs not competing in the marketplace.
- Identifying areas that might be addressed by the Apex catalog so it becomes the desired source for purchasing wallpaper.

The Discussion Guide opposite addresses the research goal and objectives and could be used to conduct the focus groups. A Discussion Guide is the road map for how the time will be spent. It indicates the topics that will be covered and the manner in which the conversation is intended to evolve. It also indicates the relative amount of time to be spent on each topic. It does not necessarily indicate the exact words that will be used by the moderator.

No two moderators prepare Discussion Guides in exactly the same way, so your job as an evaluator or preparer of a Discussion Guide is to be sure it meets the overall goal and specific objectives of the research.

The Discussion Guide is a road map, but as the saying goes: "The map is not the territory." This means that once the group starts, reality takes hold. Respondents may jump to a topic sooner than expected and the order of discussion will need to be changed. A planned topic produces very little response and new material needs to be added, or the moderator discovers a very promising line of questioning not originally envisioned. Or someone in the viewing room has an idea for a follow-up question that is sent into the moderator.

These and more always take place. Focus groups are organic; they are living dynamic creatures and rarely correspond perfectly to the way the Discussion Guide is constructed.

Discussion Guide

1. Background:

   - introductions, etc.;
   - likes/dislikes in purchasing wallpaper from catalogs;
   - whether recently purchased/considering purchase of wallpaper;
   - factors in determining whether to purchase from a catalog versus going to a retail store.

2. Catalogs:

   - When wallpaper catalogs arrive in your home, what catches your attention? What makes you decide to look at some catalogs and not others?
   - What is it about the cover that grabs your attention? What is it about some catalogs that causes you to look through them, while others are just glanced at?

Probe importance:

   - of a well-recognized name in the decision to inspect a wallpaper catalog when it arrives;
   - of products being new, unique, and different from what might have been seen elsewhere;
   - of price, clear descriptions;
   - of companies that have their own credit plans in addition to normal credit cards;
   - of being able to track the status of order by phone or online.

---

3. Catalog companies:

- Which wallpaper catalog companies are you aware of? Which companies have you purchased from? Why those?
- Which wallpaper catalog companies are you aware of, but have not purchased from? Why those? What causes some to be purchased from but not others?
- List catalogs purchased from/aware of. Compare how they differ in terms of:
  - quality of merchandise;
  - ease of shopping;
  - offering good prices/good promotions;
  - customer service;
  - reputation;
  - price.

4. Apex versus competition:

- Pass out two Apex and two competitors' catalogs. Allow respondents 15 minutes to review. Have respondents make notes as to what they liked/disliked about each catalog.
- Rank the catalogs in terms of most to least compelling. Which catalog did you find most compelling? (Choose the most compelling.) Why that one? List the areas liked/disliked.

Probe:

- Does the catalog allow making a buying decision easy?
- In what ways is the catalog helpful?
- Is the catalog easy to read? In what ways?
- Is the catalog unique/different from the others? In what ways?
- How do you feel about the manner in which the products are shown and described? What about the quality of the photographs/product colors being true?
- What about the merchandised categories/depth and breadth of selection?
- What about the prices?
- If you want to place an order, could you do so without calling the number given for help? If not, what would you need to know?
- What additional information would you need to make a decision to purchase from the catalog?

Repeat the above process for the other three catalogs.

The results of these focus groups allow the company to develop a list of areas that could be addressed to make the catalog more competitive. This list could then be researched through a second research survey designed to determine which ones would provide the greatest competitive advantage.

SETTING UP FOCUS GROUPS

There are a variety of things to consider when planning focus groups: the composition of the groups, how many groups, whether certain locations are better than others, and whether a male or female moderator would be more appropriate.

The question of male versus female moderator is an interesting issue. Years ago, there was pharmaceutical client that marketed birth control pills. All its focus groups had been conducted among female respondents by a female moderator, which seemed fitting. The company liked the way we moderated focus groups for its headache products and asked if we'd be willing to moderate a couple of birth control focus groups among women – just to experiment.

The rationale was that a male moderator could play dumb and the women would express things that they might think would be obvious to a female moderator and, therefore, not express. We reluctantly agreed to conduct the groups.

The groups were uncomfortable for the moderator and difficult for the women. He blushed and was embarrassed when asking the women highly personal questions about their sex lives. The women were squirming in their chairs and reluctant to give more than curt answers. At the end of each group, the women were told we were experimenting and asked how they felt about having a male as a moderator. The answer we remember most came from a beautiful, 25-year old, single woman, who said: "Well, you were very professional, but you just don't get it. Men wouldn't."

Most of the time, though, it really doesn't matter whether the moderator is male or female. A competent moderator can effectively address the objectives of any Discussion Guide.

Consider the following. We have conducted groups among nuclear physicists without an engineering degree, among pharmaceutical researchers without a biology degree, among a wide variety of physicians without a medical degree, among teens and children even though we've long passed that age group, and among avid fishermen though we prefer to buy fish rather than catch it. The examples could fill this page.

The reason we have been successful is that familiarity or technical expertise with a topic are not as important as are: 1) understanding what the marketing problem is, 2) knowing how the research is supposed to provide information to help make a decision and, 3) getting people comfortable enough to talk openly and honestly about a topic.

If you have a particularly sensitive topic, just use your common sense in deciding whether a male or female moderator is more appropriate to ask the questions.

Keep respondents as homogeneous as possible

Once you have developed your research goal and objectives, you must determine the customer or prospect targets who would provide you with the greatest opportunity for growth. Do you want to persuade heavy users to spend even more? Light users to become heavy? Users of your competitors' products to become users of your products? Do you want to attract younger customers, higher-income customers, or men more than women?

Set priorities. Don't try to learn everything about everybody all at once. When you conduct groups among respondents who have similar backgrounds, it is far easier to crystallize a perspective about that target.

When you mix targets in the same group, it's more difficult to determine whether answers that come from one target influence the answers from another. You may fail to get consistent points of view because you have such different respondent lifestyles and demographics, and this can get in the way of clear learning.

There are certainly times when it might be productive to mix respondent types: mixing perhaps older and younger respondents, men and women, or heavy users and light users. Doing this will generate a wide and disjointed range of attitudes, perspectives, opinions, and preferences, which might be the best thing to do given your focus group goals. Just realize that, when you interview disparate targets at the same time, it is more difficult to develop cohesive theories about any one target.

Here's a trick of the trade you might try. When combining different segments in one group, you can keep straight who is who by using different color name badges or by seating one type of respondent on one side of the table and a second type on the other.

Always conduct more than one group of a type

If you decide you want to understand attitudes of heavy and light users better, conduct at least two groups for each type. If you want to focus on the attitudes of younger vs older respondents, conduct at least two groups for each. Remember, it is always prudent to conduct more than one session for each type rather than to rely on the attitudes of a single group.

This truism comes from the fact that, even though respondents have been recruited to have similar characteristics, it doesn't mean they will have the same attitudes and perceptions. In fact, it is not surprising to hear diametrically opposed attitudes from a first group to a second group. The trick, in fact, may be trying to figure out why respondents who have similar characteristics have such different opinions.

You'll also find that a first group provides the broad strokes. It allows you to begin to understand attitudes and productive lines of questioning. By then following the most productive lines of questioning in follow-up sessions, your learning builds dramatically. Taking them together, you develop a richer understanding and appreciation of the issues.

As moderators like to say, conducting only one group for a particular target can produce idiosyncratic results. Therefore, always conduct a minimum of two of a type to ensure your first wasn't a bunch of eccentric or peculiar respondents.

Consider multiple locations

Assuming you do business in more than one area, consider at least two geographic locations for your focus groups. Because attitudes and perceptions usually differ geographically, it is prudent to represent at least two areas. In the US, the north vs the south, the old northeast and the new west, and urban vs rural areas are good examples. Geography matters because the history is different, the weather patterns are dissimilar, the natural resources and industrial bases vary and, as a result of all these, so do culture and the resulting behavior. And if you learn that markets do differ by geography, of course, you'd have to consider different business approaches.

Focus group facilities

Focus group facilities are available to rent in every major market and in many secondary ones as well. These facilities exist for the main purpose of supporting qualitative research, especially focus groups. (Some also rent their facilities for meetings, etc.) If you need a moderator, most will provide one (for a fee, of course) or refer you to moderators with whom they have worked, including those with appropriate ethnic backgrounds, if necessary. The facilities provide a range of services including:

- Renting discussion rooms with accompanying observation suites that allow clients to observe the groups without being seen by respondents.
- Recruiting the types of respondents needed for your groups and making sure they show up when they are scheduled.

- Providing foreign language moderators, if you are doing groups in multiple countries, and, of course, translating the Screening Questionnaire (see below) and Discussion Guide into one or more languages as well as providing simultaneous translations during the sessions.
- Providing specialized respondent recruiting such as medical doctors, business executives, people with certain medical conditions, high-tech respondents, children, older people, ethnic respondents, etc.
- Handling the incentives (usually cash) that respondents receive for participating in the groups.
- Providing test kitchens.
- Providing audiotaping, videotaping, and/or DVD recording of the sessions, including camera operators, if desired, and other audio and video equipment that you might need to use in the sessions. Some facilities have the capability of linking to the internet for remote viewing and storage of recordings.
- If needed, providing special connections and equipment to allow you to better understand how customers navigate through websites.
- Providing simple business services like copying and faxing and making a broadband connection available while you are visiting.
- Ordering and serving refreshments or meals to respondents and clients/observers.

Working with focus group facilities is very easy. A person is assigned to your project who will work with you on costs and then make sure that all aspects of your focus group study proceed smoothly.

Finding a group facility is also simple. There is a directory called *Impulse Survey of Focus Facilities* that is published every year. The directory lists hundreds of focus group facilities throughout the US as well as internationally. Each facility is rated by moderators who have used the facility in the past. An overall rating is provided, as are individual ratings regarding the quality of recruiting, staff, the facility itself, location, food, and value.

You can browse through a number of facilities in an area and call the ones that are convenient or have the highest ratings. The cost of the directory is $85 per year in the US, and you can get it by phone (310–559–6892), fax (310–839–9770) or from its website (http://www.impulsesurvey.com). You can also check out www.quirks.com. In the US, listings of focus group facilities can also be found on www.bluebook.org and www.greenbook.org.

Facility costs

Focus group facilities provide cost estimates for each of the services provided. Costs are broken down as follows.

1. *Room rental.* In the US you can expect a fee of $400 to $500 for a typical two-hour focus group. Multiply this by the number of groups you will be conducting. The cost includes the focus group conference room, an easel for writing, pens and paper for the respondents, and audiotaping of the group. It also includes the cost of the observation room, where six to 12 people can sit comfortably and watch the group unobserved, as well as a host or hostess to make sure everything runs smoothly.

    Increasingly in the US the cost of videotaping (but not DVD recording) is also included in the price. Also always included are snacks such as cookies, crackers, popcorn, pretzels and candy and a wide variety of non-alcoholic beverages.

2. *Recruiting.* This cost is variable and can range from a low of about $70 per "normal" respondent to as high as $200 per respondent. Average cost is about $100. This means that, if you are recruiting 10 people to attend your group, you simply multiply your cost for recruiting that group by 10. If you are conducting four groups, you then multiply by four.

    Recruiting costs can vary by how easy or difficult the facilities feel it will be to find the types of respondents you want for your groups (see the next section on focus group Screening Questionnaires). Business-to-business groups, where professional people are required, or medical groups requiring MDs, dentists, and so forth are more costly. Most focus group facilities have a database of people (often including professionals), who have indicated a willingness to attend groups, and the majority of group studies use respondents who are screened and recruited from these databases for at least part of the required sample.

    The facilities can also recruit respondents from lists you might provide. Perhaps you wish to conduct groups among your customers and have customer names, phone numbers, and zip codes available. Or, depending on your precise need, facilities can recruit respondents using local phone or other directories or even by placing small ads in local newspapers.

3. *Incentives.* It is customary for respondents to be paid a monetary incentive for attending groups. Incentives are generally in the same range as recruiting costs. If it costs $70 per recruit, a $70 incentive usually will suffice. If the cost is $200 per recruit, the incentive will be in the $200 range. If you recruit 40 respondents for four groups

with a $70 incentive, you could end up paying out $2,800 if all 40 respondents actually show up for the group.

Usually, though, two to four respondents per group will fail to show, and you will not be charged incentives for the no-show respondents. Occasionally, other incentives are used (products, coupons, big discounts when purchasing from certain stores, etc.), but these are usually less effective in motivating respondents to participate and ensuring that they actually show up.

Often you don't want attendees to know in advance who is sponsoring the research, so offering your products as incentives would clearly not be a good idea. At the conclusion of the group you can always create goodwill by giving respondents whatever you wish.

4. *Other costs.* There are other variable costs that will be itemized in the estimate a facility provides. These include food and refreshments that you order. Some facilities include free videotaping as part of the room rental fee, but not all, and special audio and video equipment such as projectors, computers, etc. are often needed and will cost extra. You will also be charged for the use of videographers, translators, note-takers and any business services you use, e.g. copies or faxes. Many facilities also have a full kitchen available if your study calls for special food preparation.

Focus Group Screening Questionnaire

The focus group Screening Questionnaire is commonly referred to as a "Screener." This is a short questionnaire that moderators develop in concert with clients and then provide to the focus group facility. The facility uses the Screener to identify the right types of consumers to be included in the groups. It provides the facility with the means to obtain a good mix of the respondents desired in your groups.

Importantly, a Screener will ask questions to eliminate respondents who might work for a competitor, who have a language barrier, or are termed "professional respondents" because they frequently attend focus groups mainly to obtain the incentive.

Screeners are real questionnaires and should adhere to all the rules of questionnaire writing (see Chapter 15). They are not casual documents. An error in the Screener will bring the wrong people to your group and, no matter how many questions you ask them, you will not learn what you need to know.

Below is an example of a typical Screener for a camera store wishing to conduct focus groups about digital cameras. Note the explanation of the various sections of the Screener.

Digital Camera Screener

Hello, my name is _____ from _____, a market research firm. I want to assure you that this is not a sales call. We are conducting a study among people concerning the purchase of cameras. May I have a few minutes of your time? Good.

1. First of all, are you, or is any member of your household, employed in the camera industry, such as a manufacturer, distributor, or retailer of cameras? IF YES, TERMINATE.

2. Do you or any member of your immediate family work for a marketing research or marketing consulting firm, an ad agency or PR firm, a direct response agency or a communications design firm? IF YES, TERMINATE.

   (*Explanation:* It is usually desirable to screen out respondents who work in or are associated with the industry in which your focus groups are being conducted as well as those involved in marketing or marketing research. This is done to ensure that atypical respondents do not participate in the groups and that a potential competitor does not become aware of your research.)

3. In the past six months, have you participated in any research studies or focus groups conducted for any company selling cameras? IF YES, TERMINATE.

   (*Explanation:* It is unwise to allow respondents into a group if they have had recent experience in the research topic, as they tend to become overly informed about the topic and therefore would be considered atypical. There are some cases, though, where familiarity with a topic is helpful and provides valuable input. In such a case, this screening question would be eliminated. The advisability of recruiting such respondents will be discussed later in this chapter.)

4. When it comes to buying cameras for you or your family, are you the primary decision maker regarding where a purchase would be made? IF NO, ASK TO SPEAK TO THAT PERSON.

   (*Explanation:* You want to speak immediately to the person whom you want to participate in your group. There is no point in screening a respondent only to find out later that the person is not the decision maker when it comes to your products or services.)

5. Do you have children of school age living at home? IF NO, TERMINATE.

6. Do you have a computer in your home? IF NO, TERMINATE.

7. Which of the following do you personally use on a regular basis? READ LIST; CHECK ALL THAT APPLY.

cell phone	_____
pager	_____
PDA	_____
laptop computer	_____

MUST USE AT LEAST TWO DEVICES; OTHERWISE, TERMINATE.

8. How interested are you in digital cameras and digital photography? Are you:

Very interested	_____
Somewhat interested	_____
Not interested	_____

RECRUIT AS MANY AS POSSIBLE WHO ARE VERY OR SOMEWHAT INTERESTED.

(*Explanation:* This series of questions is intended to include only respondents who have children living in their home and are technologically savvy. As you will surmise from the screening questions that follow, the goal of this group is to explore attitudes toward the purchase of digital cameras. These questions will ensure that respondents are in the desired target group. Of course, you would have to decide what questions would be appropriate to ask when recruiting for your particular study.)

9. In the past 120 days have you personally gone to a retail store and shopped for or purchased a camera? IF NO, TERMINATE.

(*Explanation:* Since the company selling digital cameras is a retailer, it is important to ensure that respondents coming into the group have personally shopped at retail stores in the recent past and not just made a decision to purchase using the internet or a catalog. If appropriate, you would use a question like this to qualify respondents for your groups.)

10. What one retail store that sells cameras do you shop at most often? DO NOT READ LIST. RECRUIT A GOOD MIX OF STORES.

Target	_____
Walmart	_____
Costco	_____
Other	_____

IF OTHER, TERMINATE.

(*Explanation:* In this case, the focus group is to be conducted among a mix of customers loyal to the above three stores. If the study was being conducted for Walmart and it wanted to identify Target customers for its groups, this question would be appropriate. The same question could be used to identify and recruit those loyal to any other competitor. A similar question could be used if you are trying to recruit your customers for the groups.)

11. Approximately what percentage of your technology purchases for your household products such as cameras, computers, PDAs, or entertainment products, are made:

At a retail store _____
   (MUST BE AT LEAST 51 PER CENT)
Using a catalog and phone or fax _____
Using the internet _____

(*Explanation:* The study is designed to determine attitudes toward purchasing digital cameras from retail stores. Again, it is important here to recruit shoppers whose primary channel of purchase is a retail store rather than another channel.)

We would like to invite you to attend a focus group discussion about purchasing digital cameras. The session will be held on [date] at [time]. The location of the group is [address]. You will be paid for your participation.

Prior to the focus group we would like you to visit a retail store near you. We would ask you to look around the digital camera department and fill out a brief questionnaire. And, again, I want to reiterate that no one will attempt to sell you anything as a result of your participation. Are you willing to attend? Good.

(*Explanation:* Prior to attending the focus group, respondents are being asked to visit the digital camera department of a retail store. Therefore, the experience will be fresh in their minds when they attend the group, and they will be better able to express their attitudes and opinions regarding how digital cameras are being sold. As previously pointed out, it is sometimes helpful to have respondents become more informed about the topic before they attend groups. Shopping assignments are a good way to accomplish this.)

I just have a few more questions for classification purposes.

12. Is your age (RECRUIT A GOOD MIX):

Under 21 _____
21 to 34 _____
35 to 44 _____
45 to 54 _____
55 or over _____

13. Are you employed (RECRUIT A GOOD MIX):

Full time _____
Part time _____
Not employed _____

14. Is your total family income before taxes:

Under $50,000 _____
(DO NOT RECRUIT MORE THAN THREE RESPONDENTS)
Over $50,000 _____

(*Explanation:* There are usually a number of demographic questions that are part of a Screener. Setting demographic quotas ensures that the group is not made up of respondents who have the same characteristics. In this case, age, employment status, and income are important for ensuring a good mix.)

15. Interviewer: Your signature below indicates that this respondent is fluent in spoken English; OTHERWISE TERMINATE. If you are not sure, ask the respondent to describe their favorite TV show and then make a determination.

Signature _____

(*Explanation:* This check ensures that the respondent will be fully able to participate in the session and does not have a language barrier.)

Please mark your calendar for [repeat date and time]. Do you want us to e-mail you the questionnaire or fax it? If fax, what is your fax number?
We will call you in several days to make sure you received the questionnaire and also to remind you of the time of the focus group. If for some reason you cannot attend, will you please call us at [number] and let us know? Thank you.

Name
Address
Phone

(*Explanation:* It is always wise to follow up with respondents to ensure that they received what might be needed for the group and to remind them to attend.)

Focus group Screeners can be relatively simple and straightforward or quite complex. Questioning should be precise enough to ensure that you are recruiting respondents whose opinions are representative of your target. Clearly, you want to avoid spending a great deal of money recruiting respondents who are not the ones you should have questioned. Whatever the number of questions it takes to accomplish this task will determine the length of your Screener.

Of course, there are times when, no matter how hard you try, your Screener fails to ask the exact questions that are necessary to identify the right target. In such cases, ending up with a few wrong respondents can be a learning experience anyway. At the least you'll then have information that will cause you to question your target market assumptions and be better able to develop the necessary screening questions the next time around.

HOW TO BE AN EFFECTIVE FOCUS GROUP MODERATOR

Should you moderate your own focus groups or should you pay an experienced moderator to conduct your groups? That's like asking lawyers if they should represent themselves in a criminal trial, with common wisdom saying they'd have fools for clients. Nevertheless, there are many lawyers who can and do argue their own cases and are quite successful at it.

If you're going to be an effective moderator, you have to start sometime. And if you have what it takes, it won't be long before you're pretty good. To decide if moderating is for you, consider the following necessities.

Suspend your ego

Good moderators have no ego involved in the topic. They don't care if respondents like something or not. They aren't interested in convincing anybody of anything. They have absolutely no position on the subject. They are neutral and allow everyone's ideas to be equally valid. They are there to learn and to ensure that everyone is heard. They are totally unbiased.

This is arguably the most important aspect in moderating successful focus groups. We have seen company presidents, marketing directors, brand managers, and market research people attempt to moderate. These are very smart people, who know a lot about their products and services, certainly far more than the respondents in their focus groups (and more than a moderator they might hire). However, they can be disasters when it comes to being effective moderators.

The minute a group gets an inkling the moderator has a position on the subject, that group is lost. Nothing will turn off a group faster than a moderator who doesn't know how to phrase questions in an unbiased manner. A moderator who seemingly invalidates a respondent's opinion because of a need either to prove the respondent wrong or to change the respondent's point of view to that of the moderator, will lose that respondent totally and most likely everyone else in the group.

To determine if you can suspend your ego when conducting focus groups, give an honest answer to the following questions:

- Can you be totally unbiased for two hours?
- Can you refrain from being defensive?
- Can you smile at respondents when you are seething inside because you don't like what you hear?
- Can you let the respondents be the experts they pretend to be even if they haven't a clue what they're talking about?
- Can you learn how to phrase questions so that respondents have the space to change an opinion, but not feel intimidated or diminished in doing so?
- Can you suspend judgment regarding silly, stupid, uninformed, or misinformed respondents?
- Can you regard every opinion as equally valid whether you like the respondent or not, or whether he or she is a pain in the neck or not?
- Can you seem relaxed and not be flustered when you get off track or hear something that suddenly throws you off?
- Can you listen effectively to respondents whom you might regard as below your social status?
- Can you suspend your vested interest in what the focus group is telling you?
- Can you refrain from being frustrated and confused when one group after another is telling you a different story or giving you a different picture?

If you answer "no" to any of these questions, consider hiring a professional moderator and studying his or her skills until you feel comfortable with your ego issues. Otherwise you'll be wasting your money trying to moderate your own groups.

Be relaxed

The first few years we moderated we would perspire in groups. We were nervous. We worried about everything. What was the client observing our groups thinking? Were we going to be able to get around to all the questions in our Discussion Guides? Were the respondents saying things we thought the client wanted to hear? Were we asking questions the right way and in the right tone? We were not relaxed moderators.

In and of itself, being on edge needn't hinder your ability to conduct an effective focus group. We were great moderators in those days even though we were very nervous going into a new study. It didn't hinder our ability to suspend our egos and trust where we were going. And it didn't compromise our ability to listen effectively to our respondents.

As we gained more experience in moderating, we learnt to relax and enjoy the time we had with each group. Two-hour groups went by in a flash. We became sharp in our ability to maintain a broad perspective when large strategic issues were being explored. And when close-in tactical issues were the focus, we became adept at exploring the minutiae of a topic.

If you can suspend your ego and learn to relax when facilitating, you can become a good moderator. The rest is simply practice. Read on.

Be aware of where you're going

One focus group is never the same as the next. If your focus group study calls for four groups, you can be assured that each group will be different from the previous one – sometimes subtly so, sometimes radically so.

Many moderators, both new and experienced, become confused when respondents who are recruited to have the same characteristics, say your best customers, express totally divergent points of view. In the first group, the best customers might talk glowingly about product quality, while in the second they might focus on great service and make little mention of product quality. The third and fourth group could be a bunch of complainers regarding product quality and service – even though they are great customers.

Remember, focus groups are *not* about achieving consensus.

Just as you are beginning to find a consistent pattern in what focus group respondents are saying, and just as you are becoming comfortable thinking you have a handle on the problem, things are likely to change. All your theories will go down the drain. And you will find yourself flustered and lost.

What is critical to remember is that a focus group study should be viewed in its entirety – and in retrospect. Just as you should suspend your ego when moderating, you should suspend judgment about what you are hearing until after all the groups have been completed. If the study calls for four two-hour focus groups, you will have an eight-hour continuum of discussion.

What takes place in the first hour is no more or less valid or important than what takes place in the last hour. The goal is to observe a range of thinking and of attitudes and then begin to analyze what you have heard.

Don't become frustrated because you can't achieve consensus. In fact, "consensus" is not a word that applies to focus groups. Be aware of where you are going, and remember being aware means knowing that:

- All the groups should be completed before you reflect totally on what you hear.
- Ideas, thoughts, and thinking patterns as expressed in one group should be explored in the next and, if you fail to receive consistent responses, the goal is to understand why this is happening.
- Exploring why you are getting negative opinions in one group, but positive opinions in another is what groups are about.
- Focus groups are never about achieving closure, but rather about observing the options.
- The more disparate the opinions and attitudes, the better the job you are doing as a moderator.

Seasoned moderators are comfortable with a lack of consistency in their focus group studies. In instances when groups concur on an issue, there is the strong temptation to think that the results will hold true for everyone – that they are projectable. Remember our earlier discussion on risk.

Survey research among a statistically reliable sample is the only way to definitively determine whether the different opinions and ideas expressed in focus groups are important or unimportant and to determine which ones are the keys to improving your business.

The warm-up

Respondents in focus groups don't know each other, and they certainly don't know you. As the moderator, it's your job to put people at ease immediately and to let them know that what they have to say is important. To accomplish this in less than 10 or 15 minutes, try these techniques for warming up a group.

The standard moderator approach

Most moderators go around the table and have respondents introduce themselves one at a time. Typically it goes something like: "Hi, I'm Bob. I've been conducting focus groups for a number of years. I'm an independent moderator and I'm hired to talk to people on many different topics.

"I want you to know that there are no right or wrong answers here. I'm just interested in your opinions, no matter what they might be. I'd like to first go around the room and have everyone introduce themselves. Susan, let's start with you. Tell me a little about yourself. Where do you live? Do you have a family? If you work, what type of work do you do?"

The moderator then continues around the table, referring to the name card in front of each respondent and addressing each by name.

The inclusion approach

Using this approach, you would introduce yourself as suggested above. Now rather than going around the room one at a time, you would say to the group: "In a minute I want you to turn to the person next to you and introduce yourself. I'd like you to find out a little bit about that person such as if they have a family, the type of work they do, whether they've had a good or bad day. Then I'm going to ask you to introduce that person to the rest of the group. OK?"

"John, say hello to Susan. Bill, say hello to Jack [and so on]." After pairing off respondents, the moderator leaves the room for a few minutes while the respondents talk to each other.

We like the inclusion approach because it immediately connects one respondent with another, forming a bond. It gives respondents the feeling that they're not alone. Most importantly, it raises the energy level in the room because everyone is engaged at once. After a few minutes of chatter, the moderator returns and asks for everyone's attention. Respondents should be told to talk one at a time because it's difficult for the moderator to follow what one person is saying when there are side conversations or when people interrupt each other. The moderator then turns to the first pair and says, "John, tell me about Susan."

The jump-right-into-it approach

Often a good way to start a focus group is to immediately tell respondents about the topic. For example, the moderator could say, "We're going to talk today about shopping for a new car. What I'd like to have each of you do is take a pencil and paper and write down what you like about shopping for a new car and what you dislike."

After giving respondents a few minutes to write, the moderator asks respondents to introduce themselves and then read their likes or dislikes about new car shopping. The moderator could also have respondents say hello to each other per the inclusion approach and have them create a list of likes and dislikes together.

The approach you use often depends on the topic and the types of respondents in the group. Professional groups (medical doctors, lawyers, and business executives) are not particularly comfortable with the inclusion approach. They often feel silly introducing a stranger in these circumstances. And trades people or blue-collar respondents are often ill at ease when asked to introduce someone they have just met. For most other types of respondents, though, the inclusion technique is a good approach for making people feel comfortable and putting them in the mood to talk.

Here are a few more hints to make people feel comfortable during the warm-up:

- Don't be too serious. Smile. Chuckle when a chuckle is appropriate.
- Share a little of yourself as long as it reveals nothing about your opinions on the topic. Tell a respondent, "I know how you feel when kids scream in restaurants. That happens to me a lot."
- Stroll around the room while people are introducing themselves. It breaks the formality of the situation.
- Dress casually. Respondents relate better to a casually dressed moderator than to one who is stiff and formally dressed.

Always call on people by name

Some moderators are great at remembering names. If you are so blessed, introduce yourself as respondents come into the room, and get their names in return. You'll find that respondents love the fact that you remembered their name and tend to be more open in their remarks as a result.

Nevertheless, don't refrain from using respondent name cards on the conference table. Just because you don't need them, doesn't mean that everyone else in the room doesn't. People in a group like to know who the other participants are. Once a session gets flowing, they are inclined to address other respondents by name to ask them questions of their own.

In every group there will be some respondents who will be more aggressive than others in giving their opinions. The bane of every moderator's existence is having one or two overly verbal, overly opinionated respondents in a group. Such respondents can dominate a group if the moderator lets them. One clue about whether there might be such a person in your group is to see if someone voluntarily sits directly opposite the moderator. The moderator is the most important and powerful person in the room; the one who wants to sit opposite is also a power-seeker.

Also, when a question is posed to the group in general, the respondents likely to offer their opinions first will be the verbal ones. For example, the moderator might say, "I'd like to talk about what it's like to open a new checking account at a bank. What are your thoughts?" If the moderator continues to ask questions of the group in general, the same two, three, or four people will be the ones who pipe up. The better approach is "I'd like to talk about what it's like to open a new checking account at a bank. What are your thoughts, John?"

Just because a respondent must be coaxed to respond to a question does not make his or her opinions any more or less valid than those of a dominant respondent. As a moderator, you must be constantly aware of the equal-time rule. At the conclusion of the group, you should be clear as to where each and every respondent is coming from on virtually each and every question. If you find that you can only recall the opinions of a few, you have not obeyed the equal-time rule. You have let the few dominate the many.

Directing questions to respondents by name not only makes the laid-back respondents feel that their opinions are as valid as anyone's, but it sends a message to overbearing respondents by quieting them down. Most importantly, though, it evens out the discussion and allows the moderator to understand each respondent's unique perspective.

Listen intently

Good moderators have an ability to pick up nuances and details that make for immensely productive groups. They are able to focus their complete attention on the respondent doing the talking. They can blank out all the other noise going on around them.

When one respondent is talking, there is a strong tendency for moderators to think about the next question or the next respondent they should call upon. It's impossible to listen carefully while thinking too far ahead. If you are overly concerned with where to go next, you will not be likely to seize on a thought-provoking comment that could trigger an extremely productive line of questioning.

Nevertheless, being able to listen intently to one respondent, while thinking two questions ahead, is important to being an effective moderator. Some moderators have a natural ability in this regard; others just never get it

To get better at listening, follow these guidelines.

Paraphrase

This means picking up on what one respondent says and using it to address another. Susan makes the comment, "I love it when my husband buys my clothes. He has a great knack for picking up on the next big trend." The comment implies that Susan likes trendy clothes but may not trust her own judgment to choose new styles. Paraphrase the thought by turning to Hilary and saying, "I hear Susan saying she likes trendy clothes and really trusts her husband to make choices for her. How do you feel about that, Hilary?" Paraphrasing is one of the techniques that will cause moderators to listen more intently.

Write it down

As respondents are talking and making points, moderators can scribble notes to themselves. We like standing at an easel and making notes right in front of the group. In addition to forcing us to listen carefully, it also makes respondents feel that what they are saying is important.

Other moderators prefer to make notes on a pad while sitting at the conference table. A combination of both also works well. While making notes, put an innocuous mark (*, !, ^) next to comments that you feel are interesting and deserve further probing or paraphrasing. By writing down respondent comments at various times throughout the group, you'll find yourself worrying less about remembering everything being said and more about the tone, manner and substance of what is being said. This will give you the space to focus on comments as they're being made.

And, remember you will have audio and video tapes to review and/or perhaps verbatim notes from a note-taker. If you choose to write your own notes as the group proceeds, be careful not to become ponderous. Stopping for long periods of time to write down your thoughts can cause the group to lose its spontaneity and for you to miss respondents' expressions and other non-verbal responses that might be important.

Recap

Recapping is a cousin to paraphrasing, but broader in scope. Assume you've just finished questioning mothers about the challenges of raising children. You have your notes and you take 30 seconds to look them over. You might recap by saying, "OK, you gave me a lot of issues. They include academic concerns, social concerns, and concerns about being well-rounded and having outside hobbies and activities." You could then turn to Emily and say, "Emily, how would you recap what everyone has said?" Recapping gives everyone a second chance to express themselves. It forces respondents to express in their own words what they've heard. By doing so, you'll find new and different takes on the subject.

Moderator reversal

Another great listening aid is to ask a respondent to be the moderator for a question or two. Have one or two respondents ask questions of the group. Often respondents have a totally different frame of reference on a topic. Say to the group, "I've asked a lot of questions about what it means to have a clean house. If you became the moderator, write down one question you'd ask the group about a clean house that we haven't discussed." The moderator would then ask various respondents to pose their question to the group, and new or fresh thoughts that emerge would be probed.

These techniques not only force the moderator to listen better, but they generate an active and involved group. They also provide snippets of time for the moderator to think ahead and plan where to take the group next.

Probing

By far the most important skill that separates great moderators from the rest is knowing when and how to probe. They know or sense when it is important to dig below the answers that respondents give because there is more to be learnt.

In every focus group, there are hundreds of opportunities to probe. After asking a general question and getting a response, probably the one probe that moderators use most with a respondent is "Why do you say that?" "Why do you say that?" is the beginning of what is referred to as a "question ladder." If you ask a respondent, "Why do you say that?" multiple times (two, three, four times), you will find a wealth of information in their remarks. For example:

Respondent: I love driving my car fast.
Moderator: Why do you say that?
Respondent: Because it gives me a sense of freedom.
Moderator: Why do you say that?
Respondent: Well, I guess because there is no one around to tell me what to do.
Moderator: Why do you say that?
Respondent: Because my wife hates it when I drive fast. When she's not with me, I can pretend I'm Mario Andretti.

"Why do you say that?" probes help to get to deeper levels of attitudes and feelings and to surface thoughts and ideas that aren't easily or quickly expressed. In this case, the comment "I love driving my car fast" is so vague that it begs for probing and clarification. The final ladder probe surfaces a whole race car frame of reference that would never have emerged otherwise.

Another example of probing is to use the answer that a respondent gives as the basis for another question. Here is an example of answer probing:

Moderator: Why do you brew coffee at home on some mornings, but go to Starbucks for coffee on other mornings?
Respondent: I don't know. Just for a change of pace.

Moderator: What do you mean by change of pace?
Respondent: On some mornings I might have a little more time to sit and relax. Even though I brew Starbucks coffee at home, it never seems to be as good. So I go to the Starbucks up the block.
Moderator: Beside the coffee, is there anything else you like about sitting and relaxing at a Starbucks?
Respondent: When I leave Starbucks, I'm more ready for the day. I just feel a little more energized than when I have coffee at home.

You can see that the moderator probed every answer the respondent gave by turning it into another question. This probing surfaced the idea of being energized when having coffee at Starbucks rather than at home, which could be an interesting advertising concept that Starbucks might wish to explore further.

When probing, it is also appropriate to question more than one respondent on a subject. Take the following:

John: I love shopping at Lands' End because the clothes fit me so well.
Moderator: Norman, what is it about the fit of clothes at Lands' End?
Norman: They fit in a way that makes me feel like I'm roaming Africa on a safari – kind of loose but relaxed.
Moderator: Harry, do you get that loose and relaxed feeling when you wear Lands' End clothes?
Harry: Not exactly loose and relaxed. I'd describe it as casual, you know, not pretentious.

Probing across respondents has the effect of keeping everyone involved in the conversation. In using this technique, care should be taken not to push respondents who find that the areas being probed have little to do with what may be important to them.

Here are a few guidelines to indicate when further probing is appropriate:

1. When you're getting the same answers over and over again – your questions are likely to be superficial.
2. When the answers you're getting fail to suggest actions that you feel you are likely to take.
3. When your gut tells you there's more to it than is being expressed.
4. When your experience indicates that what respondents are saying will fail to result in added sales.
5. When you know that answers really exist in nuanced attitudes.
6. When you are looking for something that might produce a paradigm shift.
7. When you simply become bored with the answers you are getting.

Probing is very much an art and is best done by feel. The greater the experience moderators have in a product category, the more they are able to pick up areas that are ripe for probing. When respondents give unusual or out-of-the-ordinary responses, these will jump out at an experienced moderator and be a cause for probing and digging deeper for the real meaning.

Being good at probing will come in time. You can speed up the process if you listen to the audiotapes of your groups. In doing so, you'll be amazed at the times you failed to seize on a respondent's remark and where probing could have added greatly to your learning.

Knowing when to change subjects

Beating a topic to death should always be avoided. When questioning and probing on a subject ceases to be productive, it is both aggravating to respondents and a waste of valuable group time. Knowing when you have reached that point is the trick. You can sense that happening when:

- You have given all the respondents a chance to respond to the same basic set of questions and feel that you can now summarize their collective feelings and opinions.
- All the respondents give basically the same response when you ask a question.
- You have tried to probe a topic by rephrasing and you don't get any new information.
- You are able to anticipate what respondents will say before they say it.
- You sense respondents getting fidgety and losing interest.

Knowing when to move from one topic to another comes from "feeling" the group. Respondents will let you know when they have more to say on a subject. They may shake their heads in agreement or disagreement when another respondent is talking, or be inclined to interrupt because they are anxious to say something. They might pick up on the comments of each other and start talking before you have to ask a question.

When any of these things happen, you'll know that the group is engaged and has more to say. In fact, when this happens, the group is actually doing much of the work. The moderator then becomes the referee whose job it is to make sure everyone gets heard.

Another important point in moving off a topic is to know how much time you have. In developing a Discussion Guide, some topics will be far more important than others. Most moderators will anticipate the time they should spend with each topic and will move off a topic when the time allotment is reached. Below is the Discussion Guide that appeared earlier in this chapter (the notes in brackets shows how the moderator broke up the time allotted to each topic):

1. Background *(15 minutes total; complete by 15 minutes into the group):*
    –   introductions, etc.;
    –   likes/dislikes in purchasing wallpaper from catalogs;
    –   whether recently purchased/considering purchase of wallpaper;
    –   factors in determining whether to purchase from a catalog versus going to a retail store.

2. Catalogs *(25 minutes total; complete by 40 minutes into the group):*
    –   When wallpaper catalogs arrive in your home, what catches your attention? What makes you decide to look at some catalogs and not others?
    –   What is it about the cover that grabs your attention? What is it about some catalogs that causes you to look through them, while others are just glanced at?

    Probe importance:
    –   of a well-recognized name in the decision to inspect a wallpaper catalog when it arrives;
    –   of products being new, unique, and different from what might have been seen elsewhere;
    –   of price, clear descriptions;
    –   of companies that have their own credit plans in addition to normal credit cards;
    –   of being able to track the status of order by phone or online.

3. Catalog companies *(25 minutes total; complete by 65 minutes into the group):*
    –   Which wallpaper catalog companies are you aware of? Which companies have you purchased from? Why those?
    –   Which wallpaper catalog companies are you aware of but have not purchased from? Why those? What causes some to be purchased from but not others?
    –   List catalogs purchased from/aware of. Compare how they differ in terms of:
        –   quality of merchandise;
        –   ease of shopping;
        –   offering good prices/good promotions;
        –   customer service;
        –   reputation;
        –   price.

4. Apex versus competition *(55 minutes total; complete by the end of the group)*:
   - Pass out two Apex and two competitors' catalogs. Allow respondents 15 minutes to review. Have respondents make notes as to what they liked/disliked about each catalog.
   - Rank the catalogs in terms of most to least compelling. Which catalog did you find most compelling? [Choose the most compelling.] Why that one? List the areas liked/disliked.

Probe:
   - Does the catalog allow making a buying decision easy?
   - In what ways is the catalog helpful?
   - Is the catalog easy to read? In what ways?
   - Is the catalog unique/different from the others? In what ways?
   - How do you feel about the manner in which the products are shown and described? What about the quality of the photographs/product colors being true?
   - What about the merchandised categories/depth and breadth of selection?
   - What about the prices?
   - If you wanted to place an order, could you do so without calling the number given for help? If not, what would you need to know?
   - What additional information would you need to make a decision to purchase from the catalog?

Repeat the above process for the other three catalogs.

Within each of the above sections there are far more questions for you to ask than time would allow. Clearly, though, the purpose of the group is to probe deeply into the questions posed in Section 4. To belabor other sections by asking superfluous or tangential questions once general attitudes have been covered would minimize time for Section 4 and would jeopardize the goal of the group.

The best way to know when to get off a topic is to know what you want to accomplish in the group. Don't be tempted to spend time on a topic that is less than critical to the goals of the group. Don't be tempted to spend time on questions when you can predict how respondents will answer.

Following the Discussion Guide

The operative word here is "guide". Discussion Guides are not questionnaires. When a questionnaire is administered to a respondent, it is done by the script; every respondent is asked the same questions the same way. When a Discussion Guide is administered in a focus group, it is done creatively and with sensitivity to the goals of the group.

When you first look at a road map you're likely to get a general picture of the route to your destination. As your journey proceeds, you'll refer to the map again to make sure you haven't made a wrong turn. A Discussion Guide is like a road map, to be referred to occasionally and to make sure you are taking the group down the intended roads.

It is impossible to follow a Discussion Guide exactly as it is written. Conversations in focus groups don't go that way. So don't even try.

Our experience with guides is that, while they are important, we don't refer to them much once a group begins. The guide will outline the areas to be covered and the general time allotted for exploring each area. It will also serve to embed in memory the variety of questions needed to be asked.

For a skilled moderator, the guide becomes almost superfluous after the first or second group of a four- or six-group study. That is, we tend to understand the patterns of thinking we're likely to encounter and vary our questions and approach. Therefore, we'll tend to rely less on the literalness of the guide and trust our experience and questioning instincts.

Not all moderators like to work this way, and it certainly is not a great approach for a new moderator. There is comfort in following the guide more closely and not risking such freewheeling in a group. Essentially it's a matter of experience and style. There is no totally right or wrong approach. That's the message here.

When all is said and done, here's our take on using Discussion Guides:

- Look at Section 1 on introductions just before respondents enter the room. Note how much time you have and wait for everyone to be seated. Each introduction will take about 30 seconds, so plan accordingly.
- Look at the time you have for the next section of the guide. As the conversation unfolds, trust that the questions in the guide will be the ones that you'll ask naturally by just listening to the conversation. If your mind goes blank on what to ask next, look at the guide.
- Take a quick glance at the guide before you leave a section. If a compelling question pops up that you haven't covered, ask it. If not, move on.
- Keep track of the time. Note the topic of the next section, scan the first area of questioning in the guide, and dive in. If your mind goes blank, look at the guide.

- Don't be afraid to skip over a section. If you have completed Section 2 and it seems natural to skip Section 3 in favor of Section 4, jump ahead. Cover Section 3 at a later time.
- If you have certain group exercises or tasks to complete, look at the guide occasionally to remind yourself what you have in front of you (see the next section on group exercises).
- Give the guide one last glance a few minutes before the group is scheduled to end. Chances are you have covered almost everything that's important. If not, you still have time to go back.

Regard each group as a time to explore thoughts and ideas about general topics. Know that explorations can follow different paths and still reach the same destination. Discussion Guides should be thought of as tools to aid in exploration, nothing more.

GROUP EXERCISES

Engaging respondents in exercises can be very productive. By exercises we are referring to periods of time in the group during which the moderator asks respondents to work on their own, in pairs, or in teams. Group exercises will change the pace of the session and are particularly useful when a group is dragging or nothing new seems to be emerging.

Group exercises can be either planned or spontaneous. If they are planned and part of the Discussion Guide, the moderator knows exactly when they should take place and how long they should last. If they are unplanned, the moderator will have to use on-the-spot judgment as to when an exercise should be tried and then instruct the group what to do.

Exercises can be productive when:

- looking for new ideas, needs, or wants;
- trying to determine the actions that you might take to change customer behavior;
- an advertisement, catalog, or other selling material is being critiqued;
- trying to develop a product or company personality;
- trying to determine product improvements.

Group exercises can also be used in a situation in which the moderator might be struggling or just be looking for a break to collect his or her thoughts on what the group seems to be saying.

Almost any exercise can be done individually, in pairs, or in teams and some can even be accomplished as a committee-of-the-whole:

- Individual exercises are valuable in forcing each respondent to think about the issues and becoming more active in group participation.
- Pair exercises are usually better in generating ideas and new approaches. Give-and-take situations are usually more productive for generating new ideas than having respondents work alone.
- Team exercises usually generate fewer ideas, thoughts, or approaches, but the ones that do emerge are usually better thought out or conceptualized.

There is no right or wrong approach here. Sometimes exercises surface the unexpected; sometimes they are totally unproductive.

Below are typical group exercises that can be done individually, in pairs, or in teams. Usually 5 to 10 minutes is appropriate for each exercise:

- *Write an ad for a product or company.* Have individuals or teams present the ad to the group and explain why they took the direction they did.
- *Create personality profiles.* Have a pile of totally disparate magazine pictures and put them in the middle of the conference table. Instruct individuals or teams to choose three to five pictures that they feel represent the personality of the company or product under study. Have respondents explain why they feel that the pictures they chose represent the personality of the company.
- *Look into the future.* Have individuals or teams write down what a company and product could do in five years that would make them want to buy. Have the ideas presented.
- *Create a wish list.* Have individuals or teams create and present wishes for the future as to how the company or product could make their life easier.
- *Critiquing.* Anything can be critiqued – an ad, catalog, product, or idea. Critiquing seems to take on greater depth when pairs or teams "conspire together." Have pairs or teams create a critique list and present their critiques and suggestions for improvements.

Group exercises are often less about the actual ideas (although sometimes a great idea will pop up) than they are about looking at the issues from various perspectives. Exercises often are best in stimulating moderator thinking and for suggesting new ideas or theories that should be explored further in the same group or with future groups.

There are thousands of ideas for group exercises and several books have been written on the subject. Of course an exercise doesn't have to be in a book for you to give it a try. The best moderators are creative on their own and if they think a particular exercise might be helpful and stimulate the discussion, they'll certainly test it out.

PRE-GROUP HOMEWORK

Sometimes it is productive to have respondents think about a topic before they attend the group. Even though respondents will be screened to represent your target market, it is unrealistic to expect them to be familiar with all the issues that you are going to question them about.

Very often it is important to get spontaneous reactions and opinions from respondents. At other times, though, it is far more productive to have respondents familiarize themselves with the topic before they come into the group. For example:

- You want to know how respondents feel about customer service in retail stores when they are shopping for diamonds, expensive electronic equipment, health foods – or anything else, for that matter. It can be extremely productive to have respondents visit several stores before they attend the group. In that way, the customer service experience will be current and fresh in their minds. They will be less speculative when making comments.
- You might be interested in how competitors package their products. If you're selling cosmetics, have respondents visit the cosmetics section of a store and purchase two packages they like and two they don't like (you would have to repay them for their purchases). When they bring their packages to the group, their task will be to compare and contrast the packages.
- You can have respondents keep a diary. Perhaps you are trying to uncover unmet needs in the kitchen. Instruct respondents to keep a seven-day diary writing down all the frustrating happenings as they go about preparing meals. It's often the little things that happen, and that are easily forgotten, that lead to breakthroughs. Having respondents keep a pre-group diary can be very productive.
- You can have respondents bring in articles. Inform them of the topics that will be discussed in the group. Instruct them to watch the newspapers, browse magazines, or surf Google, and collect two articles that they find interesting about your topic. Use this material to stimulate conversation.
- You can provide respondents with materials to review prior to the session; you can have them take pictures of their garage, for example, if you are a maker of garage storage systems, or their laundry area or their kitchen pantry area.

Forcing respondents into your issues before they attend the group can prove extremely productive. Remember, they aren't thinking about your problems the way you are. By encouraging them to do so, your learning curve will peak.

There really is no limit to the kinds of pre-group tasks you might consider and might help your study be more insightful.

BUILDING FROM ONE GROUP TO ANOTHER

A focus group study is a series of dynamic building blocks. Each group will unveil new information and new ways to think about the issues. As moderators proceed from one group to the next, they're sensitive to the ever-changing and often inconsistent attitudes that they hear.

What is always interesting is to explore from group to group the new theories that emerge. There's a challenge of figuring out why respondents with seemingly similar profiles have different attitudes and perspectives. Further, it is constructive to take concepts and ideas that one group thinks are good and explore them in subsequent groups. Always keep in mind that to conduct each group exactly the same way is missing the point.

A focus group study is about learning as you go. If that means deviating from the Discussion Guide, changing your approach to reflect what you are learning, or trying different group exercises, you should not hesitate to do so.

RECALL RESPONDENTS

Recalling respondents simply means having the same respondents return for a second or third session – or perhaps even more. This is not a popular focus group technique, but that does not negate its potential effectiveness, especially when you are trying to get below the surface to uncover new needs, wants, wishes, desires and emotions that customers have, such as when developing new products or services or looking for ideas to improve your business.

When you bring respondents in for a first group and question them, they'll express what spontaneously occurs to them in those two hours. For most focus group studies, this is enough. When it comes to digging at unmet needs, wants, wishes, and desires though, you won't be likely to get much that is new in those first couple of hours.

For the vast majority of purchases customers make, and particularly for less costly products, they aren't particularly concerned about your company, your products, or your services. Occasionally, they may read your sales materials or the labels on your products. Most of the time, their purchases are by rote. They certainly don't think much about improvements you could make and, when asked in two-hour focus groups, they rarely think beyond the obvious.

When you clue in respondents and tell them what you are trying to accomplish, you pique their interest. You surface their awareness of your issues. You make them more sensitive to what you could do for them if you wish to improve your company, products, or services and make them more loyal to you.

Think of it this way. If we were to give you two hours to come up with a great new product that addresses a need that you don't even know you have, do you think you'd come up with much? Probably not! However, if we gave you four, six, or eight hours and told you to take your time and be more aware and observant of your needs, do you think your chances for discovering new possibilities will improve? We do.

At many levels, two-hour focus groups are only a superficial probing of consumer attitudes and behavior. Try giving one or two groups diaries to complete or homework assignments after their first group, and then recall them in a week or two for a second session. At the recall session discuss their diaries, homework, and your issues. You'll be amazed at the new information that surfaces. You'll get ideas and suggestions that those same consumers didn't express in the first group simply because the ideas didn't occur to them at the moment you asked.

Consumers are experts in their own lives. And every time they make a purchase they express their expertise. Recall groups help you get closer to understanding what makes them tick and how to change their attitudes and behavior. To not take advantage of that expertise is a qualitative research waste.

TYPES OF QUALITATIVE RESEARCH

When considering the type of qualitative research best for your situation, there are a number of options. Listed below are the various qualitative methodologies and the advantages and disadvantages of each.

Traditional focus groups

Characteristics

- Usually scheduled for two hours in length.
- Consist of eight to 12 respondents.
- Tend to focus on homogeneous customer or prospect targets for each group.
- Consist of four groups for the typical study although six, eight, or even more can be beneficial.
- Are conducted in more than one location.

Advantages

- Allow give-and-take interaction, dynamic.
- Provide a learn-as-you-go atmosphere – new ideas and theories evolve and are quickly explored, improved, or discarded.
- Allow a wide number of topics to be discussed and probed.
- Great for providing background or "first blush" information on topics of interest.
- Fun, and allow easy observation by others in the company and fodder for decision making.
- Can be completed quickly, usually in less than a month.
- Less expensive than some survey research techniques.

Disadvantages

- Tendency to jump to conclusions.
- Not projectable – more than limited decision making is risky.
- Can be biased toward "groupthink" in that some respondents are swayed by the opinions of others.
- Can be dominated by respondents who are overly opinionated or verbal.

Mini focus groups

Characteristics

The same as focus groups, except that each mini group consists of four to six respondents instead of eight to 12.

Advantages

- The same as focus groups, but lower number of respondents per group, making them less expensive.
- Lower cost per group, and, therefore, more economical to add additional target segments that might otherwise be unaffordable.

Disadvantages

- Lower number of respondents per group can render the session somewhat less dynamic.
- Information provided could be less robust.
- Fewer participants means less variety in responses.
- If going to multiple markets, the travel costs may equal the cost of the research.

Recall focus groups

Characteristics

- The same characteristics as traditional or mini groups.
- Respondents recruited to attend two or more groups.
- Homework assigned between groups.
- Incentives not paid to the respondents until the completion of the final group.

Advantages

- Respondents become more aware of why they behave as they do.
- More effective at surfacing unmet needs, wishes, wants, and desires that are not immediately evident.
- Greater rapport developed with respondents so that they become comfortable expressing themselves and their ideas.
- More effective than traditional focus groups when developing new ideas, products, or services.

Disadvantages

- Expectation should be tempered – sometimes recall groups don't produce anything new or worthwhile.
- Take longer to complete than traditional focus group studies.

One-on-one interviews

Characteristics

- One respondent at a time is interviewed.
- Usually scheduled for one hour or less in length.
- Typical study can consist of anywhere from 12 to 48 or more interviews.

Advantages

- Sensitive and personal topics more easily explored.
- Lack of group pressure provides an atmosphere in which respondents can express their thoughts honestly and independently.
- Allow greater in-depth probing of each respondent.

Disadvantages

- Lack of dynamic interchange – ideas and theories expressed are not as easily explored or challenged.

- Time-consuming.
- Moderator and observer boredom are real issues.
- Analysis takes longer.

Dyads or triads

Characteristics

- Respondents interviewed two or three at a time.
- Usually scheduled for one hour or less in length.
- Typical studies can consist of anywhere from 12 to 24 dyads or triads.

Advantages

- Can be more dynamic than one-on-one interviews, as thoughts and ideas of one respondent can be commented upon by another.
- Lack of traditional group pressure – provide a more easy-going atmosphere in which respondents can express their thoughts honestly and independently.
- Allow greater in-depth probing of each respondent.
- More economical to explore the attitudes of a wider number of targets.

Disadvantages

- Lack the full dynamics of traditional focus groups – ideas and theories expressed are not as easily explored or challenged.
- Time-consuming.
- Difficult to schedule.
- Analysis takes longer.

Internet focus groups

We would be remiss if we didn't also discuss a relatively new form of qualitative research, which is often described as the internet focus group. Technology has made such a qualitative procedure available only recently, but our digging around already lists 70 providers of internet focus group services.

As with regular focus groups, the idea is to gather together a group of respondents, but rather than coming together physically at a focus group facility, respondents join in electronic space.

Internet focus groups currently take one of two main forms. One is kind of a chat room in which the moderator posts a written question and participants respond by typing their responses. Those who do not type well often are not able to fully participate – which becomes one problem with this approach. Typically chat room focus groups are done in real time and can last as long as an hour and a half.

The other method is to conduct the group while seeing respondents and listening to them. This, of course, requires that respondents have video cameras and microphones attached to their computers and appropriate software – which in and of itself is a problem as most customers and prospects don't have the required software. This problem aside, though, a moderator can now be seen and heard asking a question and the group participants can respond one at a time and can be seen and heard doing so.

This effort can be quite useful when it is difficult, too costly or will take too long to gather a group together in a single location. A good example here would be conducting international groups with respondents in different countries. Further, it is a good substitute for an older but similar form of research often referred to as "the telephone focus group," which is just another version of a conference call. Under these limited circumstances, the internet focus group can be a useful research tool.

A company called Insights On-Line, based in Point Arena, California, lists a number of additional positives associated with conducting research online. They include:

- *Responses are more objective.* Respondents participating in online focus groups tend to be more objective and straight to the point when they are not communicating face to face. They can remain a bit more anonymous and do not tend to "beat around the bush" since they are typing their responses rather than speaking them.
- *Cost effective.* In most cases, online focus groups are less expensive than traditional methods because they eliminate phone expenses, facility rental expenses, and transcriber expenses. Further, it is considerably more expensive to incentivize people to come to a central location for a focus group than to ask them to join one virtually.
- *Can recruit from a wider geographic scope.* It can be very difficult to find enough qualifying respondents for a select group inside a 25 mile radius. During an online focus group, participants can join us simultaneously from multiple locations around the globe. Also, some hard to find groups such as webmasters, MIS, network administrators, etc. are much easier to contact online than via other means.
- *Less intrusive.* Inviting someone to participate in an online focus group via e-mail or web methodologies is much less intrusive than contacting them via telephone or mall-intercept.
- *Faster turnaround.* Online focus groups can be turned around much faster than traditional methods mainly because the recruiting

process is shorter and there is no need to record and transcribe the sessions.

In spite of these positives, common wisdom is that internet focus groups have not reached the stage where they are a good substitute for a live focus group, and shouldn't generally be considered as an alternative. Should you wish to explore in greater depth why we feel this way, we'd refer you to a terrific article by George Silverman who is President of a Company called Market Navigation, Inc. Go to http://www.mnav.com/online.htm.

Essentially, our problem stems from the fact that there is no real interaction between moderator and the respondents – or between respondents – especially in the chat room version. Further, most group exercises are hard to use, non-verbal reactions are minimized and it's very hard to observe anyone in the group other than the person talking. As such, the body language and expression of respondents goes unseen and, with it, the chance to probe areas that could prove extremely productive.

Perhaps at the heart of the problem is the fact that with online focus groups there is a lost sense of community and sharing among the respondents. Also, important interaction between the moderator and a client observing the group can be compromised. As the personal interaction becomes less, the dynamic nature of the group is minimized. And with it goes the very intimacy that is the centerpiece of a great focus group study.

This is a rapidly evolving area and we expect that further technological developments will enhance the utility of online focus groups. At this time, though, we will repeat our feeling that they are of limited value.

"QUALIQUANT"

We have already spoken about the desirability of combining qualitative and quantitative research in order to truly understand a marketing problem. In fact the research community is almost universal in stressing the importance of using both qualitative and quantitative information. This is so attractive an idea that methods have been developed to accomplish this and have been termed "qualiquant."

The oldest and easiest way to do this is to treat responses to open-ended questions in surveys as qualitative data. This requires simply providing open-ended answers as verbatims. When analyzed by a skilled researcher, they can be just as useful as a transcript from a focus group.

More typical is for open-ended responses to be converted into quantitative data by creating codes that capture the breadth of the data and then counting how often a coded answer is given. In other words, the richness of the qualitative data is enhanced by converting it to quantitative projectable data.

Another easy way to combine the benefits of qualitative and quantitative research in a single study is to have skilled interviewers conduct a short duration qualitative interview, i.e. 10 minutes or less, among a projectable sample of respondents. Here again the responses are prepared as verbatim transcripts and/or can be coded and tabulated. The analysis is conducted the same way as for a focus group, but when complete can be projected to the target audience.

For several years now researchers have looked at patterns within survey responses and then re-contacted some respondents who meet specific criteria. This is another form of qualiquant, only here the quantitative data preceded the qualitative.

An example would be if a survey is being conducted on the internet and the respondent answers a sequence of questions in such a way that suggests that adding questioning and probing outside the interview might be beneficial. In such an instance, a notice is inserted into the survey at that point indicating the respondent might be phoned at a later point in time to answer a few additional questions in person. (For more information, go to www.iModerate.com.)

CREATIVE CONSUMERS

A great deal of research has been conducted on the subject of creativity. Edward de Bono's book *Serious Creativity* (Harper Business, 1992) is a wonderful read. You can also go to www.synectics.com to find out everything you might want to know from one of the earliest pioneers on the subject of creativity.

Almost anyone can be trained to be more creative. Given the right circumstances and training, most people can generate more new ideas than they ever thought possible.

Nevertheless, some people are more naturally gifted in creative thinking – quicker on the creative trigger. Finding such creative thinkers among focus group respondents is not that difficult. About 15 to 20 per cent of respondents who qualify for your focus groups will also qualify as being creative consumers.

If you are conducting qualitative research to develop new products, services, or ideas, or are just seeking a deeper level of understanding regarding unmet consumer needs, you should consider recruiting one or more groups with creative respondents.

To do so, first screen your respondents to make sure that they are in your target. Then, using the questionnaire shown in Table 11.1, ask respondents the extent to which they agree or disagree with each statement.

Table 11.1 Recruiting creative respondents

	Agree strongly	Agree somewhat	Disagree somewhat	Disagree strongly
1. You are a very energetic person	4	3	2	1
2. People say you have a great sense of humor	4	3	2	1
3. You are comfortable discussing concepts or ideas you may not be familiar with	4	3	2	1
4. You are more open to new ideas and activities than other people	4	3	2	1
5. Others describe you as persistent	4	3	2	1
6. You often dream or fantasize	4	3	2	1
7. You enjoy the uncertainty that often comes with working through a problem	4	3	2	1
8. You always like to be the first in your area to try something new	4	3	2	1
9. You would describe your childhood as unpredictable	4	3	2	1
10. You often think of solutions to problems when you least expect them	4	3	2	1
11. You often say things spontaneously without thinking	4	3	2	1
12. You enjoy making up stories	4	3	2	1

Total respondent score ___ Maximum score = 48 (12 statements × 4).

A respondent must score 36 or more to qualify as being a creative thinker.

What you will find with creative consumers is that they are more verbal, expressive, and able to speculate about issues. They are more aggressive and opinionated than normal respondents. As such, keeping a group of creative consumers under control can be a challenge for new moderators.

Nevertheless, the ideas that emerge from creative consumers often provide extraordinary fodder, especially when you are trying to stretch beyond the obvious. This can be extremely useful when your study calls for exploring emerging trends or trying to determine the needs, wants, wishes, and desires that are below the surface.

In summary

Qualitative research is an extremely valuable research tool, especially for those new to research. It can surface the many issues that might be addressed to grow a business and it can do so inexpensively. Importantly, it can focus attention on both the short- and long-term issues that need attention and, in doing so, can provide impetus for growth. However, it is an easy tool to abuse.

In developing a research program for your company, use qualitative research prudently. Understand its value and its limitations. Don't be lulled into thinking that because you have conducted focus groups or other qualitative research you have done all your homework.

What you have done is to begin the research process. For that, we offer congratulations. At the same time, we hope you won't end your search at this point.

DIGGING DEEPER

Quantitative survey research works best when its rules are obeyed. This means the rules of sampling, sample size, statistical inference, validity of scales, questioning formats, data collection methods, and analytical tools conform to well-accepted guidelines. Sophisticated practitioners of quantitative research would agree you have to know the rules before you know which ones to break and when to break them.

In contrast, sophisticated practitioners of qualitative research might say the only rule is that there are no rules – except getting the job done in a professional and creative manner. In fact, qualitative research can be characterized as more nimble and offering greater flexibility than quantitative research.

We'd like to end this chapter with a series of examples of successful qualitative research – which we define as having satisfied client needs – that didn't follow traditional approaches.

The proof is in the pudding

A well-known manufacturer of locks wanted to cross over into automotive security and compete with the best-selling steering wheel security devices. The issues were determining which of its ideas for a new device would be perceived as effective and compete most strongly with the industry leader. It also wanted to know how its ideas could be improved.

The solution was to add a live clinic to the standard focus group. First, sitting around the table, we explored issues relating to automotive security. Then we went to specially lighted parking garages and had consumers drive their vehicles to us. With a videographer catching the action, we asked consumers to try to put the new security prototypes on their vehicles and to talk through what they were thinking as they engaged in the task. We finished by going back inside the facility to wrap up.

Powerful findings resulted – stream of consciousness remarks were noted, facial expressions, voice tones, extent of fumbling behavior and instant product assessments were observed. This all provided a strong framework to understand which security device concept might be the strongest.

Mother and child reunion

An ad agency was pursuing a toy client and seeking to find something new to say about the category. The agency was seeking to gain insights about toys that the prospect didn't already know.

We conducted after-school focus groups simultaneously among mothers and their younger children using two different moderators – one who specialized in conducting groups with children, the other a traditional moderator. Many topics were explored including how new toys were learnt about, shopped for and selected. Then participants were given cash and sent shopping at a nearby toy store.

Each parent–child pair, another example of a dyad, was accompanied by a video camera operator to capture interactions during the shopping spree. Following the shopping trip, respondents came back to the focus group facility and the mothers in one group and children in the other were reconvened to discuss what happened.

The major learning was that children's role in the purchase process was less important than the kids expressed, but more important than the mothers thought. This nuance, along with interesting clips of film from the shopping experience, became the centerpiece of the new business pitch.

Getting the word out

Here's a case that can be generalized to many situations.

Public relations firms are regular users of qualitative research. Apart from the typical marketing insights, they often seek something special from their research – a way to get input on what would make an interesting story and the best way to tell it.

We used the projective technique of asking respondents to write a brief letter about the topic to their best friend. Here respondents were given the chance to think independently, without the influence of others in the group. Common responses that appeared in their letters and the use of similar words were good places to look for stories and headlines.

The moderator has left the house

A good qualitative tool is the sorting task. The idea is to ask respondents, collectively or individually, to sort objects – brand logos, real products, product attributes, names, etc. – into categories.

In this instance, the client acquired information about how consumers viewed products in the market, how they saw them as the same or different, and the features that characterized some products but not others. A twist was that the moderator actually left the room during the sorting process, saying: "I'm going to leave the room so that no one will say I've influenced your work." Of course, he just went to the observation room and missed nothing. Doing this forced a higher level of interaction, freed up quiet respondents and generally raised the energy level.

The result was a fresh view of the market and led to the development of new advertising approaches.

A picture is worth a thousand words

Picture-sorts are another familiar qualitative technique. Here a number of pictures from magazines or other sources are scattered on a table. Respondents are asked to complete any number of tasks by arraying the pictures. They could array pictures alone by themselves or in concert with other respondents.

One approach is in regard to Brand Personality. Here respondents are shown a sequence of pictures by the moderator and asked to collectively agree on the ones best associated with the companies, brands or products being studied. Respondents are asked to explain why the pictures chosen are better associated with one company, brand or product than another.

The picture-sort exercise helps respondents project their attitudes and feelings beyond what might be normally expressed. In doing so, it provides another approach for getting below the surface.

I've got, got, got no time

It used to be that pulling together respondents for a focus groups study could be completed more quickly than quantitative research. Today the reverse is often true.

In the past it was common for it to take six to eight weeks to write a questionnaire, conduct the interviews, code and process the data, analyze the data and write a report. Today, a national probability study on the telephone or via the internet can be executed and the data available in a few days. A week or so later, an experienced researcher could effectively analyze the data and make recommendations.

Some internet panel providers even turn out twice weekly studies among a random sample of consumers. Here clients can buy a few questions in these weekly surveys and obtain results plus all the demographic information quickly and at a minimum cost.

In contrast, the time necessary for conducting a focus group study hasn't changed much as it's still necessary to prepare a Screener and Discussion Guide, recruit respondents, moderate the groups and prepare a report. Travel may be involved as well.

So here's an idea when time is of the essence and a qualitative study is the right approach. Find a focus group moderator who is an expert on a subject and willing to be your respondent. Interview that individual about your product category.

Like an expert witness, many moderators (but not all) who specialize in certain areas are willing to charge a consulting fee for telling you what they know. In fact, you can go to www.quirks.com, Quirk's Marketing Research's website, and scan various category listings for moderators who focus on particular areas. This is not only a fast approach to collecting qualitative insights, but is also less expensive than conducting a full focus group study.

We have used this approach to learn about heavy users of beer and to explore an automotive concept designed to appeal to teen boys.

Man on the street

One-on-one personal interviews are another qualitative research tool. Who's to say, however, that these interviews need to be conducted at a focus group facility or over the telephone?

For a beer client we conducted "man on the street" interviews outside popular drinking establishments. Imagine an interviewer with a microphone in hand as well as a camera operator and soundman. People thought they were going to be on TV so cooperation was easy to obtain.

While this approach is not generally in the research rulebook, remember that when it comes to qualitative research there are no hard and fast rules. You are only limited by your imagination and the funds that you have available.

12

Research into emotions

It's a fact. Emotions play a major role in determining why customers purchase the products they do. Human beings are not perfect calculating automatons, logically processing data to make purchase decisions – not even the most professional of purchasing agents. The emotions and feelings customers have about companies, brands and their consumption experiences are likely to be pivotal when they vote yes to one offering and no to another.

The fact that emotions play a role in consumer decision making does not come as a bolt of lightning. It's just common sense that if you feel good about a product, you are more likely to try it and then buy it over and over again. And if a product has a way of irritating you, you aren't likely to buy in the first place – or stay with it very long, even if you give it a try.

Psychologists and marketing researchers have been studying the role emotions play in influencing consumer choices for decades. Back in the 1950s motivational research began the process of trying to uncover the hidden emotions that drive purchase decisions. This was followed by a wave of research that attempted to use physiological measures.

One such technique was referred to as "galvanic skin response research." Here consumers were hooked up to a lie detector type of device that purported to measure the emotional responses resulting from being shown advertising or other marketing materials.

There were also physiological measurements that tracked facial muscle twitching, eye pupil widening or voice pitch changes, all in an effort to assess whether people were emotionally aroused by ads, packaging, logos, promotional materials, brand names and the like.

The reason such non-verbal, physiological approaches had appeal was that emotions and feelings were thought to occur automatically and were not under the control of the person being studied in the research – unlike rational answers consumers give when asked specific questions by an interviewer. The thinking was that if a particular ad, package or brand name aroused a strong non-verbal emotional response, such a reaction would relate to future purchase behavior.

While these techniques are still around today, they are used less often. The problem is researchers have not found a correlation between strong non-verbal emotional reactions and purchase behavior. Further, they couldn't tell if the response signaled a positive or a negative emotion.

By the way, it is worth pointing out that the emotions we are talking about can come about from customers who may have purchased and used a product or service, or from those contemplating purchase. Getting prospects to become emotionally attached to a company or brand is a powerful tool for motivating them to purchase for the first time. To coin a term, this might be referred to as the creation of "brand longing," and applies to many aspirational products such as luxury automobiles or expensive watches. And certainly, once a product or service has been purchased and used, emotions play a particularly strong role in influencing continued loyalty.

There is no doubt that the stronger the emotional connections to a company or brand, the stronger the loyalty. And don't be lulled into thinking that it's only advertising or other marketing communication materials that drive emotion. The purchase experience itself, post-purchase experiences and, especially, whether the product or service satisfies purchaser needs all play strongly into customers' emotional connections.

Recognizing this as an important marketing issue presents a major research conundrum. That's because the emotions and feelings customers have toward companies and brands are often unconscious. Using traditional research, you're fooling yourself if you think you can simply ask customers to recite the emotions they have about a company or brand and always expect to get a meaningful and useful response.

To repeat – customers are often not fully aware of the emotions they have toward companies and brands and, when asked directly about them, often have trouble verbalizing anything that is meaningful.

To illustrate, try answering these questions. "How does buying a tube of Crest toothpaste make you feel?" Or, "What were your emotions when you picked up clothes from the dry cleaner?" Or, "What tugs at your heartstrings when you purchase a forklift?"

As a result, researchers are sometimes reluctant to study customer emotions, particularly in business-to-business situations where emotion is considered antithetical to making rational decisions.

Further, there hasn't been an agreed upon body of knowledge that dictates the best research approaches for getting at emotions and feelings. For the most part, researchers and marketers alike have been more comfortable posing rational questions, obtaining seemingly rational responses and basing their marketing programs on these results.

To get below the surface, knee-jerk responses obtained in traditional research studies, and to uncover the emotions at work requires new, untested and experimental research approaches. Happily, researchers are becoming more creative and finding approaches to better explain the roles emotions and feelings can and should play in differentiating their companies and brands.

A LITTLE MORE HISTORY

Guerrilla Marketing Research was written in 2006. In the book there is little mention of the importance of studying emotions. In the few years since, however, several researchers and marketing consultants have begun to espouse the critical role that emotions play in motivating consumers.

As we mentioned, the importance of understanding that emotions play a strong role in the personality of a brand goes back to the mid-1950s. More recently, in 1982 Trout and Ries published *Positioning, The Battle for Your Mind*. In it they make the eloquent case that positioning begins with the product, but is really about what is happening in the mind of the consumer. They say, "the consumer's mind reacts to the high volume of advertising by accepting only what is consistent with prior knowledge and experience" about the company or brand.

Although we don't know this to be fact, we're pretty sure that Trout and Ries would agree that consumers have a great deal of trouble expressing the emotional differences that exist in their minds when it comes to describing companies and brands. And even when pressed, they would have trouble explaining why a brand like IBM, for example, evokes a positive emotion for some, but a totally negative emotion for others.

In his 1997 book, *The Way of the Guerrilla*, our co-author Jay Conrad Levinson cites 10 emotional responses that can influence a person to buy. They are:

1. Achievement – Does your product/service contribute to the customer's sense of achievement or in the accomplishment of something notable in life?
2. Pride of ownership – Does your product/service contribute to the pride the consumer would feel from ownership?
3. Security – Does your product/service offer your customer a sense of security? This is a blanket emotion that includes money, love, acceptance, power and control.

4. Self-improvement – Does your product/service appeal to a sense of improvement?
5. Status – Does your product/service contribute to the status your consumer achieves or realizes or can show to others?
6. Style – How does your product/service fit or enhance or manifest your consumer's sense of style?
7. Conformity – Does your product/service offer the comfort and safety of the crowd? Does your product or service command a group following?
8. Ambition – How does your product/service help customers to get more out of life, to get ahead?
9. Power – In what ways does your product/service offer a customer more power or control over things?
10. Love – This is the granddaddy of them all. In what ways does your product/service allow the consumer to feel or express love?

The literature actually has dozens of such lists, most of which bear a similarity, but all of which also differ slightly. The Levinson list is not all-inclusive. For example, many lists contain the negative emotion of fear, which is frequently used by insurance companies and has been successfully employed in differentiating the Volvo brand.

EVOKING EMOTIONS IN MARKETING

So important are emotions that any modern discussion of branding always includes the notion that a brand must seek to create an emotional connection with its user. For example, in his book, *Emotional Branding*, published in 2000, Daryl Travis says: "Thinking about the value of a brand in terms of its emotional equity – how it makes your customers feel – requires the use of intuition, which makes some execs feel like a fearful fish out of water."

Here's an example. We were conducting qualitative research on new logos being considered by a maker of outboard motors for marine use. One option was quickly rejected by participants and we were struggling to understand why. In this case, a consumer helped us immeasurably when he said: "That logo is angry; this brand would never be angry."

In his course, Building Your Own Brand Foundation, long-time marketing consultant Art Katz says, "It is commonly understood that strong brands virtually always have some common emotional connections to the customer – if the brand represents something that differentiates it from other brands."

Rather than the 10 emotions Levinson lists, Katz uses a model of 29 core emotions that was developed in collaboration with Dr Paul Ekman of the University of California, San Francisco Medical School, and that

Katz refers to as "emotives." This model puts forth a more detailed emotional language that can be specifically applied to categorizing the emotions consumers have toward companies and brands.

Vadim Kotelnikovÿ, founder, Ten3 BUSINESS e-COACH, advises:

> Emotional marketing is better in many instances than rational marketing that focuses on product attributes. Capturing minds is one thing; *capturing hearts* is quite another. Build emotions in your marketing strategies; don't always chase "share of wallet" – chase "share of heart". Employ strategies that would make decisions very emotionally driven and remove the rational questions that might drive the prospect elsewhere.

All in all, the role that emotion plays in positioning companies and brands is not one that needs to be debated. Look at any national brand – Coca-Cola, Citibank, Rolex, Neiman-Marcus, Walmart, Mercedes Benz, *The Wall Street Journal* – and you can quickly find an emotion that largely defines that brand. In Levinson's model the following emotional connection are easily identified: Coca-Cola = conformity, Citibank= security, Rolex and Mercedes Benz = status and pride of ownership, Neiman-Marcus = status, Walmart = conformity, *The Wall Street Journal* = power and self-improvement. The travel industry often uses self-idealization, i.e. the extent to which a product helps us express who we are, as the defining emotion when promoting exotic places to visit or vacations in which consumers experience things like the rain forest.

However, emotions are not just the unique provenance of national brands. If you don't think that consumers in your neighborhood make emotional connections when choosing where to spend their money, you're mistaken. The Guerrillas who own the local automobile repair shop, dry cleaner, restaurant, or pest control service similarly develop emotional connections with consumers. By the way, this happens whether they plan an emotional connection or not. If you are dealing with consumers, you are dealing with emotions.

THE RESEARCHER'S DILEMMA

Researchers would be the last to deny the importance of emotions in positioning brands. However, if they were honest, they would likely be the first to admit difficulty in uncovering the emotional connections that customers have toward companies and products – particularly when those emotions are sometimes unconscious or partially unknown.

When conducting focus groups, in-depth one-on-one interviews or following other qualitative approaches, there are two common probing questions that moderators typically use when probing consumer responses. Take these examples.

Example #1

Consumer: I don't like shopping at Walmart.
Moderator: Why do you say that?
Consumer: Because I can't find anyone to help me.
Moderator: Why do you say you can't find anyone to help you?
Consumer: I told you. There's no one around when I have a question.
Moderator: Can you tell me more about why you say that?
Consumer: I don't know anything about electronics and would never buy a TV or even a printer for my computer without talking to someone.

Here the probe "Why do you say that?" achieves a certain depth of response from the consumer and a logical conclusion would be that for Walmart to compete more strongly in electronics or computer areas, it would be necessary to have knowledgeable sales staff on hand. Here the consumer gave rational responses to rational questions and the rational conclusion might be to hire more staff.

Example #2

Consumer: I don't like shopping at Walmart.
Moderator: How does shopping at Walmart make you feel?
Consumer: It makes me feel like I'm just one of the herd.
Moderator: How does being one of the herd make you feel?
Consumer: Like Walmart doesn't really need me as a customer.
Moderator: When you think a company doesn't need you as a customer, how does that make you feel?
Consumer: It makes me feel my money isn't really important to them.

Here the probe "How does it make you feel?" surfaced the feeling that money from yet another customer wouldn't make much difference to Walmart. One conclusion here would be that Walmart should depart from fulfilling a need for conformity and to instead focus on Levinson's emotion of pride of ownership and strive to communicate that for Walmart every customer is valued and cherished.

These probes are typical and both are used to uncover rational needs as well as deep-seated emotions. Do they work equally well in both instances? Are the answers they elicit complete? Do they accurately reflect the consumer's experience or is the consumer simply projecting his or her rational thoughts about Walmart? Are there any rational issues more important than the ones raised?

And is the emotion the key one for the consumer or only one that surfaced at the moment the questions were asked? In our opinion, these questioning sequences just scratched the surface.

In Chapter 11 on focus groups, we discussed how important it is to dig below the surface and to always consider using projective techniques, homework assignments and recalling respondents for follow-up sessions in an effort to get below the surface. And we advised that the typical probes when questioning consumers will only take you so far.

We've stressed that to unearth needs, wants, wishes and desires that consumers don't know they have takes new approaches and fresh insights into the way research is designed. And if creative thinking and new approaches are necessary to uncover the more rational needs that consumers have, they certainly are essential if we are to ever find the real emotional drivers of behavior.

WHERE ARE WE TODAY?

When it comes to understanding emotions, many of today's marketing researchers are largely out of their element. Most have education in general business, marketing, marketing research, or statistics. We've even run into a few with liberal arts, history or literature backgrounds.

Fewer have been trained in social sciences like psychology, sociology and anthropology – the very disciplines that focus on emotions, feelings and cultural influences in seeking to understand and explain why we behave as we do.

Research as practiced today is outstanding at explaining the rational. And we are not about to cast aspersions on the value of understanding rational behavior. In fact, we strongly believe that by understanding rational decision making we have traveled a long way in making the research profession an integral and valuable marketing tool.

Now it's time to take things a step further and, fortunately, some are.

For example, Daryl Travis' company, BrandTrust, has developed a fine reputation for combining traditional marketing research skills with the perspective of expert social scientists. It offers clients a fresh approach to understanding the feelings customers have toward brands and how those feelings can be effectively integrated into traditional marketing programs.

And Art Katz, in his *Building Your Own Foundation*, offers a particularly useful and affordable course for Guerrillas. For a very minimum expenditure he provides a detailed roadmap that explains how emotional positioning can be used to set your business apart. This is a great do-it-yourself course.

There is a company that's using hypnosis to get at customers' deep-seated emotions. Another firm is using a self-administered, web-based word association approach that profiles customer emotions toward brands and advertising approaches. In fact, if you do a web search using the key words "emotional marketing research" you'll come upon dozens of research companies purporting to conduct some form of marketing research that delves into customer emotions.

What we find interesting and hopeful is that researchers are branching out and seeking new approaches. Whether any prove to be breakaway methods for understanding customers' emotions will remain open for now. What is clear though is that if you fail to recognize the importance of customer emotions and are reluctant to delve into the emotions they have toward you, you are putting your head in the sand.

IT'S NOT ALL OR NOTHING

In stressing the importance of emotion in positioning a company or brand we are by no means minimizing the role that rational approaches play in motivating customers. We are not making an "either/or" argument. Customers are not sold by emotion alone any more than they are sold by rational arguments alone.

Look at most any large company and you'll see how they combine emotional and rational sales messages in their marketing programs. The following are a few examples:

- When Home Depot advertises, "You can do it. We can help," it makes a very strong self-improvement emotional appeal. When it stresses the variety of products it carries, great customer service and low price, it makes a strong rational appeal. One approach strengthens the other.
- Budweiser claims to be the King of Beers, which is a very strong appeal to the security emotion. What guy wants to walk into a strange bar and order a brand of beer that might have others snickering at him? Budweiser also relies on the rational by stressing beachwood aging and its long heritage as the US's best-selling beer. Bud is a leading brand in the world because it knows how emotional and rational appeals work together.
- Apple has built a mega-brand around the pride of ownership and self-idealization emotions. It actually has followers rather than customers, who will drop everything at a moment's notice to tell you Macs are far better than PCs. That doesn't mean Apple doesn't pound home rational features like its design superiority or unique graphic capabilities and the stability of its operating system.
- McDonald's evokes the emotion of conformity. You know you can walk into any McDonald's in the country and be assured you are getting the exact meal you expect. McDonald's is also consistent in stressing the great taste of Big Macs, its fast service and low prices. It's safe to say McDonald's has effectively used and integrated both emotional and rational appeals.

We realize Guerrillas don't have the resources of Home Depot, Anheuser-Busch, Apple or McDonald's. We also have the firm conviction you don't need them. Communicating your emotional position can start simply with a logo on your stationery or it can be in the way you greet your customers. As you grow and add more marketing clout, you'll find everything you do can easily find its way into the same emotional position.

Be it a sign in the window, a small ad in a local newspaper, a mailing announcing a sale, the way you design your website or a national ad you can finally afford to run during the Super Bowl, your focus on one consistent emotion will differentiate you from your competition and drive your business.

WHERE TO GO NEXT

What we also know about emotion in marketing is that it isn't just about the customer. Call it what you want, but if your company doesn't have a clearly stated vision, mission, purpose or reason for being that you and your employees embrace, you're not going to be successful in executing an external emotional position to customers.

Companies seeking an emotional position based on pride of ownership better make sure their employees take pride in their jobs. Or if you are seeking to allow customers to manifest power, better take care that decision making isn't confined to one or two offices. Or if you're seeking to motivate via the comfort of conformity, better start with making the day-to-day, location-to-location experience that customers have with you predictable and consistent.

Don't ever forget that achieving a viable emotional position is a two-way street. It goes from your company to your customer or prospect and from your customer or prospect back to your company. You do indeed reap what you sow!

In fact, one of the best places to search for a strong emotional position is with your employees – which sounds to us like a great place to start your research.

For now, though, we'll leave you with this Levinson question: "What's the best single thing you can talk about with a prospect?" And the answer is: "How they'll feel after they've made the purchase."

DIGGING DEEPER

What is a Brand Personality and why does it matter?

We want to expand on the topic of emotional positioning by discussing Brand Personality. This is a very interesting topic, which, when properly understood, can help Guerrillas make a major strategic breakthrough in marketing communications. The idea applies equally well to any market and every marketing setting.

In this discussion we do not differentiate between Brand Personality and company personality. Microsoft is the name of a company, but it is also the name of a brand. Kraft is the name of a company, but it is a brand name as well. Therefore, a company will have Brand Personality traits just as the branded products of that company have their own unique personality traits.

There is a wonderful Chicago expression, "comes with" as in "dessert comes with," and is included for free. The point is you don't get to make a decision about whether to develop a Brand Personality. You already have one; it "comes with" the very act of being in business and having customers and prospects.

A Brand Personality will develop because a business is defined by its various constituencies – most particularly its customers. The Brand Personality, therefore, is a function of every public contact made: the corporate logo, advertising, public relations, packaging, website, name, sales force appearance and behavior, customer service, office décor, building architecture, and certainly the design and performance of the product or service being sold.

To reiterate, you, as a Guerrilla, do not get to decide whether your brand should have a Brand Personality. Whether you like it or not, one will emerge. The issue, then, is to understand what your brand's personality is and how it differs from those of your key competitors.

Only by understanding your Brand Personality can you decide whether it is helping or hindering you in achieving your sales and profit goals.

Old brands sometimes have out-of-date personalities. Struggling brands sometimes have inappropriate personalities. Remember Oldsmobile's last ad campaign, "Not your father's Oldsmobile"? They had the right idea, only it came to them too late.

Sometimes even established brands have bland or underdeveloped personalities. This is a finding by itself and usually is a sign of trouble. Typically it means they have spent too little on marketing communications or have failed to effectively communicate the personality positives associated with their brand.

The point of view of the customer

When developing a Brand Personality, the point of view of customers and prospects is critical. Without first determining how the brand is perceived, it would be guesswork to decide whether and how the Brand Personality should evolve.

Most brands enjoy positive personality traits that resonate with customers and prospects and should be enhanced. Likewise, they suffer from negative traits as well, which should be addressed lest they hinder the brand from realizing its full potential.

Brands develop strongly out of both emotional and rational connections that customers and prospects attribute to them. Simply put, by conducting research about the current personality landscape of your brand from the customer's point of view, you stand a far better chance of molding the kind of personality that works, than by trying to do so by conjecture alone.

Developing a Brand Personality

There are a number of factors that are important to consider when developing a Brand Personality. Listed below are the ones that are important to understand before writing a Brand Personality profile:

- What are the physical, functional and character depictions of the brand and how do they produce a psychological bond with customers and prospects?
- What are the emotional attachments, feelings and perceptions attributed to the brand?
- What words and phrases do customers express when describing the brand?
- What is the "who" of the brand or the human personality traits that are ascribed to it?
- What is the attitude the brand takes in its advertising and marketing efforts?

As a practical matter, Brand Personality can easily be explored in qualitative research. The question below would be one way a moderator might question a focus group when exploring the personality of a brand:

Moderator: I'd like you to imagine that Caterpillar was not a large manufacturer of earth moving equipment. Instead I'd like you to imagine Caterpillar as though it were a person. If Caterpillar were standing in the corner of the room, how would you describe it as a person? What physical characteristics would it have, what age, what gender, what hobbies and interests would Caterpillar have?

Respondents have no trouble engaging in this task and the discussion would yield the "who" of the company or the human personality traits that make up the personality of the brand.

The history of Brand Personality

It turns out that the Brand Personality tool has a long history.

In 1954, one the pioneers of motivational research, Dr Ernst Dichter, in an article entitled "Your product's personality determines its sales," wrote:

> Each time a consumer sees an ad, a package, a point of purchase display, hears about a product, speaks about a product, or tries a product, the consumer is building an impression of that product. In the process, the consumer perceives the personality of the product, and this, more than any single factor, will decide whether the consumer does or does not buy the product.

In 1958, Pierre Martineau authored *The Personality of the Retail Store*. He opined:

> What is it that draws the shopper to one store or agency rather than another? Clearly, there is a force operative in the determination of a store's customer body besides the obvious functional factors of location, price ranges and merchandise offerings. I shall show that this force is the store personality or image – the way in which the store is defined in the shopper's mind, partly by its functional qualities and partly by an aura of psychological attributes.

The above two quotes from early marketing researchers indicate that they understood the concept of Brand Personality very well. In fact, marketers have been engaging in corporate and brand image studies for decades now.

One of the early applications of this type of thinking was to use celebrity endorsements. Clearly, the intent is to have the personality of the star become a surrogate for the brand in that the personality traits of the star spill over to the brand. Further, any time that characters are licensed or "critters" are invented, the notion of brand image and personality is paramount.

While the idea is not so new, the formalization of thinking about Brand Personality as a creative tool is relatively new.

Is Brand Personality a strategic communications issue?

In marketing communications, "strategy" refers to determining what will be said and "execution" refers to how it will be said. As we've noted before, only when you determine what you want to say can you effectively execute how to say it. There are three primary situations when Brand Personality is a strategic issue:

1. When all brands in a category are at functional parity and there is little performance variation.
2. When a brand is being introduced for the first time and is new to the world.
3. When it has been determined that the personality of a brand is no longer appropriate and it must be changed.

When all brands are functionally similar, Brand Personality may be the best and only means of differentiating your brand from competitors. Of course, when a brand is born, its personality must be defined. Often, unfortunately, Guerrillas have a tendency to take this task lightly or ignore it altogether.

Finally, as customer tastes change over time, as new competitors come and others go, as technology alters the marketing landscape, it may become necessary to change the personality of a brand. The strategic questions here, and ones that cry for research to delve deeply into customer emotions, are "Change to what?" and "To accomplish what?"

Hint: in our opinion your Brand Personality should not change very often. Imagine how your friends and family would feel if your personality changed frequently. It would drive them crazy. The same applies to the personality of a company or brand. While the marketing tactics and executional elements could easy change over and over again, the basic Brand Personality need never change.

For example, we can cite several brands that have continued to succeed without ever changing their core personality. Budweiser, Coca-Cola, Dr Pepper, Hooter's Restaurants, Harley Davidson, Apple and Harvard University are all examples of brands whose personalities have never changed. The way they communicate about their brands changes frequently, but their basic identity has not wavered.

On the other hand, Marlboro changed gender from feminine to masculine and Cadillac has added a harder edge and gotten younger in recent years. Both personality changes have enhanced the brands.

Brand Personality may be not a strategic issue at other times. For example, when a brand offers benefits to customers that are either unique, more important, or in greater number than what the competition provides, the best strategy might be to focus on these rational differences.

However, even if not a strategic consideration, ignoring Brand Personality issues when creating marketing communications is a mistake. There are many tactical issues that must be considered when building or maintaining the personality of a brand. Whether it's a new advertisement, redesign of a website or changing a logo, the question should always be how such a change will enhance the brand and its personality.

Hint: one way to use the Brand Personality tool is to conduct research from time to time and ask customers if a brand would behave in a certain way. Recall our earlier example: of an exploration of new logotypes for an established brand. A consumer remarked: "That brand would never have that as their logo: it's angry; this brand is never angry."

Similarly, when making major changes to your marketing programs, research into the personality of your brand is important to ensure that you haven't strayed from who you are or who you want to be. And, if research can't be afforded, the next best thing is to mentally ask the brand if it would behave that way.

How to write a Brand Personality

Brand Personalities come to life by writing them down. Your Brand Personality can be the result of research you've conducted or evolve from your thinking, experience and intuition. Either way, as we've emphasized, it must be done from the customer's point of view.

To us, writing a Brand Personality is a creative act in itself. And we have found the use of pictures, illustration and analogies, mixed in with a little humor, helps a personality develop. It makes it easier for everyone, from customers and prospects to company employees and vendors to understand the personality you are trying to achieve and to provide input to make it better.

Hint: a Brand Personality need not have a single line of usable advertising copy in it. It is a planning document meant to guide the developing of your marketing communications programs. In fact, the only time customers might see a written version your Brand Personality is when you conduct research to help in its development.

When developing your Brand Personality, you can use a variety of techniques. Try these:

Conduct focus groups or individual interviews with customers and prospects and challenge them to write a personality description of your brand. Do the same thing yourself, with key executives, employees or vendors. In doing so, challenge everyone to consider:

- What kind of personality the brand would have if it were a person and why do they see it that way?
- The age, gender, income, education and marital status of the brand and why those demographics are seen as part of its personality.
- The kind of car the brand drives and why.
- What magazines does the brand read and why those?
- What hobbies and leisure time activities interest the brand and why those.
- What personality traits do competing brands have that are different or unique from your brand and why?
- Who are the brand's friends?
- What actor or actress, celebrity or person from fiction or history could play the role of your brand and why?

Once you have gathered all the personality information, summarize the common elements into as detailed a personality description as you can.

An example: Caterpillar's Brand Personality

The Caterpillar Brand Personality was derived from six focus groups conducted among men, all of whom either owned or operated the kind of equipment that Caterpillar manufactures. The researcher took the many verbatim comments that emerged from the focus groups and worked them into a series of paragraphs. Here are some of the verbatims that were developed:

- Cat is a "hard livin," "bourbon drinkin," "stompin," "always on the go," "drivin," "rugged" guy who "never gets sick," who is "always there to work" and is "there when you need him." "You can count on him" and he "always gets the job done." "You don't have to worry about Cat," because "when the going is tough, he'll be there." He's definitely an "American" but he does "a lot of international traveling." His favorite color is "yellow."
- Even though he is an "older" man, perhaps "in his 60s," maybe even "in his 70s" and a "founding father" of his industry, Cat is, nevertheless, "in tune with the times" and is thought to be "old but still young." Perhaps that's because he's a "weight lifter," "a body builder" who "works out in the gym." He is a "charismatic" "leader," an "innovator" and "trend setter" of whom it is said: "people follow him" and "he can do just about anything." Caterpillar is "reliable," "dependable," "durable," and "has always got what you need;" he's "always ready to work" and "doesn't mind gettin' his hands dirty." "Very professional" and "well-respected,"

Cat "charges a lot for what he does." In sum, he is considered "outstanding" and thought to be a "great person."

- Caterpillar is "well established," "organized," and a "good investor;" he could have been a "banker" and brings to mind "dollar signs" when he is seen. He personally has a "lot of money" because he "knows how to run a business," is "stable," and "strives for excellence." When he "went to college," he "played football – a big fullback." Cat "wears a lot of gold" and "fancy boots," but "not three piece suits." He is a "classy guy" but is "extravagant" and has "expensive hobbies like racing cars" and "drives a Cadillac." Cat also "owns his own airplane."

The best actor to play the role of Caterpillar clearly is John Wayne (mentioned in most sessions). If he wasn't available, then Clint Eastwood, Charleton Heston or Arnold Schwarzenegger could fill in. Robert Mitchum, Sean Connery and Charles Bronson could play the role, too. Strong men all.

Given the verbatim comments above, a precise Caterpillar Brand Personality was worked into a coherent whole. Here is the summary Brand Personality that evolved:

Caterpillar, who is usually called by his nickname, "Cat," is a "big," "strong," "husky" man, a "heavy weight." He's about "6' 4"," "weighs 240–250 lbs" with "chiseled features, a dimple in his chin and a flat-top haircut." In fact, he is the "biggest and strongest" man ever seen by many of those who know him… and he is "known by almost everyone" because he was the "most popular guy in the class." He is "self-assured" and "confident" to the point of being "arrogant" and "cocky." He has been referred to as "The Big Dog," "Top Dog," "Number 1," "The Big Man," and as a "high roller." "Hanging around Cat is almost like a status symbol."

Given this succinct personality summary coupled with the support paragraphs, it is easy to see how advertising and other marketing communication can now flow and support the personality traits of the Caterpillar brand.

13

Surveys and quantitative research

Quantitative research puts numbers behind the issues. Unlike qualitative research – focus groups and the like – quantitative research will tell you how many people think or feel or behave one way or the other.

Table 13.1 shows the differences between qualitative and quantitative research.

Even though surveys are, by far, the dominant form of quantitative research, the term "quantitative research" is not synonymous with survey research.

For example, a museum may want to know how many people visited a particular exhibit. For exhibits requiring special tickets, they need only look at the number of tickets sold in its system. And even for exhibits not requiring special tickets, gathering quantitative data is easy. The museum can put an observer at the entrance and simply use a clicker to count visitors. Both of these are quantitative methods.

Counting cars in parking lots, noting the states on the license plates, tabulating returns of coupons or observing and coding in-store shopping behavior are other examples of quantitative studies that are not surveys. You may recall shopping and being asked to indicate your zip code at the end of the transaction. These data will be used to understand the drawing range of the store and the proportions of customers who come from various geographies.

The options for quantitative behavioral research are actually limitless and not all forms of quantitative research require a sample and a questionnaire. The kinds of research we focus on in the following chapters, though, do require development of a questionnaire, determination of

Table 13.1 Features of qualitative vs quantitative research

Qualitative: Focus groups, etc.	Quantitative: Surveys, etc.
The goal is to develop the factors, ideas, theories and hypotheses that are at work in the market	The goal is to determine which factors, ideas, theories and hypotheses should be followed to drive business
The aim is a complete, detailed description and discussion of the factors that exist in the market	The aim is to classify features, count them, and construct statistical models in an attempt to explain and prioritize the important factors
Researchers may only know roughly in advance what they are looking for	Researchers know clearly in advance what they are looking for
Usually most effective during earlier phases of research projects	Usually used in the latter phases of research projects when the factors that need to be measured are clear
The research design is dynamic, often emerging as the study unfolds	All aspects of the research design are carefully constructed before data are collected
Researcher questions are often unstructured and formed on the spot. Responses to questions are open-end	Researcher uses structured and precise questions to collect close-ended numerical data
Findings are verbal and can also be explained by pictures, objects and symbols	Findings are in the form of numbers, graphs, charts and statistics
Subjective – researcher interpretation of information is important and based on the analyst's experience and point of view	Objective – researcher seeks precise measurement and analysis; numbers and statistics can be compared to normative or previous data to observe trends
Qualitative data is more "rich," time-consuming, and less able to be generalized	Quantitative data seeks to test the importance of factors, ideas, hypotheses and theories and can be generalized to the population
Researcher tends to become subjectively immersed in the subject matter	Researcher tends to remain objectively separated from the subject matter

the best targets to interview, and making a decision on the proper sample size and best approach for collecting data.

Again, focus groups and other qualitative studies will highlight potential issues, such as customer service, price, or product variety, as being the ones that could be addressed to increase sales. A survey will tell you which one of the issues is the most important to increasing sales, which is second most important, which is third most important, and so forth.

Ultimately, it does you little good simply to know that there is potential for more profits if you were to take action to improve customer service, change your product, or lower your price. Without knowing which one would have the greatest impact, you would have to take action to improve all of them at the same time. Why, for example, would you cut prices without knowing that it would motivate only 10 per cent of your customers to buy more, whereas improving customer service would motivate 50 per cent? You wouldn't – or you shouldn't.

Quantitative survey research is projectable research. That means that the results can be generalized to the population as a whole. From a survey that might question as few as 150 respondents, you can confidently predict what is important for many thousands. That, in turn, means that you can determine which actions will be most potent in motivating which targets – and to what extent.

Surveys allow you to set priorities based on the number of customers or prospects in your target market who would be most influenced by your action.

TYPES OF SURVEYS

As previously discussed, there are two general areas of survey research: strategic and tactical. Strategic studies provide a global understanding of the marketplace. They generate essential learning regarding attitudes, images, and perceptions that consumers have about the companies, brands, and products that compete against each other. They determine the extent to which the needs, wants, wishes, desires and emotions of customers and prospects are being met, and which companies are doing the best job of meeting them.

The information generated from strategic studies forms the basis for determining the marketing direction a company should take – the position that, if achieved, offers the greatest opportunity for success.

Tactical studies address specific questions and issues. Once the overall marketing strategy and desired position are determined, there are many smaller elements that contribute to ultimate success. Tactical studies determine which elements are strongest in achieving the strategy or where changes should be made to reinforce the strategy.

Consider just some of the many tactical studies that you might conduct:

- Customer satisfaction studies, which determine how customers and prospects are being served and what should be done to serve them better.

- Tracking studies, which determine whether you are achieving your desired image, position, and strategy, and how your competition might be hindering your success.
- Product development studies, which determine the new products or services that reinforce your strategic direction.
- Product improvement studies, which determine what can be done to improve current products and services to keep them up to date and competitive.
- Pricing studies, which determine how much you can charge for your products or services.
- Attitude and awareness tracking studies, which determine whether your advertising messages are being seen, heard, and remembered, and whether the advertising is motivating customers to purchase more frequently and/or changing the attitudes of prospects so that they'll soon begin purchasing.
- Advertising communication studies, which determine the strongest messages for communicating your company, brand, or product strategy and for motivating purchase.
- Premium or promotion studies, which determine the best kinds of special offers that will motivate purchase and reinforce your strategic goals.
- Packaging studies, which determine the strongest package and graphic approach that will contribute to your strategy to motivate purchase of your products.
- Naming studies, which determine the strongest name for your company, product, brand, or service and is in keeping with your strategic direction.
- Screening studies, which determine which among a number of potential new products or services offers the best option for expanding your marketplace and reinforcing your strategy.

While tactical studies are important, strategic studies are the essential building block to understanding the marketplace and how to compete effectively. Think about it as if you were taking an exam without first doing your homework. Maybe you'll pass, but the odds of achieving a high grade are greatly diminished. Without a well-structured strategic research study, without doing basic homework, your decisions are often a best guess or, even worse, based on conjecture and hope.

And remember, hope is not a strategy.

Tactical studies are most effective if they are conducted within the global context provided by a strategic study. To determine the best package that communicates quality, for example, is moot if strategy dictates that the most effective package should be one that communicates low price.

As we've said before, if you don't know where you're going, any road will get you there.

STRATEGIC STUDY GOALS AND OBJECTIVES

Assume you have decided that you want to conduct a strategic study to understand your marketplace "drivers." You want to determine the factors that are important in keeping your customers or attracting your competitors' customers. Strategic studies are referred to as "segmentation studies," "usage and attitude studies," or "market structure" – or you can simply call it your "homework study."

To get started with your homework study, develop a short statement of the strategic goal. This will help you focus your study emphasis. You can refer back to Chapter 2, Setting Research Goals and Objectives, and Chapter 8, The Research Plan, or follow the example below, which is written as the strategic goal for a window air-conditioner study.

Example: window air-conditioner

Strategic goal:

> To determine the attributes that are important when consumers purchase window air-conditioners. An additional objective is to determine how my company and my competitors perform on the important attributes.

Stating the strategic goal in this way focuses the study in two areas: 1) determining the important air-conditioner attributes for customers in general; and 2) determining company performance on those attributes.

An alternative strategic goal might be:

> To determine what customer segments exist in the air-conditioner marketplace, and which attributes are important in appealing to each segment. An additional goal is to determine whether some companies do a better job of appealing to a certain segment of customers than to others. For example, differences between those who live in big homes as opposed to small apartments.

Stating the strategic goal in this manner broadens the scope of the study in that it must now: 1) seek to determine the existence of various segments in the market and array the attributes by two or more customer segments; and 2) determine whether some companies perform better when appealing to the various segments than others.

Whatever the strategic goal, it should be the preeminent purpose of the study. Only when you are clear on the strategic goal can you elaborate by stating the secondary objectives of the study.

The following are good examples of secondary objectives for a strategic study of the window air-conditioner market:

- Determine what specific attributes are most important and least important when it comes to the purchase of window air-conditioners.
- Learn which brands are purchased.
- Discover how each brand is rated on its perceived ability to deliver the various attributes.
- Identify attributes not being strongly addressed in the marketplace to provide an opportunity to gain a competitive advantage.
- Understand what brands are weakest in delivering important attributes to their customers and, therefore, would be most vulnerable to a competitor.

Developing clear and concise objectives is not an academic exercise. It is essential in determining your final study methodology and its likely cost. If you are crystal clear on the information that you seek, you will not over-spend in collecting superfluous data or under-spend and find out later that the research only took you half way.

DETERMINING YOUR TARGET RESPONDENTS

A critical step in designing a survey research project is the determination of whose opinions are important – that is, determining the profile of your desired targets. Do you want to gather data on men vs women or younger vs older respondents? Perhaps the attitudes of respondents who have purchased from your company once as opposed to those purchasing many times are important. Or maybe you want respondents who are heavy buyers of your products compared to light buyers.

There could be dozens of target respondents who are important to study. Without careful determination of your targets, you could end up with a wealth of data among respondents who offer little potential for growth.

Often the target to be sampled will be determined by where you are having trouble, for example, among customers who returned items, or among those who stopped being customers.

Often, too, it will be determined by where you think there are opportunities, for example current heavy buyers, customers of competitors, people who recently moved into your neighborhood.

In some cases the target is obvious, for example everyone living within three miles of your store, those who purchased online in the past three months, everyone with an Irish last name if you are an "Irish" gift store, everyone who has visited a casino in the past six months and who lives near a planned new casino.

And sometimes the target is more subtle.

For business-to-business situations you'll need to distinguish between decision makers (those who can say "yes") and influencers (those who can't say "yes," but might say "no" and/or act as gatekeepers) and interview both.

Even in consumer research, targets can be subtle.

In the case of a children's cereal, for example, the father may be very interested in healthy foods and insist that no sugar-coated "junk" come into the house (decision maker); the mother is the one who goes to the store, finds the item and puts down the money (shopper); and the child is the one who consumes the product. Who should be the research target? Well, it depends, doesn't it?

A packaging study for the children's cereal might target the mother because she's the one who has to spot it on the shelf. A taste test might target the child, who needs to like it or she or he won't eat it. And an advertising study might target the father because he's "the person in the home most responsible for influencing the types of cereal that are purchased."

In Chapter 8, on developing the research plan, we listed a number of questions that you should ask yourself when determining your target respondents. It's appropriate to repeat that list here:

1. What targets offer you the best opportunity of increasing your business the fastest?
2. What targets would be important for longer-term growth?
3. What targets would be least costly to convince to buy more from you?
4. What targets actually have the information you need to know?
5. What targets would provide nice to know information, but would be too costly to attract?
6. If you knew the attitudes of one particular target, could you extrapolate to other targets without having to study them?
7. Do you have the research budget available to cast a very wide net across a number of targets?

Further, the customers you target for your survey can be viewed demographically, firmographically, behaviorally or attitudinally. Here are some examples of each.

Demographic/B2B firmographic targets

- Customers in various age groups (e.g. 21–34, 35–44, 45–54, 55–64, 65+).

- Customers in various income groups (e.g. under $50,000 yearly income, $50,000 to $99,000, $100,000 +).
- Customers with varying educations (e.g. high school graduate or less, some college, college graduate, postgraduate work).
- Customers who fall into various ethnic groups (African-American, Caucasian, Hispanic, etc.)
- Customers from large, medium or small organizations.
- Customers with various titles/functions (purchasing, engineering, physicians, nurses, etc.)
- Customers in one region or sales district vs others.

Behavioral targets

- Customers who purchased within the product category in the past 12 months.
- Customers who purchased within the product category once, twice, three or more times in the past 12 months.
- Customers who purchased at least once within the product category in the past 24 months but have not purchased within the past 12 months.
- Customers who have purchased certain brands within the product category in the past 12 months.
- Customers who have never purchased within the product category but would consider purchasing.
- Customers served directly by you vs those served by distributors.
- Decision makers who can make a capital decision vs influencers who cannot make a capital decision.
- Customers who attended a trade show vs those who did not.
- Customers who require financing.

Attitudinal targets

- Consumers who feel price is the most important reason to purchase.
- Customers who feel quality is the most important reason to purchase.
- Consumers who like the adventure of travel.
- Consumers who feel that they have financial security.
- Consumers who feel their better days are in the future.

The above lists are simply representative. Targets must be determined in light of your overall study goal, secondary objectives and, of course, your budget.

If you are conducting your first strategic study, it is incumbent upon you to choose the target or targets whose responses are most important to driving your business growth in the next 12 months. As you take marketing actions against your "close-in" targets, and achieve success, you can move to studying targets of lesser immediate potential.

To reiterate, good research requires asking the right people, the right questions, the right way.

14

Types of surveys

There are five major approaches for collecting data for quantitative studies. They are:

1. The internet.
2. Telephone.
3. Mail.
4. Personal interviews.
5. Panels.

Additionally, these five approaches can be used in tandem. Sometimes respondents are first contacted by phone, questioned, and asked to complete a follow-up mail or internet questionnaire. The same is true for respondents first questioned by the other approaches.

The point is that, once a person has agreed to be interviewed using one technique, a relatively high percentage will be willing to be interviewed on the same topic using another approach. Determining the best single or dual approach for collecting the needed information is what's ultimately important.

THE INTERNET

In the past few years, conducting research over the internet has become extremely popular. In 2008 Pew Research estimated that 55 per cent of US homes had broadband internet access and an additional 10 per cent had dial-up connections. This alone has eliminated much of the concern researchers earlier expressed that it was not possible to generate a representative sample of consumers when using the internet to collect data.

In fact, CASRO (The Council of American Survey Research Organizations) estimated that while 24 per cent of survey research was conducted over the internet in 2004, that figure had jumped to 38 per cent in 2007. And Greenfield On-Line, a leading provider of internet research services, estimates that 35 per cent of all research dollars in the US are spent online.

While there is little disagreement that the internet offers many advantages over other methods of collecting research data, most notably speed, flexibility and low expense, there remains one large disadvantage. It is difficult to generate a representative sample among the 65 per cent of the population with internet access.

Think about all the spam you get in your e-mailbox and how quickly you delete e-mails that look suspicious or hold very little interest. An invitation to complete a survey is usually met with just such a reaction. Because of this, it becomes extremely important to understand how the internet should be used to conduct a survey.

Response rates to questionnaires that are randomly e-mailed to respondents who have not opted in are most problematic, sometimes generating less than a 5 per cent response rate. We were involved in one such attempt where the response among subscribers to a trade magazine was one half of 1 per cent after two e-mail blasts.

Response is also influenced by the length and complexity of the questionnaire, familiarity with the company sponsoring the study, the nature of the topic, the size and type of the incentive and the manner in which you invite respondents to complete the questionnaire in the subject line of the e-mail.

Our experience is that the use of the internet to gather data works best with people who have a strong relationship with you. Highly loyal customers, purchasers of expensive items like cars, retailers, distributors or sales reps who sell your products would be examples, as would alumni, members of an association and people who have made donations to you.

Unless you are very careful, conducting a study over the internet, even with your best customers, can be worse than not conducting one at all.

As with any quantitative market research study, it is important that results be representative and projectable to your targets. If you invite 1,000 of your best customers to complete an internet survey about their satisfaction in doing business with you, and only 10 per cent respond, you have a real problem. Are the 90 per cent who failed to respond different than those who did? And how will you find out?

Further, if you put a banner ad on your website that invites visitors to complete a questionnaire, and thousands respond, you still need to be suspicious. Assume a banner invitation or e-mailing to bulk addresses generates 1,000 responses to your questionnaire – a large number indeed and one that might give you a feeling of confidence. As discussed in Chapter 17 on sampling, it is not the number of responses you generate as much as assuring the response is representative of your target(s).

Strangely enough, there are apparently many consumers who enjoy spending hours clicking on banner invitations or responding to e-mails urging them to complete a survey – sometimes more than once. You must always be concerned whether they are the consumers whose opinions are important to you.

Most reputable market research companies and consultants are experienced when it comes to conducting research over the internet. However, as with any research situation that is new or unfamiliar to you, it is prudent to first consult with several research suppliers or consultants who have experience with this mode of data collection.

Make sure you do your due diligence by determining:

- Cost. There are various cost elements when creating an internet survey. They include the programming and hosting of your questionnaire – which can be more expensive if your questionnaire includes pictures, exhibits, sounds, motion, or complex skip patterns. If you aren't using a house list, you might have to pay to acquire a list of e-mail address and execute an e-mail blast. And your contract will require that you provide an opt-out option for e-mail recipients.
- Incentives are almost always required to generate a representative sample (the cost here is not just the incentives, but also administrative expenses associated with distributing them) and the cost of processing the data using a research tabulating service should be considered.
- Whether they have their own software readily available for conducting online surveys or if they have created internet questions using some of the popular internet sites such as www.surveymonkey.com, www.zoomerang.com or www.instantsurvey.com.
- The response rate they have achieved when using the internet and an explanation of what they did to achieve acceptable rates of response.
- How they recommend obtaining the respondents you want for your survey.
- How they recommend obtaining a representative and projectable sample of respondents.

If you are so inclined, go to www.surveymonkey.com, www.zoomerang.com or www.instantsurvey.com for information and approaches to creating internet surveys yourself. We would note that at present surveymonkey.com provides free data gathering if your survey sample is small – up to 100 respondents and 10 or fewer questions.

To recap, below is a list of the advantages and disadvantages of using the internet for surveys.

Advantages

- Cost: using one of the many legitimate sites, the cost of creating and hosting an internet questionnaire is very reasonable, often less than $1,500. Cost of tabulating responses to internet questionnaires is extremely low, often less than $500.
- Ability to generate large sample of respondents for minimal cost and the cost of a survey does not greatly increase when additional respondents are added. The computer doesn't care whether 100 or 1,000 answer a question.
- Allows showing color pictures, illustrations, detailed product descriptions and complex ideas in simple, easy to grasp formats. Additionally, can incorporate sound and motion including full TV commercials.
- Questionnaire is easy for respondents to complete.
- Ability to control the order in which respondents see questions.
- Based on how respondents answer one question, they can be easily skipped to next appropriate question.
- Allows respondents to complete an interview at their own pace and at a time of their choice.
- Usually faster to collect data than other survey approaches.
- No interviewer bias in how questions are phrased when asked.
- As soon as the respondent answers, the data are in the computer. There are no data entry errors.

Disadvantages

- Sampling issues previously discussed.
- Lack of control over who fills out the questionnaire. Answers might not come from the person for whom the interview was intended.
- Difficulty reaching low income and older targets, who don't have internet access, are uncomfortable with the internet technology or don't like to complete self-administered questionnaires.
- Open-ended questions where respondents are asked to write in an answer usually result in superficial, incomplete and unproductive responses as well as entailing added cost for coding respondents' answers.

Finally, even though the internet is considered to be faster and less expensive than using the telephone, it would be prudent to estimate your study both ways. In a world where many marketing research studies are outsourced, interviewing may originate from India, the

Canadian Maritimes or the Dominican Republic and, as a result, may be very economical to conduct. The telephone may be a better means of conducting your survey. And if the costs are higher, they might be only marginally so.

TELEPHONE INTERVIEWING

Telephone interviewing is a frequently used approach for collecting data, although its popularity is decreasing. CASRO estimated that in 2004, 49 per cent of research was conducted over the phone. In 2008, that number decreased to less than 35 per cent. Telephone data collection is still considered the "gold standard" however.

There are two primary reasons for this. First, there is less of a "non-response problem." The proportion of those contacted who agree to participate in telephone research is quite high – often 40 per cent or more. Thus there is less of an issue regarding whether those who refused to participate in an interview or could not be reached were any different than those who did participate in the survey. Data collection via the internet or mail rarely produces the same level of cooperation as the telephone, even after incentives are applied.

Second, telephone interviewing services do the work of connecting to the respondent. And they do the work of asking questions and recording responses. The respondent doesn't have to read any questions or check any boxes on a questionnaire or write down answers to open-ended questions. This accounts for the higher degree of cooperation and explains why open-ended questions are best asked over the phone (or in person). Respondents can be probed for more information if an inadequate or unclear answer is given.

There are many interviewing services that specialize in telephone interviewing for market research purposes. They hire and train interviewers and administer questionnaires written by professional researchers. They, themselves, don't employ professional market research people. Their sole purpose is to complete the desired number of interviews among a designated population group, as instructed by their professional research clients.

There are in addition many market research companies that hire and train telephone interviewers as well as provide professional services. These tend to be the large, full-service research suppliers that can design your survey, write your questionnaire, conduct the interviews, process the data, and analyze your results.

Simply go to your favorite search engine using the key words "telephone interviewing services" and add your country to your search instruction. You can also find either full-service suppliers or telephone interviewing suppliers throughout the world by going to www.quirks.com, www.bluebook.org or www.greenbook.org. Finally, companies that do this work are so numerous that any good-sized city will list several in the *Yellow Pages* under "market research."

Advantages

- Along with panels, telephone is considered the best approach for generating a projectable sample of respondents and there is much less of a non-response problem.
- It is a very efficient approach for interviewing large numbers of respondents.
- It allows the collection of a great deal of information quickly.
- The level of detail for open-ended questions is the best.
- Generally, no incentive is required for consumer studies or even when conducting shorter business-to-business studies.
- It is economical, especially when the respondents to be interviewed are a large percentage of the population and/or when incidence levels of product usage are high.

Disadvantages

- Generally, the longest you can keep a person on the phone is 20 minutes. Interviews that are longer might require an incentive for the respondent to complete the interview and still might result in drop-outs well into the interview, but before it is completed.
- It can become expensive to find small population groups, when fewer than 10 per cent of the population might qualify as potential respondents.
- As consumers have become inundated with calls from marketing research companies, and as telemarketing services attempting to sell are often lumped together with legitimate market research services, more consumers simply hang up. It is now estimated that as many as 30 per cent of all consumers receiving calls to participate in a legitimate telephone survey will immediately hang up. This means, even by telephone, it has become a bit more difficult and expensive to interview a representative sample of the population.
- It is estimated that over 10 per cent of households (and growing) in the US are now using a mobile phone as their primary telephone rather than a land line. In other parts of the world this proportion is even larger. This adds to the difficulty of interviewing a representative sample of the population.
- Further, because directories of cell phone numbers do not exist, it is virtually impossible to generate a random selection of these cell-only users. Also, if you happen to reach a person on their cell, cooperation rates tend to be very low and respondents may even become angry if they have to pay for the incoming call.

- The telephone can't be used for certain kinds of questioning procedures in which a respondent is required to see lists or pictures or manipulate objects in order to give meaningful responses. Although it is costly, we note the phone-mail-phone approach can solve this problem. Here respondents are recruited over the phone, mailed a package to be opened at the time of the survey, and then phoned again for the interview.
- Respondents often have difficulty grasping long drawn out product descriptions, concepts or ideas when read over the phone by an interviewer.
- Interviewers can exhibit bias in how they ask questions or they may have accents and be hard to understand.
- In telephone surveys with large samples in which the data are entered into a computer as the interview takes place, a special programming fee is required to get the questionnaire onto the computer.
- And in small surveys where the data are gathered on paper, there is a subsequent data entry process, which not only adds cost to the survey, but allows error to creep into the data.
- Most business-to-business and professional respondents require an incentive to ensure their participation.

Telephone interviewing costs

Table 14.1 gives an example of costs for conducting telephone interviews in 2008. It illustrates the cost per interview (CPI) for a 5, 10, 15, or 20 minute interview as well as for various incidence rates. The incidence rate refers to the percentage of consumers who are expected to qualify as the respondents you wish to interview.

If 100 per cent of people in your sample qualify to be interviewed (which is rarely the case), and you are going to question them for only 5 minutes, you would pay $7.50 for each completed interview or $750 for 100 interviews, $7,500 for 1,000 interviews, etc. On the other hand, if only one in 10 people qualify to be interviewed – a 10 per cent incidence – and you want to interview them for 20 minutes, you would pay $72.50 for each completed interview.

These figures are only the cost for collecting the data. They don't include what you would pay a full-service supplier for writing your questionnaire, processing your data, or analyzing your results. Of course, if you undertook all the activities of a full-service supplier yourself, your only expense would be the telephone service.

Table 14.1 Example of per-interview costs when estimating a telephone interview

Incidence %	5 minutes $	10 minutes $	15 minutes $	20 minutes $
100	7.50	12.50	18.50	24.50
90	8.00	3.00	19.00	25.00
85	8.50	3.50	19.50	25.50
80	8.75	13.75	19.75	25.75
75	9.25	14.25	20.25	26.25
70	9.75	14.75	20.75	26.75
65	10.25	15.25	21.25	27.25
60	11.00	16.00	22.00	28.00
50	12.75	17.75	23.75	29.75
40	15.50	20.50	26.50	32.50
30	19.75	24.75	30.75	36.75
25	23.50	28.50	34.50	40.50
20	28.75	33.75	39.75	45.75
10	55.50	60.50	66.50	72.50

Source: APC Research, Chicago (2008)

MAIL SURVEYS

Depending on the response rates, mail surveys can be a very economical way to collect data. They are particularly efficient for collecting large quantities of information among large samples of people. As a rule of thumb, mail data collection is about half the cost of telephone data collection.

Most important when using a mail survey is to ensure that you are generating a representative sample of respondents.

Let's say you send out a four-page questionnaire on the topic of life insurance to 2,000 men at random. Even if you included a postage-paid return envelope, you would be lucky if 5 per cent responded. Although you would have 100 completed questionnaires, the low response rate would invalidate the data. You'd be left wondering whether the opinions of the 1,900 who didn't respond are the same as those of the 100 who did. This is the non-response problem we referred to earlier.

Some marketers won't use mail survey data unless at least 50 per cent respond. Such a result is exceptionally rare. In our experience, a 35 per cent response rate will generate reliable data; that is, if the study were to be conducted a second time with a 35 per cent response rate, results would be within the statistical error range that was observed in the first study.

There are a number of ways to stimulate higher response rates. They are:

1. Always use money as an incentive. Include a $1 bill, or better yet a $2 bill, when you mail the questionnaire. With a four-page questionnaire, offer an additional $10 when the completed questionnaire is returned. For a longer questionnaire, offer more (i.e. $20 for eight pages).
2. Along with the money, identify yourself as the sponsor. People are far more likely to respond if they know who is sponsoring the study. However, care should be taken here. When respondents know who is sponsoring a study, some may be overly critical while others may be overly complimentary. Always weigh these considerations before deciding to identify a sponsor.
3. Do step 1, or steps 1 and 2 after you have sent out a letter announcing the study. This alerts people to the fact that the questionnaire is on the way and provides additional legitimacy. And if an incentive is necessary, alerting respondents that money is coming their way will make them more likely to open the envelope containing the questionnaire rather than discarding it as junk mail.
4. Do all the above steps and provide a lottery bonus. Offer an additional $200 if the respondent's name is chosen from the names of a pool of people who respond.
5. Always provide a date for return. From the approximate date of receipt of the questionnaire, give no more than three weeks to respond.
6. Even the best planning might not generate a good response. Therefore, consider pilot-testing your questionnaire. Sending out 200 questionnaires is enough to determine if you are hitting your response goals. If not, consider increasing the incentive, shortening the questionnaire, doing both, or even switching to an alternative data collection method.

There are certainly other factors that influence response rates. They include the nature of the topic, the ease with which the questionnaire can be completed, and the time of year it is sent. For example, mailing around holiday periods like Christmas is always a terrible time. Nevertheless, the incentive that you offer and the length of your questionnaire are always the most important.

Advantages

Mail questionnaires have advantages when:

- You have a great deal of information to collect, i.e. a long question-naire.
- It is important for respondents to complete the questionnaire at their own pace. This may be necessary when there are pictures, illustrations, longer product, concept or idea descriptions that take time to comprehend before being evaluated, or when information needs to be looked up.
- You are familiar with designing an easy to read, simple to complete questionnaire.
- You can easily access the names and addresses of people whose opinions are important.
- You can afford the extra four to six weeks that it takes to conduct a mail study as opposed to a phone study.

Disadvantages

Mail questionnaires are at a distinct disadvantage when:

- You have open-ended questions. People will easily check boxes, but if you ask them to write in why they feel a certain way, don't expect much more than superficial responses or none at all.
- You want to control the manner in which questions are seen. If seeing one part of the questionnaire is important before seeing other parts, using a mail questionnaire poses a problem. Respondents will often read the entire questionnaire and view all the questions being asked before filling it out.
- You have a complex questionnaire. Respondents can follow very simple instructions for skipping from one question to another or one section of the questionnaire to another section. If complex skip patterns are required, respondents can become confused and frustrated and give up the questionnaire altogether or answer it incorrectly.
- You don't have confidence that the person answering the question-naire is the person you intend to answer. Since you have no control over who fills out a mail questionnaire, you can never be 100 per cent confident it is filled out by the right person.
- You obtain low response rates. Every questionnaire mailed out includes the cost of printing, stuffing, postage and incentives. This can be a huge waste of money if a large proportion of recipients do not respond.
- You need answers quickly and can't afford the four to six extra weeks it usually takes when collecting data by mail.

IN-PERSON INTERVIEWING

Years ago interviewers would go door to door to administer questionnaires. They would follow a complex series of instructions to determine what neighborhood to go to, what street to start on, and the exact house to go to, all in an effort to generate a random, projectable sample of respondents. Today, in-person, door-to-door interviewing is both unsafe and economically impractical, except in the case of the government when it conducts the Census of the Population every 10 years.

This doesn't mean that in-person interviewing is an unpopular approach for collecting data – quite the contrary. In survey research, personal interviews are most often conducted when it is necessary to show respondents exhibits, have them taste food products, or interview them before giving out products to take home and use.

In every major city in the world there are market research field services located in shopping centers. Go to www.bluebook.org, www.quirks.com or www.greenbook.org for a listing of such facilities. These central location mall facilities are the primary source for conducting in-person interviews.

You may have encountered interviewers in the shopping centers that you frequent. They would generally approach you with a clipboard and ask a series of questions to determine whether you qualify to be interviewed. If so, you may be interviewed on the spot or asked to accompany the interviewer to a nearby research location.

Sometimes, respondents are pre-recruited by phone and paid $25, $50, or more and given an appointment time to be interviewed at the mall facility. And, on rare occasions, an interviewer might go to the respondent's home to conduct the interview. Obviously, these approaches make for a more expensive study, but, depending on the information you need and the characteristics of respondents, they may be the best approach for addressing your research objectives.

One-on-one personal executive interviews are also common. Here the researcher makes an appointment at a time convenient to the executive and travels to his or her office.

Advantages

Central location mall intercept interviewing is optimal when it is necessary for respondents to be presented with something before they are asked to respond. This could be:

- ads, concepts, storyboards, new product idea boards, promotion materials, catalogs;
- packages, packaging graphics, package sizes and shapes;
- products to observe and comment upon;

- products to taste before commenting;
- products to take home and use;
- product displays, etc.

Additionally, there are research studies such as those on very sensitive topics or those that require complex interviewing approaches that make it necessary for the interviewer to be physically present to ensure that the interview is undertaken properly.

Disadvantages

Mall intercept interviewing has a number of problems associated with it. They include:

- Not generating a nationally projectable random sample. Say you collect 150 mall interviews in one city and 150 in another. Even though you have collected 300 interviews, which is a robust sample, you really are only representing the opinions of shoppers in those cities who shop at those malls. Your findings might not represent the attitudes of people who shop at other malls in those cities, much less those of people who live and shop in other cities.
- Finding low-incidence respondents. If you need to interview consumers who might be difficult to find (e.g. men with size 13 feet or larger, women who wear four-inch heels), it might take a long time to find the right people. This can be very costly.
- Consistency from one mall location to another. In any research study, you want to control as much as possible the manner in which interviewers administer the questionnaire. You don't want them going at it one way in one location and another way in another location. This is always a challenge when conducting mall intercept studies in a number of markets.

PANELS

In the early 1950s consumer mail panels were formed for the purpose of conducting market research studies. The early panels consisted of several hundred thousand people. Panel members were solicited by mail, asked if they would like to participate in market research surveys from time to time, and promised products or other incentives to participate. The early panels were very successful.

Today, panels are extremely sophisticated and a great way to collect information, often quite inexpensively. Panels consist of millions of members in many different countries who can be used to survey almost any consumer product and many business-to-business products or services. Panel members can be interviewed using telephone, mail, or the internet.

Because members are pre-screened for their willingness to participate in surveys, response rates are extremely high. This allows panel studies to be easily designed to be representative and projectable.

What is particularly useful about panels is that they already have large databases of information about their members. All member demographics are on file, as are many other characteristics such as brand/product category usage for automobiles, financial products, health care, information technology, packaged goods, etc. This allows easy access to specific panel members whose opinions are important and to people who might be difficult to locate when conducting a random survey. Hard-to-find respondents can be people with certain diseases or ailments, those who drive a particular make of car, men over 65 who like deep-sea fishing, or others who undertake unique activities.

Additionally, some panels conduct monthly, weekly, and even daily "omnibus" surveys that allow clients to purchase one question at a time. These omnibus studies are conducted among nationally representative samples balanced to US Census regions with typical sample sizes of 1,000 or 2,000.

Omnibus studies allow you and other clients to purchase a limited number of questions – as few as one to as many as 10. And because panels have previously collected the demographics of their members, answers can be sorted by region, gender, income and other characteristics.

The obvious advantages of using an omnibus study are speed and cost. For example, panels allow you to send in your questions on a Monday and have your results before the end of the week, and even in some cases overnight! The cost per question is typically less than $500 per 1,000 respondents.

When all is said and done, though, panels are not a panacea. They are not useful for collecting information from customers or from in-house databases. And while costs for some types of studies can be very reasonable, for others they can be quite high. There is also an occasional concern that some panel members participate in too many research studies and thus no longer are "average" respondents.

There are a relatively small number of panels that collect data over the internet as well as by phone and mail. There are four providers operating in the US as well as in various countries throughout the world using all three means for data collection: synovate.com, tns-global.com, ipsos-insight.com and surveypro.com.

Also, in the US there are additional panels that focus primarily on internet data collection. Examples are harrisinteractive.com, greenfieldonline.com, e-rewards.com, commonknowledge.com and marketingtools.com

In-person, mail, internet, and panel interview costs

There are so many factors affecting costs when conducting in-person, mail, internet, and panel studies that it is difficult to provide detailed figures that can be compared to the telephone costs shown in Table 14.1. Nevertheless, we have found the following to be generally true:

- Costs for mail surveys are highly dependent on the incentives that must be used to generate respondent cooperation. Nevertheless, if response rates are high, mail studies can cost almost 50 per cent less than telephone studies on a per interview basis.
- Costs for conducting personal interviews via random mall intercepts are approximately the same to 15 per cent higher than telephone costs.
- Costs for conducting internet interviews are also highly dependent on the incentives that must be paid to generate respondent cooperation. You can usually figure, though, that you will save 25 to 50 per cent over telephone interviewing costs.
- Panel costs tend to be unpredictable. Sometimes they are extremely low and other times very high. Omnibus surveys, if applicable to your situation, are exceptionally cost-effective.

Since panels ensure the privacy of their members and will not release their names, you must use their in-house interviewing staff when conducting telephone interviews. Costs here tend to be 15 to 25 per cent higher than using a regular telephone field service.

Costs for panel mail studies can be quite reasonable and run almost 50 per cent lower than using a regular telephone field service. Panel interviewing using their internet panel is about 20 per cent lower than using the panel for telephone questioning.

Now that you have completed this chapter we suggest you read Chapter 17 on sampling and then review it again.

DIGGING DEEPER

IVR (Interactive Voice Response) is now readily available as a purchased service from the larger research organizations. The basic idea here is that the respondent uses a telephone touchtone keypad as a data entry device.

Consumers call an 800 telephone number and hear a pre-recorded survey read to them in their language of choice. They punch in their answers using their touchtone keypad. Open-ended responses are simply spoken and recorded. Because the data are entered into a computer automatically, there is no data entry issue.

One popular application for IVR technology is for restaurants wishing to assess customer satisfaction. When customers pay their bill, they are given a card that requests their participation and gives them directions for completing an IVR questionnaire. If they do so, they are given a code at the end of the survey that qualifies them for a free dessert, for example, on their next visit to that restaurant.

For Guerrillas, IVR can be very cost-effective and should be a consideration when conducting customer satisfaction studies, or other kinds of research where having respondents know your identity isn't a problem.

15

Writing questionnaires

When writing questionnaires, it is worth keeping this advice in mind:

> Never ask a question because it might be good to know or because you've seen other questionnaires with the same question. Only ask those questions for which you know what decision you will make when the data come in and where the findings will influence marketing decision making or customer behavior. Asking any other questions only wastes money and time – your money and the time of the respondents.

A survey cannot be completed without a questionnaire. Unlike a focus group Discussion Guide that is employed dynamically to question respondents, a survey questionnaire is precisely structured and must be followed exactly. When an interviewer administers a questionnaire, it is done precisely as it is written. There can be no deviation from the questionnaire or room for interpretation. Questions must be asked exactly as they are written – every time.

There are two major types of questionnaire: 1) the questionnaire will be administered by an interviewer directly with the respondent; and 2) the questionnaire will be completed by the respondent without assistance from an interviewer – a self-administered questionnaire.

An interviewer-administered questionnaire can be quite complex. Because interviewers are trained in the flow of the questionnaires they administer and will conduct a number of practice interviews prior to confronting a respondent, developing a complex, interviewer-administered questionnaire is not a problem.

Often interviewer-administered questionnaires will have skip patterns that jump a respondent from one section of the questionnaire to another based on his or her responses. Sometimes, particularly with face-to-face interviews, the questioning process might also involve showing respondents certain products or exhibits during the interview, or having the respondents read concepts or ideas based on how they respond to various questions.

Often, too, when large numbers of respondents are required, the interviewer will take advantage of a computer-managed display screen from which the questions are read and the answers displayed as they are entered. This makes the use of even more complex skip patterns possible without any pause in the questioning. It also eliminates the need for most subsequent data entry.

Self-administered questionnaires, on the other hand, need to be simple, straightforward, and logical. Question 2 should follow question 1. Question 3 should follow question 2, and so forth. The going-in assumption with self-administered questionnaires should be that respondents will not complete a questionnaire when the pages are crowded or hard to read, or when instructions for completion are overly complex.

It's been estimated that as many as 50 per cent of respondents starting a self-administered questionnaire will not complete it because they become irritated and annoyed at the way it is constructed. Therefore, when writing a self-administered questionnaire, care must be taken to ensure that it is easy to complete. Such questionnaires should be written with a child's mentality in mind.

A word of advice

It is not easy to write an effective questionnaire. It takes practice and experience, but that doesn't mean you shouldn't try. With a careful reading of this chapter, you will have the tools to write a workable questionnaire.

However, you should always consider hiring a research professional to review your questionnaires to check for clarity and flow, and to ensure you are asking the kinds of questions that address your study objectives. It shouldn't take a professional more than a couple of hours, and the money will be very well spent.

TYPES OF QUESTIONS

Survey questionnaires are primarily close-ended in nature. That is, the answers are pre-structured. Close-ended questions are those where the interviewer reads the question and the response options are predetermined. Here is an example of a close-ended question with the optional answers:

How would you rate Exxon as a company? Do you feel it is: (READ LIST; CHECK ONE)

an excellent company _____
a good company _____
a fair company _____
a poor company _____

As is evident, there are only four possible responses to the question.

Other survey questions could be open-ended in nature. With open-ended questions there are no structured answers. The interviewer records the respondent's verbatim response to the question. An example would be: How do you feel about Exxon as a company?

Both questioning techniques allow answers to be tabulated and the exact number of respondents giving particular answers can be reported. In the case of the open-ended question though, an additional procedure is required. Verbatim answers to each question are examined looking for common responses. Codes are then developed that allow common responses to be grouped together. Subsequently, all the verbatim responses are coded so that the frequency of these common responses can be recorded just like the answers to structured questions.

As you read the remainder of this chapter, keep in mind that there are only two types of survey questions: close-ended and open-ended.

QUESTIONNAIRES FOR TELEPHONE AND PERSONAL INTERVIEWING

Telephone and personal interview questionnaires have a distinct flow – or distinct phases. They are:

1. The cooperation phase.
2. The respondent qualification phase.
3. The main body of the questionnaire phase.
4. The demographic phase.
5. The thank you phase.

1. THE COOPERATION PHASE

Step 1 involves gaining the respondent's agreement to be interviewed. Because respondents are usually skeptical when first approached, what you say and how you say it can make the difference between a quick "No, thanks" and the opportunity to complete an interview.

First, with telephone interviews, the person who answers the phone may not be the person you want to interview, e.g. a man answers and you want to interview a woman, or perhaps a child answers. The best approach is to ask to speak to the male or female head of household. If the person answering asks who is calling, simply say that it is about doing a market research interview.

Once you have a male or female who might qualify for the interview, you can use several approaches to gain respondent cooperation:

> Introduction #1. Hello, my name is _____ from [insert the name of the research company conducting the interview], a national market research firm. I want to assure you that this is not a sales call of any kind, and no one will try to sell you anything as a result of your cooperation. May I have a few minutes of your time? Thank you.

Comment: The goal here is to quickly assure the person that you aren't selling anything. While this is a standard approach and is usually effective, should you feel that different wording would be better to accomplish this goal, you should use it.

> Introduction #2. Hello, my name is _____ from [insert the name of the research company conducting the interview]. We are conducting a market research study on the topic of [insert the topic] that will last about [insert the time frame]. I want to assure you that this is not a sales call of any kind, and no one will try to sell you anything as a result of your cooperation. May I have a few minutes of your time? Thank you.

Comment: Most researchers prefer to be up front with a potential respondent about the topic and length of interview. While some respondents will terminate an interview when they learn of the topic or when they learn how long the interview will take, it is better that a respondent doesn't start the interview than hang up when it is half-completed because it's taking too long. We generally prefer to use introduction #2.

> Introduction #3. Hello, my name is _____ from [insert the name of the research company conducting the interview]. We are conducting a market research study for [insert the sponsor of the research]. The topic of the study is [insert the topic], and the interview will last about [insert the time frame].

Comment: Revealing the sponsor of the study to the respondent will usually enhance cooperation. However, in many cases it is desirable to keep the name of the sponsor confidential, as will be discussed later in this chapter. Where confidentiality is not an issue or it is perhaps even desirable to disclose the sponsor's identity, use introduction #3.

2. THE RESPONDENT QUALIFICATION PHASE

Once you have respondent agreement for an interview, there will be a series of questions to determine whether, in fact, you have a qualified respondent. This is referred to as "screening." Just as in focus groups, most survey questionnaires have a critical industry screening question. This immediately eliminates people whose attitudes might be biased or who are in a competitive industry and might use the fact that you are conducting a survey to their advantage. For example, if you were conducting a study among customers who shop for computers, you would use the following critical industry screening questions:

Are you, or any member of your household, employed in the computer industry, such as a manufacturer, distributor, or retailer of computers? (IF YES, TERMINATE)

Are you or any member of your family employed in marketing consulting, direct marketing, public relations, advertising, communications design or the marketing research industry? (IF YES, TERMINATE)

Comment: In this case, the study is about computers and the types of people indicated above would be deemed inappropriate for interview. You would, of course, have to determine whether either of these screening questions is necessary for your study and insert the appropriate wording.

Once you have eliminated critical industry respondents, you may still have other screening questions to make sure that the person is qualified to complete the questionnaire. Below is a screening question that might be used if you were conducting a study for a bank about checking accounts:

Are you the person in your household who is most responsible for determining the bank you use for your checking account? (IF NOT, ASK TO SPEAK TO THAT PERSON)

Comment: If necessary for your study, now is the time to ask whatever questions are appropriate to make sure you are talking to the right person. Whether it's a consumer, professional, or business-to-business interview, you don't want to waste time questioning a respondent further only to find that the person isn't the decision maker.

At this point, you have generated respondent cooperation and determined that the person doesn't pose a critical industry problem and is indeed the decision maker. So far, so good!

There still may be a number of additional screening questions that should be asked before you reach the main body of the interview. These questions reflect your target market requirements and your determination of who is important to interview. There can be any number of screening questions necessary to qualify a target respondent. The following are some examples:

> Additional screening question #1. In the past 90 days, have you personally purchased office products or supplies for your household? (IF NO, TERMINATE)

Comment: If you are representing an office products company, you might want to interview only respondents who have purchased office products and supplies in the past 90 days. Therefore, screening question #1 would be asked, which qualifies the respondent as appropriate to interview.

> Additional screening question #2. Are you between the ages of 25 and 45? (IF NO, TERMINATE)

Comment: If you want to interview only respondents in a certain age range you would use an age-screening question such as question #2.

> Additional screening question #3. What one brand of gasoline do you use most often? (IF THE SPONSOR YOU ARE REPRESENTING (e.g. SHELL) IS NOT MENTIONED, TERMINATE)

Comment: Often the study will call for the interviewing of respondents who use a certain brand or product. In such a case, a brand-screening question would be asked, like additional screening question #3.

> Additional screening question #4. In the next three months, are you very likely or not very likely to shop for a new computer? (IF NOT VERY LIKELY, TERMINATE)

Comment: If you want to interview respondents who are likely to take some kind of purchase action in the near future, a screening question is required. In question #4, the goal is to interview only respondents who are very likely to shop for a new computer in the next three months. You would, of course, choose the screening time frame most appropriate for you.

> Additional screening question #5. In the past six months, have you spent at least $200 purchasing wine for use in your home or to give as a gift? (IF NO, TERMINATE)

Comment: You might want to qualify respondents who have committed a significant amount of money to purchasing products in your product category. Additional screening question #5 indicates that the target respondent must have spent at least $200 on wine in the past six months.

Again, to identify a target respondent, there are often several screening questions that are required. You might want your respondents to be in a certain age group as well as to be heavy users. You could qualify respondents as having a certain favorite brand, but also likely to try a new brand in the next three months.

In determining your target respondents, you should use as many screening questions as are necessary to identify only those people whose opinions you seek.

Setting quotas with screening questions

Many market research studies are designed to develop information for two or more targets – that is, for two or more groups that have different screening qualifications. In such cases, quotas are determined. Quotas refer to the number of interviews that you want to collect among various target segments.

Screening questions will also allow you to determine the appropriate quota group for a respondent. For example, look at additional screening question #3 again:

What one brand of gasoline do you use most often? (IF SHELL IS NOT MENTIONED, TERMINATE)

Your study might call for conducting 150 interviews among people indicating Shell is the brand that they use most often and 150 interviews among people indicating they purchase another brand most often. While your screening question would be the same as originally written, instead of terminating the respondent you would have a different instruction, as follows:

What one brand of gasoline do you use most often? (QUOTA: COMPLETE 150 INTERVIEWS AMONG SHELL MOST OFTEN AND 150 AMONG OTHER BRANDS MOST OFTEN)

Take another example in which the goal is to screen a variety of targets:

When you use copying and printing services outside your home, do you usually use:

Alpha-Graphics or other printing chains like Kwik Kopy, PIP, Sir Speedy, etc.
Kinko's
OfficeMax
Office Depot

Staples

A local print shop

(QUOTA GROUP #1: CONDUCT 150 INTERVIEWS AMONG THOSE WHO USUALLY USE KINKO'S. QUOTA GROUP #2: CONDUCT 150 INTERVIEWS AMONG THOSE WHO USUALLY USE A LOCAL PRINT SHOP. QUOTA GROUP #3: CONDUCT 150 INTERVIEWS AMONG THOSE WHO USUALLY USE ALL OTHERS)

In both of the above examples, every person initially screened will qualify to be interviewed and will fall into a quota group. Respondents will only be terminated when 150 interviews in a quota group are collected and a respondent is identified who is no longer needed to fill a quota.

As you can see, the qualification phase of the questionnaire can be an involved process. It can require any number of questions and often takes several minutes to complete. Careful thought about the screening process is essential for a successful survey.

Once you have written your screening questions, always go back and check them against your target respondent requirements. If they do not precisely identify the types of respondents you wish to interview, add or reword questions until they do.

3.　THE MAIN BODY PHASE

Now that you have obtained respondent cooperation and determined that the respondent qualifies for the interview, you are ready to begin the main phase of questioning. Quantitative research studies use a variety of questioning approaches and scales to collect information.

Structured questioning approaches are:

- stand-alone;
- in a series; or
- in a string.

Stand-alone questions are simply isolated questions or questions that don't connect to an inquiry pattern. Here are some examples of stand-alone questions:

- What one brand of beer do you purchase most often?
- When you think of brands of forklifts, what are all the brands you can think of?
- The last time you bought gasoline, did you purchase other products at the gas station?
- How knowledgeable are you when it comes to the mechanics of keeping your car running?

Questioning in a series might best be thought of as branching questions. When a respondent answers a question a certain way, it triggers the next question – or the branch. The branch question is only asked as a result of the answer given to a previous question.

Question 1a below has two branch questions. Questions 1b and 1c are the branch questions and would only be asked if the answer to 1a were Yes; otherwise the respondent is skipped forward:

1a. In the last 30 days have you seen or heard any advertising for discount stores?

Yes.
No. (IF NO, SKIP TO QUESTION 2)

1b. Which of the following discount stores have you seen or heard advertised most often? (READ LIST; CHECK ONE)

Costco   ____
Sam's Club   ____
Sears   ____
Target   ____
Walmart   ____
Other   ____

1c. Where did you see or hear advertising for [mention store shopped in Question 1b]? (READ LIST; CHECK ONE)

TV   ____
Newspaper ad   ____
Flyer in mail   ____
Radio   ____
Other   ____

Questioning in strings is a frequently used approach. Here are some examples of question strings:

I am going to read you a series of statements about buying from a catalog. Please indicate whether you agree or disagree with each statement. (CHECK EACH ITEM AGREED WITH)

Buying from catalogs is fun   ____
Buying from catalogs usually saves me money   ____
It is more convenient buying from catalogs than going to a retail store   ____
You can find unique products when buying from catalogs   ____
It is difficult to return products when you buy from catalogs   ____

Here the string of statements would be read by the interviewer one at a time – and should be in a rotated order so that there is no position bias in the responses.

Here is another example of a string question:

> I am going to read you a list of statements about catalog companies. Please indicate how important or unimportant each is in determining the catalog companies you purchase from. Do this by using a five-point scale where "five" means "very important" and "one" means "not at all important." Or you can use any number in between.
>
> They provide free returns   ____
> You can easily contact them with questions   ____
> They carry products that you can't find elsewhere   ____
> Their products are always in stock   ____
> Their products are the highest quality   ____

A string question can list dozens of statements, attributes or characteristics. Usually each statement can be read by the interviewer and answered in about 10 to 15 seconds. A 25-statement string question can usually be completed in five minutes or less, which makes it a very fast technique for generating information about many issues. Long strings are almost always presented in a rotated order so that each respondent replies to a different sequence thus eliminating a position bias.

Open-ended questioning

In addition to structured questioning, quantitative surveys may contain open-ended questions. Open-ended questions are unstructured and do not anticipate a particular response. They allow respondents to use their own words when answering a question. The following are examples of open-ended questioning:

1a. Do you recall seeing advertising for Walmart?

Yes. (ASK QUESTION 1b)
No. (SKIP TO QUESTION 2)

1b. What do you recall that Walmart's advertising said or showed?

Comment: The interviewer would record the respondent's response to question 1b exactly as expressed.

Another example is:

1a. Have you purchased from catalogs in the past 30 days?

Yes. (ASK QUESTIONS 1b AND 1c)
No. (SKIP TO QUESTION 2a)

1b. What do you feel are all the advantages, if any, of purchasing from catalogs?

Comment: The interviewer would record the respondent's response to question 1b exactly as expressed.

1c. What do you feel are all the disadvantages, if any, of purchasing from catalogs?

Comment: The interviewer would record the respondent's response exactly as expressed.

2a. How would you rate purchasing from catalogs? Do you think it's:
   – An excellent way to buy products?
   – A good way?
   – A fair way?
   – A poor way to buy products?

2b. Tell me why you said purchasing from catalogs is [insert answer from question 2a].

Comment: The interviewer would record the respondent's response to question 2b exactly as expressed.

As respondents answer open-ended questions, interviewers record their comments verbatim. The main goal of open-ended questions is to allow information to surface that might not be addressed in structured questions.

When you ask open-ended questions, a person called a "coder" must read each answer and code the response(s) into answer categories. That is, each response is put into a category that captures the essence of the remark. The codes are then tabulated and the percentages of respondents giving particular answers are reported.

Scales

Scales are one of the most important tools used in surveys. Scales gauge the degree to which an opinion is held or the extent to which respondents have feelings one way or the other about an issue.

Attitudes held by consumers are rarely all positive or all negative. There are many scales at your disposal that measure not only the most positive or most negative attitudes that are held, but also assess the shades of gray that exist.

Scales should be balanced. That is, they should evenly represent both positive and negative attitudes. Consider this question and the scale:

How do you like this chapter of *MORE Guerrilla Marketing Research?* Do you:

Like it very much?
Like it somewhat?
Neither like nor dislike it?
Dislike it somewhat?
Dislike it very much?

The response options are evenly balanced and unbiased. Respondents can choose a totally positive or negative response as well as a positive leaning or a negative leaning response. There is also a middle option if the respondent simply doesn't have an opinion.

Consider this question posed another way:

How do you like this chapter of *MORE Guerrilla Marketing Research?* Do you:

Like it very much?
Like it fairly much?
Like it a little?
Dislike it a little?
Dislike it a lot?

There is a decidedly positive bias to these response options. There are three positive and only two negative response options. Even the response "Dislike it a little" has a biased positive tone.

Take another question:

Think about the last time you flew in a plane. Would you rate the carrier you flew as being:

Excellent?
Good?
Fair?
Poor?

The four response options represent equanimity. There is neither a positive nor a negative bias.

Look at the scale used below:

Think about the last time you flew in a plane. Would you rate the carrier you flew as being:

Excellent?
Very good?
Good?
Fair?

Clearly, these responses pose a positive bias. Even the "Fair" response suggests that not all is bad.

There are several popular scales used in survey research that are unbiased. Scales are referred to as four- or five-point scales depending on the number of options provided. Four-point scales force respondents into leaning one way or the other on a question. Five-point scales provide respondents with a middle ground.

Here is a four-point agreement scale. In this case, the question is:

To what extent do you agree with the statement that you enjoy life to its fullest. Do you:

1. Completely agree.
2. Agree somewhat.
3. Disagree somewhat.
4. Completely disagree.

Using a five-point scale, you would have the same response option plus a middle ground, as follows:

1. Completely agree.
2. Agree somewhat.
3. Neither agree nor disagree.
4. Disagree somewhat.
5. Completely disagree.

Whether you use a four- or five-point scale is usually a matter of personal choice. One school of thought says that consumers usually lean one way or the other no matter what the question, so a four-point scale that forces them into a direction is the best. Others say it is equally legitimate for respondents not to have an opinion and, therefore, providing a mid-point is the best way to go.

Often it will depend on who you are surveying and the nature of your questions. If you feel your target respondents are unlikely to have an opinion, as might be the case when you are interviewing respondents who may know very little about the subject, go with the five-point scale. If you are interviewing past customers who have had some experience with your company and products and are likely to have opinions, you might prefer a four-point scale.

Consistency is what is ultimately important. You shouldn't have a four-point scale for some respondent targets and a five-point scale for others. This would make it impossible to compare findings across the targets.

Also, if you have a questionnaire with a number of question strings, it is usually best to stick to one scale; otherwise respondents tend to become confused when going back and forth from a four-point scale to a five-point scale or vice versa.

Here are some additional four- or five-point scales, all of which are unbiased and, depending upon your questions, are good options for your questionnaire.

A four-point importance scale:

Extremely important.
Somewhat important.
Not very important.
Not at all important.

A five-point importance scale:

Extremely important.
Somewhat important.
Neither important nor unimportant.
Not very important.
Not at all important.

A four-point liking scale:

Like very much.
Like somewhat.
Dislike somewhat.
Dislike very much.

A five-point liking scale:

Like very much.
Like somewhat.
Neither like nor dislike.
Dislike somewhat.
Dislike very much.

A four-point satisfaction scale:

Completely satisfied
Somewhat satisfied.
Somewhat dissatisfied.
Completely dissatisfied.

A five-point satisfaction scale:

Completely satisfied.
Somewhat satisfied.
Neither satisfied nor dissatisfied.
Somewhat dissatisfied.
Completely dissatisfied.

A four-point purchase scale:

Definitely would purchase.
Probably would purchase.
Probably would not purchase.
Definitely would not purchase.

A five-point purchase scale:

Definitely would purchase.
Probably would purchase.
Might or might not purchase.
Probably would not purchase.
Definitely would not purchase.

Anchor scales are another popular approach to scaling. Anchor scales, as the name implies, use a top and bottom word or phrase to anchor the scale. Here, respondents are read both ends of the scale and asked to choose the number best describing their attitude. The question here would be:

> On a five-point scale with five being "Definitely would purchase" and one being "Definitely would not purchase," what number between five and one best describes your likelihood of purchasing from the Apex catalog?

> Definitely would purchase 5 4 3 2 1   Definitely would not purchase

Researchers like anchor scales because they don't have to worry about whether the mid-points of a scale represent a fair balance. For example, the wording "Probably would purchase" might have a different impli-cation to one respondent than it has to another. Using an anchor scale with only the most positive and most negative points expressed eliminates the vagueness of mid-point wording.

Anchor scales are particularly valuable when it is difficult to write a balanced scale. For example, assume you were judging the taste of a new candy bar and you wanted to evaluate the level of sweetness. With the question "How would you rate the sweetness of the candy bar you tasted?," a five-point balanced scale might use the words:

1. Much too sweet.
2. A little too sweet.
3. Just about right.
4. Not quite sweet enough.
5. Not at all sweet enough.

An anchor scale might be:

Much too sweet   5 4 3 2 1   Not at all sweet enough.

As you can see, both scales evaluate sweetness, but come at it differently. If using the wording "A little too sweet" or "Not quite sweet enough" in the balanced scale provides clear direction, use that approach. The wording, though, might have different meanings to your R&D people, who are working to get the right levels of sweetness. In this case, the anchor scale might be easier to interpret.

Another good use of anchor scales is when you are looking for more subtle levels of difference. Assume that you want to evaluate consumer attitudes toward Home Depot and Lowe's on the issue of price. Take the question "Please indicate the number that best describes your attitudes toward the way Home Depot and Lowe's price their products." You could use a five-, seven- or nine-point anchor scale, like those illustrated in Figure 15.1.

All three scales can be used effectively to evaluate attitudes toward price. However, because of the additional number of rating points on the seven- and nine-point scales, there is a greater opportunity to observe subtle differences. As a generalization, more points on a scale means more differentiation in the findings. Then, too, some like 10-point scales because the averages seem easy to interpret. An average score of eight on a 10-point scale is intuitively more understandable than a seven on a nine-point scale.

Overall, when choosing scales to use in your questionnaire, keep the following in mind:

● Deciding on a particular scale is more often a matter of personal preference than scientific principle.

5-point		
Home Depot prices are extremely high	5 4 3 2 1	Home Depot prices are extremely low
Lowe's prices are extremely high	5 4 3 2 1	Lowe's prices are extremely low
7-point		
Home Depot prices are extremely high	7 6 5 4 3 2 1	Home Depot prices are extremely low
Lowe's prices are extremely high	7 6 5 4 3 2 1	Lowe's prices are extremely low
9-point		
Home Depot prices are extremely high	9 8 7 6 5 4 3 2 1	Home Depot prices are extremely low
Lowe's prices are extremely high	9 8 7 6 5 4 3 2 1	Lowe's prices are extremely low

Figure 15.1   Anchor scales

- Once you have chosen a particular scale, you should be consistent and stick with it. If you want comparative data from target to target and from study to study, you must keep the scales constant.
- Sometimes your choice of scale is determined by the type of study you are doing. For example, if you are researching customer satisfaction (see Chapter 16) and want to use the "net promoter" score, you'll use an 11-point scale that runs from 0 to 10. Or you may want to compare your results to those from another study done outside your company. In this case you'll have to use the same scales they did.
- Sometimes it's impossible to create a scale that is totally balanced or in which the anchors represent both ends precisely.

If your scale has a positive or negative bias, using the scale over and over again from study to study will at least produce a constant bias. You'll be interpreting the data from the same point of view, which is always advisable anyway.

The main body of your questionnaire

There are a number of important things to keep in mind as you write a questionnaire:

- If respondents become aware of the study sponsor, there may be a positive or negative influence in the way they answer subsequent questions. Carefully consider if or when you reveal the sponsor.

- If unaided questions are important, do not give clues about the study sponsor until after such questions are asked.
- Questionnaire flow is usually from the more general to the more specific.
- Demographic questions and other "sensitive" questions should be asked at the end of the questionnaire.

Sponsor awareness

Earlier, we discussed gaining the cooperation of respondents by informing them of the study sponsor. This is appropriate when you are conducting studies in which the nature of the study isn't such that mentioning the sponsor might bias answers either positively or negatively. If you are conducting a satisfaction study among your own customers, for example, respondents are more likely to give honest, straightforward opinions when they know you are the study sponsor. Not knowing the sponsor makes them suspicious and less cooperative.

It would also be appropriate if you are evaluating new products, services, or ideas and the company or brand identity and personality would be an important part of potential success or failure of the effort. One of the greatest research fiascos in history resulted when Coca-Cola failed to identify itself in the taste testing it conducted when trying to determine the response to the "Pepsi Challenge."

By doing blind taste tests in which respondents did not know what brands they were tasting, Pepsi "proved" that people preferred the sweeter test of Pepsi to that of Coke. These tests were done on camera and became the basis of Pepsi advertising. Coke thought its challenge was to develop a competing sweet product. When it found it, it went to market as New Coke.

New Coke foundered and so did the flagship "Classic" Coke. The company lost its status as the number one cola. It quickly dropped New Coke and remarketed Classic Coke and became number one in the category again.

Its subsequent analysis was that people don't just drink a cola when they drink Coke. They participate in a deep relationship with the brand going back generations.

What Coke failed to do in its initial research was to consider the power of the Coca-Cola name. When subsequent research identified to consumers what they were testing, "Classic Coke" ratings improved dramatically. This was a case where identifying the sponsor was critical to the success of the research.

Another situation where naming the sponsor would be appropriate is if the subject matter is highly sensitive, and respondents might not be totally forthcoming without knowing who is using the information.

However, for most research studies, the information being collected dictates that respondents are kept in the dark about the sponsor, at least for a portion of the interview. These studies include:

- When you want top-of-mind spontaneous responses to questions, e.g. "When you think of makes of automobiles, what is the first name that comes to mind?" or, "Please tell me the names of all the banks you can think of in your community."
- When you are comparing your company, brand or product to one or more competitors.
- When you feel that knowledge of the sponsor up-front might bias the respondent either positively or negatively, e.g. your company did something that was in the news and mention of it might stimulate comments that wouldn't otherwise surface.

Unaided questions

Surveys may feature a series of questions regarding company awareness, attitude, or image. In this case, asking questions in an unaided manner is important. "Unaided" simply means that the respondent has not been provided with any information by the interviewer that would help him or her answer the question. Consider the following unaided questions:

- What are the names of all the places you can think of that sell home improvement products?
- What are the names of all the places that sell home improvement products that you have seen or heard advertised in the past 30 days?
- What one place that sells home improvement products do you feel gives you the best value for your money?
- What one place that sells home improvement products do you shop at most often?
- Considering all the home improvement stores you shop at, approximately how much do you spend per year at each?
- What are the most important reasons you chose to shop at one home improvement store over another?

Conversely, aided questions are also important. "Aided" questioning means that the interviewer has given the respondent information to answer the question. Consider several of the previous unaided questions and their aided counterparts:

Unaided: What are the names of all the places you can think of that sell home improvement products? (DO NOT READ LIST. CHECK ALL THAT ARE MENTIONED)

Ace Hardware   _____
Home Depot   _____
Lowe's   _____
Menard's   _____
Tru-Value Hardware   _____
Other mentions (WRITE IN)   _____

Aided: (FOR ALL THE PLACES NOT MENTIONED IN THE UNAIDED QUESTION, THE INTERVIEWER WOULD ASK THE RESPONDENT): In the past 30 days, have you seen or heard advertising for any of the following?

Ace Hardware: Yes _____   No _____
Home Depot: Yes _____   No _____
Lowe's: Yes _____   No _____
Menard's: Yes _____   No _____
Tru-Value Hardware: Yes _____   No _____

Unaided: For all the home improvement places you shop at, approximately how much do you spend per year at each? (DO NOT READ LIST. CHECK ALL THAT ARE MENTIONED)

Ace Hardware   _____
Home Depot   _____
Lowe's   _____
Menard's   _____
Tru-Value Hardware   _____
Other mentions (WRITE IN)   _____

Aided: (FOR THOSE PLACES WHERE NO SPENDING WAS MENTIONED IN UNAIDED QUESTIONING, THE INTERVIEWER WOULD ASK THE RESPONDENT): In the past year, how much have you spent at any of the following?

Ace Hardware   _____
Home Depot   _____
Lowe's   _____
Menard's   _____
Tru-Value Hardware   _____
Other mentions (WRITE IN)   _____

Unaided recall is usually regarded as a stronger indication of share of the consumer's mind than is aided recall. Often the order in which the unaided mention occurs is noted and included in the analysis. The higher in the order, the better. Ideally, your brand would be recalled on an unaided basis by 100 per cent of the respondents and named first among all brands mentioned.

However, simply because a respondent fails to mention a company, brand, or product when asked on an unaided basis, does not prove that the respondent holds it in less esteem. Aided prompts trigger additional recall. Taken together, unaided and aided questioning provides a more complete picture of respondent awareness, attitudes, and behavior. Usually unaided and aided results are summed in the analysis to create a new variable as well, total brand awareness or total advertising recall, etc.

Phrasing questions

When phrasing questions, follow the guidelines below.

- Avoid biased phrasing at all costs.
- Consider the question, "What do you like about driving a car?" There is a built-in assumption in the question that the respondent will like something about driving a car. When asked this way, it tends to force respondents to mention something they like.
- Consider the question written in an unbiased manner: "What, if anything, do you like about driving a car?" By simply using "if anything" as part of the question phrasing, the respondent is not put on the spot to find something to like.

Here are other examples of biased and unbiased questions:

- Biased: There are many factors that are important when buying over the internet. Tell me which ones you feel are most important. *This assumes there are factors that are important.*
- Unbiased: There are many factors that may or may not be important to you when buying over the internet. Tell me which, if any, you feel are important.
- Biased: How often do you just hang up without listening when somebody calls you on the telephone and tries to sell you something? *This assumes the respondent will hang up.*
- Unbiased: Consider the last 10 times somebody might have called you on the telephone and tried to sell you something. How many times out of 10 would you say you've just hung up on the person calling without listening?
- Biased: The last time you shopped for groceries, which soft drink brands did you purchase for your home? *This assumes soft drinks were purchased on the last shopping trip and on a trip to a place that also sold groceries.*
- Unbiased: The last time you purchased soft drinks for your home, which brands did you buy?

When phrasing questions, don't assume the respondent holds particular attitudes or behaves in a certain way.

Limit questions or statements to a single thought

A dual-thought question would be, "What, if anything, do you like or dislike about your dentist?" With such a question, respondents tend to focus first on the strongest likes or dislikes. If it happens to be something they like, they will give less thought to what they might dislike, and vice versa. It would be better to split this into two questions, one focusing only on likes and the other on dislikes.

String questions are easy to inadvertently write with multiple thoughts and, therefore, can be problematic. Consider this string question:

I am going to read you a list of statements that describe what people look for when they choose a bank. Please tell me how important or unimportant each is to you.
The bank should have friendly and knowledgeable people. *Friendly is one thought; knowledgeable is another.*
The bank should be open long hours and at night. *Long hours is one thought; open at night is a second.*
The bank should offer extra services such as being able to buy and sell stocks or being able to buy life insurance. *Buy and sell stocks is one thought; buying life insurance is a second.*
The bank should offer free postage when I want to bank by mail as well as free internet banking. *Free postage is one thought; free internet banking is another.*

When you ask a dual-thought question, you are unable to interpret the result. It's probably a good idea that a bank should have both friendly and knowledgeable people, but it may not be necessary. Being just the friendliest bank could set it apart, as could just being the bank with the most knowledgeable people.

Phrase questions as directly as possible

Questions should be precise and to the point. They should not be wordy or verbose. If it takes more than two sentences for an interviewer to pose your question, it's probably too long. Here is a ridiculous and real example of a question from a telephone questionnaire:

The following statements I am going to read to you deal with attitudes you may have toward buying from catalogs. In this sense, we mean buying from a catalog where you have mailed or telephoned in your order and your merchandise was delivered to your home, office, or elsewhere, or by some type of delivery service. We do not mean where you may have ordered by mail or phone and then gone to a retail store or outlet to pick up the merchandise yourself. For each statement please tell me how much you agree or disagree that the statement describes how you feel about buying from catalogs.

Let's use a five-point scale where "five" means you agree strongly that the statement describes how you feel about purchasing merchandise through a catalog and "one" means that you disagree strongly that the statement describes how you feel about purchasing merchandise through a catalog. Of course, you may use any number in between, depending on how much you agree or disagree that the statement describes how you feel about buying from catalogs.

The question could be more succinctly phrased as follows:

I am going to read you some statements about buying from catalogs where your order is delivered to your home or office. Each statement can be rated on a five-point scale with "five" meaning you agree strongly with the statement and "one" meaning you disagree strongly.

Here is another overly wordy question:

People can describe companies many different ways. There are different words and phrases that are more commonly used than others. Some are positive, some neutral, and some negative. I am going to read you the names of several companies, one at a time, and then read words and phrases to describe that company. After each word or phrase, simply say "yes" if you feel it describes the company and "no" if you feel it doesn't describe the company.

This question could be easily pared down:

I am going to give you the names of several companies. Simply say "yes" or "no" if you think the words or phrases I read describe that company.

Keep in mind that respondents can have difficulty remembering or understanding long and involved questions. While you may think that length is important to asking a question, short and simple usually works just as well.

Self-administered questionnaires

Most self-administered questionnaires arrive by mail or are accessed via the internet. On occasion, they may be handed out or filled out at computerized kiosks at trade shows and county fairs, for example. Questionnaires that are filled out by the respondent without interviewer assistance should follow many of the same guidelines previously discussed. However, there are specific issues to consider when writing self-administered questionnaires, as set out below.

Simplicity, simplicity and simplicity

It is very easy for respondents to become confused when filling out a questionnaire. To cut down on confusion, follow these guidelines:

1. The main instructions for completing the questionnaire should make the task seem effortless, e.g., "The questions in this survey can be answered by simply placing an 'X' where indicated. Be sure to answer each question. Don't skip any questions. Thank you for your time."
2. Use at least 12-point typeface to enhance readability.
3. Use bold type and/or underline to highlight important elements in a question, i.e., "How many times have you purchased from a retail store in the *past 30 days?*"
4. Place at least one line space between questions.
5. Don't have questions that run from one page to another.

Reduce question skipping

Don't jump respondents around. Keep questions in sequential order. As much as possible, one question should follow the next. Believe it or not, up to 20 per cent of respondents will fail to read or follow an instruction that tells them to skip from question 1 to question 3.

There are times when the answer to one question must dictate the next question to answer. If you have to skip respondents, assume that a child is filling out the questionnaire. The following example illustrates this mentality:

1a. Have you ever gone to a flea market? (Check one.)

Yes. (IF YES, ANSWER QUESTION 1b)
No. (IF NO, GO TO QUESTION 2)

1b. (IF YES TO 1a) How often do you go to flea markets? (CHECK ONE LINE ONLY)

Once a week or more often ____
Two to three times per month ____
Once a month or less often ____

Provide an instruction for each question

Each and every question should tell respondents exactly what you want them to do. See these examples.

Example 1:

1. Put an "X" next to the one statement below that best describes you. (PLACE AN "X" ON ONE LINE ONLY)

I'm an avid collector	_____
I only have a passing interest in collecting anything	_____
I don't collect anything	_____

Example 2:

1a. In the past 12 months, how many times have you purchased a gift? (PLACE AN "X" ON ONE LINE ONLY BELOW IN COLUMN 1A.)

1b. In the past 12 months, how many times have you purchased a gift from a discount store? (PLACE AN "X" ON ONE LINE ONLY BELOW IN COLUMN 1B.)

	Question 1a Gift purchase	Question 1b Discount store
Have not purchased a gift	_____	_____
Purchased 1 time	_____	_____
Purchased 2 or more times	_____	_____

Example 3:

1. Listed below are statements about purchasing gifts. For each statement, place an "X" on the one line that describes the extent to which you agree or disagree with the statement. (REMEMBER TO "X" ONE ANSWER FOR EACH STATEMENT.)

	Agree strongly	Agree somewhat	Disagree somewhat	Disagree strongly
You always look for unique gifts	—	—	—	—
You like nostalgic gifts	—	—	—	—
You like to give high-quality gifts	—	—	—	—
You like to give art as gifts	—	—	—	—

Avoid open-ended questions

In a self-administered questionnaire respondents tend to skip open-ended questions. If they do answer them, they won't provide more than superficial comments. Questions like, "Why do you like visiting Mexico?" or, "What do you recall about the advertising?" will generate little more than one- or two-word answers. Spending money to tabulate such responses is rarely worth the effort.

Questions in self-administered questionnaires should be 100 per cent structured. All the respondent should have to do is check a pre-listed answer. If you think you have to ask a "Why?" or essay-type question, you haven't done your homework or are being lazy. The fact is that you should know the responses you want to quantify before you collect data using a self-administered questionnaire.

Consider the issue of questionnaire control

You have no control over what respondents will do before they fill out a self-administered questionnaire. They may first read it over completely. In doing so, they will become aware of the issues your questioning is addressing, which could influence how they respond. They might also fill it out over a couple of days with those issues in mind.

Again, think about lack of control. If you think a question might possibly be misinterpreted, assume it will be and rewrite it. If you feel that answering certain questions first might affect how respondents answer subsequent questions, you are probably right. Reconsider the order. If confidentiality is important, you should make sure that you are hiding the study sponsor as best you can.

Questionnaire length is not the issue

Motivating the respondent to complete a self-administered questionnaire, no matter what the length, is job number one. (Gaining respondent cooperation is discussed in detail in Chapter 14, on types of surveys.)

Our experience has been that respondents will fill out a 40-page self-administered questionnaire if it is well written, easy to complete, and interesting. And they will toss a two-page questionnaire away if it is cluttered and complex.

Question context for interviewer and self-administered questionnaires

Much of the art of developing an effective questionnaire lies in creating the context within which you pose a question. Context is the point of view the question presents. Here are several different questioning contexts or points of view for generating unaided awareness of places that sell clothing:

1. When you think of buying clothing for yourself, what outlets come to mind?
2. When you think about outlets that sell upscale clothing for yourself, what comes to mind?
3. When you think about places that sell upscale clothing for yourself by catalog or the internet, what comes to mind?

Each of the above questions provides a different context and could generate different answers. The first context is very general – only about outlets to buy clothes. The second narrows the context to upscale clothing. The third is even narrower, referring to upscale clothing via catalogs or the internet.

When writing questions, it is very important that the context of the questions is clear to you. You must be convinced the question will give you the information you seek. The worst feeling in the world is looking at how respondents have answered and realizing that the question is irrelevant because you have not posed it in the right context.

The contextual questions in the following sections are provided as guidelines for writing a questionnaire. They should be helpful when writing questions that deal with a variety of topics. Use them as you deem appropriate.

Notes of clarification: the following contextual questions are written to reflect companies that sell retail-oriented products. When it comes to other consumer-oriented companies, or business-to-business firms, the wording of the questions should be altered to reflect the marketplace. That is, consumers don't buy checking accounts; they choose a place to open a checking account. Executives don't buy accounting firms; they choose an accounting firm, etc.

The following questioning context examples are most appropriate for interviewer-administered questionnaires. In self-administered questionnaires, in which response options are shown as part of the question, you could not, for example, consider answers to be unaided. If you are writing a self-administered questionnaire, the questioning contexts should be altered to reflect the previously discussed self-administered questionnaire guidelines.

Generating top-of-mind unaided responses

For brand awareness:
When you think of [insert your product category], what is the first [insert brand / company / product type] that comes to mind?

What other [insert brands/companies/product types] come to mind?

For advertising awareness:
When you think of [insert your product category], in the past [30 days or whatever time frame is appropriate], what is the one [insert brand/company/product type] that you have seen or heard advertised most often?
What other [insert brands/companies/product types] have you seen or heard advertised in the past [30 days or whatever time frame is appropriate]?

For brand loyalty:
When you buy [insert your product category], what one [insert brand/company/product type] do you buy most often?
What other [insert brands/companies/product types] do you buy?

For brand attrition:
What [insert brands/companies/product types] would you not consider buying?
The above brand loyalty and brand attrition unaided questions should include a list of brands, companies or product types so that the interviewer can simply place an "X" next to the answers rather than writing in responses.

Generating aided responses

Note: aided response questioning is appropriate (with obvious wording changes) for both interviewer-administered and self-administered questionnaires.

For brand awareness:
I am going to mention a list of [insert brands/companies/product types] one at a time. After I read each, tell me if you have heard of it.

For advertising awareness:
I am going to mention a list of [insert brands/companies/product types] one at a time. After I read each, tell me if you have heard or seen it advertised in the past [30 days or whatever time frame is appropriate].

For brand loyalty:
When you buy [insert brands/companies/product types], have you purchased any of the following [read the brands/companies/product types one at a time] in the past [30 days or whatever time frame is appropriate]?

For brand attrition:
For each of the following [insert brands/companies/product types] that I read, which, if any, would you not consider buying?

When generating aided awareness, the interviewer should mention only names that were not previously chosen or marked with an "X" when asking the question on an unaided basis.

The following context questions are written for a string series of statements.

Note of clarification: five-point scales are used in the context questions below. Other scales are equally appropriate, e.g. 7-, 9-, or 10-point scales. Please refer to the scale section earlier in this chapter for additional options.

Generating importance

When you want to determine how important a number of characteristics are to purchasers, use the following context question:

> I am going to read you a list of statements regarding [insert product category]. For each statement, how important or unimportant is it to you when it comes to buying [insert product category]? A "five" would mean it is extremely important, a "one" not at all important, or you can rate it any number in between. The first statement is [insert statement].

Generating agreement

When you want to determine whether respondents agree or disagree with statements regarding your products or your competitors' products, use the following context question:

> I am going to read you a list of statements regarding [insert product category] and I would like to know the extent to which you agree or disagree with each. A "five" would mean that you agree strongly with the statement, a "one" means that you disagree strongly with the statement, or you can rate it any number in between. The first statement is [insert statement].

Generating company or brand profiles

When you want to determine profiles of companies or brands via a series of statements, use the following context question:

> I am going to read you a list of statements regarding [insert the company/brand]. For each statement, please tell me the extent to which you agree or disagree that the statement describes the [company/brand]. A "five" means you agree strongly that it describes the [company/brand], a

"one" means you disagree strongly that it describes the [company/brand], or you can rate it any number in between. The first statement is [insert statement].

Generating summary measures

It is common for surveys to include an overall attitude question – one that captures the respondent's summary feeling about the company, brand, or product. Overall attitude is often used as a dependent variable when analyzing data (the use of a dependent variable is explained further in Chapter 17).

Consider the following context questions for generating overall attitude:

Taking everything you know into consideration, would you rate [insert the brand / company / product] as being:

Excellent	____
Good	____
Fair	____
Poor	____

Taking everything you know into consideration, how would you rate [insert the brand / company / product] on a nine-point scale? A "nine" would be the best, "one" would be the worst, or you could rate it anywhere in between.

Note of clarification: the scales used on the context question above can be changed to a seven- or five-point scale, as you deem appropriate.

Anchor questions

Anchor questions are particularly appropriate when generating company or brand profiles and when evaluating reactions to products. Anchor questions are more easily answered when respondents can see the question and "X" a response. The context examples below illustrate this. Of course, you should insert the words or phrases that are appropriate to your brand or company:

Listed below are word pairs with opposite meanings. For each pair, please place an "X" on the line in the position that describes how you feel about [insert the brand / company / product]. Be sure to mark an "X" on a line for each pair:

	5	4	3	2	1	
Exciting	—	—	—	—	—	Boring
Contemporary	—	—	—	—	—	Old-fashioned
Unique	—	—	—	—	—	Common
Friendly	—	—	—	—	—	Impersonal
Fun	—	—	—	—	—	Dull
Classic	—	—	—	—	—	Trendy

Note of clarification: when administering anchor questions by phone, you can use telephone-type wording (e.g. "You would choose a 'five' if you felt that the company was exciting, a 'one' if you thought it was boring, or you can use any number in between."). Also consider using scales that have only two anchor points, as follows:

More of an exciting brand	____	or More of a dull brand	____
More of a contemporary brand	____	or More of an old-fashioned brand	____
More of a unique brand	____	or More of a common brand	____

Forced-choice questions

If you are comparing two or more alternatives and you want to determine whether there is a clear winner, forced-choice questions should be considered (i.e. when comparing products, ads, promotions, premiums, etc.) Here are several examples of context questions in forced-choice situations:

Please look at both of these premiums that you would get free if you purchased a new brand of coffee you had not tried in the past. Which one would most likely cause you to purchase the new brand?

Premium #1   ____
Premium #2   ____

A new flavored cola drink is coming on the market. It could come in three flavors. Which one flavor would you most likely buy first?

Chocolate   ____
Lemon   ____
Cherry   ____

Here are two advertisements for Sears. Please read both and choose the one that you find most believable.

Ad #1 _____
Ad #2 _____

Price

There are many questions that you can ask to determine how much consumers will spend on a product. The problem with pricing questions is that if you ask respondents a direct price question, their answers usually over- or underestimate reality.

Take the question, "How much would you be willing to spend for a new computer?" Whatever answer you give might be totally unrealistic compared to the actual price you would have to pay given your needs.

It is always better to put pricing questions in a context. If you were trying to determine how much a person would be willing to spend for a weekend night at a luxury hotel, you could frame the question as follows:

> Luxury hotel rooms vary in price. During the week you could spend as little as $200 for a luxury hotel room or as much as $600 for a five-star, top-of-the-line hotel. If you wanted to spend a *weekend* night at a luxury hotel, how much would you be willing to spend? (RECORD AMOUNT:____)

Another way to determine the price of a luxury hotel room would be using a bracket approach. Here's an example:

> Luxury hotel rooms vary in price. During the week, you could spend as little as $200 for a luxury hotel room or as much as $600 for a five-star, top-of-the-line hotel. If you wanted to spend a *weekend* night at a luxury hotel, would you be willing to spend $200?

Yes _____
No _____

(If yes, ask the respondent if he or she would be willing to spend $225. If yes, ask if he or she would be willing to spend $250, and continue higher in $25 increments until the respondent is unwilling to go higher. If no, ask if the respondent would be willing to spend $175. If no, ask if he or she would be willing to spend $150, and continue lower in $25 increments until the respondent gives a "yes" answer.)

The up/down bracket approach to determining price is popular. It sets a realistic context at the outset and then tests the respondent's tolerance for paying more or less. Remember, with pricing questions, the closer you can get to describing your products and benefits, i.e. setting a realistic context, the closer you'll come to getting the real price that consumers are willing to pay.

We would caution that, if your prime research objective is to determine the price that customers will pay for your product or service, and if the success of your company hinges on getting good results, you should hire a research professional. Getting a realistic assessment of what customers will pay is one of the most difficult tasks in survey research and not an area for novice Guerrilla researchers.

Questionnaire flow

Questionnaires have a flow to them. Following the qualification phase, the main questionnaire usually flows from the general to the specific. However, the types of studies you can do vary greatly, as do the goals of every questionnaire, so there are no hard-and-fast rules for the flow or sequence in which questions should be asked. Nevertheless, the following guidelines are suggested:

- Keep the respondent in one mindset at a time. If at all possible, complete all your questions about a topic before moving on. For example, don't ask about a favorite place to shop, then about brands used, and then go back to additional questioning on a favorite place to shop.
- Ask the easy questions first. Simple questions regarding behavior, such as frequency of buying, brands purchased, or places shopped at, are easy for respondents to answer because these don't require a lot of thinking or pondering. Because of this, respondents quickly get comfortable with the interview.
- More involved or introspective questions should be asked after the easier questions. Be prepared to transition to questions that require thought and consideration after only a few minutes of the interview, once the easy questions are out of the way. Respondents don't mind giving more thought to complex questions once they are comfortable with the interview process.
- If it's important to tell respondents who the study is for, do so at the last possible moment. Sometimes you'll have to identify the sponsor at the beginning, but when this isn't necessary keep the respondent in the dark. Once respondents know who is doing the research, every answer they give will be with that knowledge in mind and will present an informed bias.
- Save sensitive questions for the end. Again, this might not always be possible but be aware that sensitive questions can alienate respondents and turn them off the entire interview process.

4. THE DEMOGRAPHIC PHASE

Demographic questions such as age, occupation, number of children, income, and other sensitive personal questions should be asked at the end of the interview. Respondents are far more likely to give personal information after they have achieved a certain level of rapport with the interviewer and the interview is about to end. When asking demographic questions, ask in generalities rather than in specifics. The following are examples:

General: Is your age: (READ CATEGORIES)

Under 21　　　　____
21 to 34　　　　____
35 to 44　　　　____
45 to 54　　　　____
55 to 64　　　　____
65 or older　　　____

Specific: Tell me your age.

General: Is your yearly family income: (READ CATEGORIES)

Under $25,000　　　　____
$25,000 to $49,000　　____
$50,000 to $74,999　　____
$75,000 to $99,999　　____
$100,000 or more　　　____

Specific: What is your yearly household income?

General: How many children do you have living at home? Do you have: (READ CATEGORIES)

None　　　　____
One　　　　____
Two or three　____
Four or more　____

Specific: Tell me how many children you have living at home.

While it may be necessary to ask certain demographic questions in the screening phase, only those that are absolutely necessary to determine if the respondent qualifies for the interview should be asked at that time.

5. THE THANK YOU PHASE

Telephone solicitation by telemarketers has hurt the market research industry and caused many people to be reluctant to cooperate with legitimate market researchers. The AMA (American Marketing Association), CASRO (Council of Survey Research Organizations), AAPOR (American Association of Public Opinion Research) and ESOMAR (European Society for Marketing and Opinion Research) all view it as highly unethical when a respondent is solicited to buy something under the guise of completing a market research interview. This is referred to as SUGGING – selling under the guise.

Interestingly, not-for-profit organizations, political parties and individual politicians also regularly commit a similar ethical breach termed "FUGGING" – fund raising under the guise of conducting marketing research. They typically use the mail for this type of abuse.

Therefore, when thanking respondents for their time and cooperation, it helps the credibility of the research profession to reiterate that respondent opinions will indeed remain confidential and that no one will contact respondents as a result of their cooperation.

16

Customer satisfaction research

Whether you are just getting your feet wet or have used research in the past, we can't stress strongly enough the need for understanding the attitudes of your customers. The marketing and sales costs of converting a prospect to a customer are so great that it's almost impossible to make money by selling to a customer just once. And it almost goes without saying that the worst mistake you can make is to spend all that money and effort converting a prospect to a customer only to lose them because they are not satisfied with your products or service.

While it's true that customers may buy from you more than once, this could be more a function of your being a temporarily convenient option than anything else. A strong connection with customers, however, leads to strong repeat, increased spending with you, more referrals, and a lower likelihood of customers switching to a competitor – even when tempted with lower prices.

APPROACHES TO ASSESSING CUSTOMER SATISFACTION

There are a number of ways to view customer satisfaction. For some companies, particularly smaller ones selling products through retail outlets rather than directly to end-users, consumer satisfaction is typically measured by product acceptance by the retailer. Large, fast moving consumer goods companies such P&G, Nestlé, Kraft, Coca-Cola, and Frito-Lay, however, generally judge consumer satisfaction by how consumers rate their products in surveys. For these larger companies, customer satisfaction among the retail outlets is assessed formally and directly, sometimes by sales people or company representatives assigned to the retailer's account and sometimes by marketing research.

When supermarkets, convenience stores, discounters, mass merchants, department stores, other retail outlets and retail websites conduct customer satisfaction studies, it's usually in terms of the customer service they provide as well as the look and feel of the store or site. This could include ratings in such areas as ease of shopping, shopping atmosphere, return policy, friendliness of employees, breadth of assortment, hours of operation, competitive pricing, and so forth. Here the determinants of customer satisfaction are more concerned with environmental and employee factors than with the products being sold.

Most B2B organizations and many others have professional sales staff and they, as do countless others firms, also employ service representatives, who interact with customers. For an increasing number of companies like these, customer satisfaction is so important that sales teams and customer service personnel are often provided with bonuses based on satisfaction ratings from surveys rather than on sales increases.

WHY CUSTOMER SATISFACTION MEASURES ARE IMPORTANT

There is so much competition in today's marketplace that losing business because of poorly conceived, designed and executed products and/or sloppy, underperforming, or inadequate customer service, a key component of customer satisfaction, is unforgivable. Here's a plaque to put on the desk of every person in your company, whether they interact regularly with customers or not:

> It costs seven times as much to attract a new customer as it does to keep a current customer.

Also, we know that if a customer is dissatisfied, a proper and timely intervention can flip that customer back into the highly satisfied column. Here is another important notice to employees where the math makes it clear how important it is to keep customers satisfied:

> A dissatisfied customer will complain to an average of nine people while a satisfied customer will tell three others about their experience.

Spending money to ensure you keep those customers you already have should be a top research priority. It should be obvious that a reliable customer satisfaction study can serve as the cornerstone for growing your business and needn't be an onerous burden on your balance sheet.

HOW OFTEN IS ENOUGH?

In Chapter 4 we discussed how to get started in research. Please recall a short paragraph that said "tracking customer satisfaction" was a good place to start. This point deserves elaboration.

Customer satisfaction is not static. Your ratings are prone to change from week to week, month to month or year to year. Changes occur for many reasons. Here are just some:

- You or your competitors change elements of the marketing program.
- You or your competitors modify products or services.
- You or your competitors introduce new products or services.
- You initiate a training program intended to modify the behavior of sales reps or customer service reps.
- You start a bonus plan for your customer service reps if customer satisfaction scores increase.
- Some customer service reps leave you and new ones come in.

For customer satisfaction research to have its greatest positive impact on your company, assessment should take place on a regular basis and be tracked over time. This allows you to see how your scores and ratings change in response to your marketing, your products, your customer service and even the actions of your competitors.

How often is enough? There is no hard and firm answer to this question. The fall-back answer would be as often as the customer satisfaction scores you generate can be acted upon.

Some companies conduct surveys every month, some every quarter, some every six months and others as infrequently as once a year. Some even conduct them after every single sale or visit, i.e. automobiles, hospitals. Jet Blue, the Guerrilla airline, interviews six passengers from every flight. We feel the more often, the better.

If you conduct a monthly tracking, you are able to quickly spot changing trends. Areas that are improving become evident and you can pour it on. Problems previously uncovered can be closely followed. With monthly tracking you can see immediately how small tactical changes you make are affecting customers.

Tracking quarterly allows you to assess seasonal (quarter to quarter) influences that might affect your business. Quarterly tracking measurements are usually frequent enough so that you are not caught unawares because a few things have turned against you and you have not acted quickly enough.

Twice yearly or even yearly measurements will at least keep customer satisfaction on the radar screen and allow you to make larger strategic changes to the way you are dealing with customers. Such a frequency will also signal to your customers and employees that you are a customer-centric company and that you are not going to allow problems to fester for very long.

Giant, multi-state home builder, Pulte Homes, Inc., tracks customer satisfaction over an extended period of time. It takes one measure immediately after the home is purchased and another one several years later to make sure buyers are still happy. According to the company (*The Wall Street Journal,* October 30 2006), such a tactic helped Pulte's repeat and referral business grow from 20 per cent in 2001 to 45 per cent by 2006. Another multi-state homebuilder, Pasquinelli Homes, assesses customer satisfaction, too, but it waits until 12 months have gone by because it considers the euphoric responses following the new home purchase to be misleading. It would rather wait until the owner really knows the house.

THE COST FACTOR

We won't presume to tell you here how much money you should spend every year on customer satisfaction research. That depends on the financials of your business as well as your inclination to make customer satisfaction one of your top priorities. Consider this scenario, though.

Let's assume you had a $15,000 budget for tracking customer satisfaction during the coming year. You determine that telephoning customers for a brief five minute interview is the best interviewing approach and will provide the data you need. You determine that you can conduct 800 interviews over the course of the year for this budget.

For your $15,000 budget you could do any of the following:

1. Conduct all 800 interviews at once and wait until the following year to conduct 800 follow-up interviews, thereby taking a full year to view your progress. This design provides "benchmark" Year 1 ratings and enables you to set 12-month goals for improving in areas of concern and to see what you've accomplished in your Year 2 ratings. Then you can set new goals for Year 3.
2. In Year 1, complete the 800 interviews over two waves. First conduct 400 interviews and set six-month goals. Conduct the second 400 interviews six months later and view your progress. Set new goals and measure your progress six months later during Year 2 and so forth.
3. In Year 1, complete the 800 interview over four waves. Conduct 200 interviews each quarter during the year. This allows you to set more immediate goals and determine your progress, while also allowing you greater flexibility to spot seasonal trends.
4. In Year 1 complete the 800 over 12 waves. With a monthly sample of 67 interviews you could spot radically positive or negative changes

than might be occurring month to month. With this approach you might also accumulate and report the data every quarter, giving you 200 interviews per quarter and more statistically reliable data.

5. If you make fewer than 800 sales per year, you might even consider contacting the customers at an appropriate period after each sale to assess their satisfaction.

6. There are other alternatives, as well. For the same $15,000 cost you could conduct fewer but longer interviews allowing you to collect richer information. Or you could cut the cost of the research by completing 600 interviews in research waves of 200 interviews every four months.

Each of these approaches has positives and negatives associated with it. The more interviews you have to analyze, the greater the statistical reliability of the data and the more flexibility you'll have to look at differences by such things as customer age and other demographic characteristics, amount of spending with you, the products purchased, and so forth.

The way you could view your data given the larger sample size would only be limited by the amount of file information you have on customers. The fewer the interviews, the less you can "cut" the data to view demographic and behavior differences. Nevertheless, smaller sample sizes are effective in spotting major problems and guiding quick action to remedy them.

DEFINING CUSTOMER SATISFACTION RESEARCH

We have talked for several pages about the importance of customer satisfaction research and now we'll stop and formally define it. The fact is you actually have to define customer satisfaction, or anything else for that matter, before you can measure it. And there are a number of ways of doing this.

The most common definition is: *Customer satisfaction is a post-consumption evaluation of performance by customers.* This simply means customer satisfaction can only be measured fully after someone has gone through the complete process of acquiring and using your product or service as well as the post-purchase issues he or she has regarding it, you or your company.

In other words, you can't measure satisfaction among prospects no matter how familiar they may be with your company because they haven't purchased from you. You can't totally measure it among those who purchased gifts for others because they may not know if their recipient had problems and had to contact your company. And you can't measure it fully even among customers who have purchased from you if the product has yet to be used. Holiday sales, for example, take a little longer to be used than sales in March.

It should not be surprising to learn there are many marketing research suppliers and consultants who specialize in working with clients on how to conduct effective customer satisfaction research. The field has become so important to companies that researchers are developing unique approaches and questioning procedures for tracking customer satisfaction. In fact, it has become so big that one short chapter here certainly can't fully cover all that can be said about the subject.

Nevertheless, we can give you a good understanding of the subject and a good place to start. And it bears repeating. Whether you are a big company or small one, keeping customers satisfied is the best offensive and defensive weapon a company can have. For Guerrillas it's essential to their existence.

Put this sign on your desk:

> Fighting a hard and often expensive battle to capture customers only to lose them because you don't live up to their expectations is a great way for a Guerrilla to quickly become a monkey.

MEASURING CUSTOMER SATISFACTION

Look at this completely made-up example using ABC Airlines.

The satisfaction question asked is, "Overall, how satisfied were you with your last flight on ABC Airlines?" This key question is called the "dependent" variable because the answer is thought to depend on everything that might be on a customer's mind in regard to that last flight.

The question might be worded like this in a survey:

1. With 10 being the highest score and 0 being the lowest, rate your overall satisfaction with the last flight you took on ABC Airlines. (Check one)

   10 __ 9 __ 8 __ 7 __ 6 __ 5 __ 4 __ 3 __ 2__ 1 __ 0 __

Once ABC is rated on this overall "dependent" variable, the customer might also rate the company on a wide variety of other "performance" variables. Ten point ratings might be applied to on-time arrival, friendliness of ticketing agents, professionalism of flight attendants, cleanliness of the airplane, and so forth.

Let's say the following mean (average) data emerge:

Overall rating of last flight	6.5
On-time arrival	9.0
Friendliness of ticketing agents	4.0
Professionalism of flight attendants	8.0
Cleanliness of the airplane	4.0
Getting a good price on my ticket	6.5

In looking at just this data, the overall rating of 6.5 might be judged as high or low so that doesn't do us much good. Over time, of course, as you accumulate more and more overall satisfaction ratings, you'll get a good sense of whether this is an acceptable result. Here it could be concluded that the relatively high ratings for on-time arrival and professionalism of flight attendants offset low ratings for friendliness of ticketing agents and cleanliness of the airplane. Perhaps ABC should focus on improving areas where the ratings are low and in doing so hope the overall rating would increase.

Let's say now that the ratings below were taken at two points in time:

	January 2009	July 2009
Overall rating of last flight	6.5	7.5
On-time arrival rating	9.0	9.0
Friendliness of ticketing agents	4.0	5.5
Professionalism of flight attendants	8.0	7.0
Cleanliness of the airplane	4.0	7.5
Getting a good price on my ticket	6.5	6.5

With these two measurements you might happily observe your overall rating has improved, as did your rating in the two areas where you were low just six months previously. Only now you might conclude your overall rating could be even higher if professionalism of the flight attendants hadn't slipped. You could also conclude that you have a way to go to bring the friendliness of ticketing agent rating up to the flight attendant rating.

In the area of ticket price, ratings have remained steady. Perhaps this has been a period where all the airlines were raising prices so this factor didn't have as much an impact on overall rating as did the other factors.

Customer satisfaction research can also serve a benchmarking purpose. You can not only capture customer ratings as shown above, but you can also capture and compare those ratings to those of the industry as a whole. Note how the wording below allows this comparison:

1. Thinking about all the experiences you've had taking airline flights in the past 12 months, with 10 being the highest score and 0 being the lowest, rate your overall satisfaction with all the flights you've taken. (Check one)

    10 _ 9 _ 8 _ 7 _ 6 _ 5 _ 4 _ 3 _ 2_ 1 _ 0 _

2. Now, with 10 being the highest score and 0 being the lowest, rate your overall satisfaction with all the flights you took on ABC Airlines. (Check one)

    10 _ 9 _ 8 _ 7 _ 6 _ 5 _ 4 _ 3 _ 2_ 1 _ 0_

If the overall airline experience rating is 7.5 and you, as ABC, rated 6.5, you are performing lower than the industry as a whole. If, though, the industry rates a 7.5 and you rate a 7.5 you are performing at a level comparable to the competition. This type of questioning and analysis could also be carried out on the performance factors.

Customer satisfaction can also mean that your customers decide whether and the extent to which they are satisfied by thinking about what they got from you in comparison to what they expected to get. This has implications for wording the questionnaire, which has to include expectations:

1. Compared to what you were expecting, overall how satisfied were you with your last flight on ABC Airlines? (Check one)

Much better than expected	____
Better than expected	____
About as was expected	____
Worse than expected	____
Much worse than expected	____

Note how the wording incorporates the comparison of performance to expectations. Similarly, other performance variables can be measured, for example:

2. Compared to what you were expecting, please rate ABC's performance regarding on-time arrival. Was it (Check one)

Much better than expected	____
Better than expected	____
About as was expected	____
Worse than expected	____
Much worse than expected	____

From studying what is known about customer satisfaction, we have also learnt that the extent to which you emotionally engage your customers is an important contributor to overall satisfaction so we also recommend an additional question or two like these:

Please indicate how much you agree or disagree with the statements listed below:

1. My most recent flight on ABC Airlines was a wise decision. (Check one)

    Completely agree   ____
    Somewhat agree   ____
    Neither agree nor disagree   ____
    Somewhat disagree   ____
    Completely disagree   ____

2. I was excited about my most recent flight on ABC Airlines. (Check one)

    Completely agree   ____
    Somewhat agree   ____
    Neither agree nor disagree   ____
    Somewhat disagree   ____
    Completely disagree   ____

3. I felt a sense of contentment when I completed my last ABC flight: (Check one)

    Completely agree   ____
    Somewhat agree   ____
    Neither agree nor disagree   ____
    Somewhat disagree   ____
    Completely disagree   ____

IMPORTANCE OF PERFORMANCE VARIABLES

Whichever customer satisfaction approach works for your company, there should almost always be a sequence of questions in which respondents are asked to indicate the importance of the performance variables.

Continuing with the hypothetical ABC example, customers would be asked to rate the importance of on-time arrival, friendliness of ticketing agents, professionalism of flight attendants, cleanliness of the airplane, getting a good price on my ticket, and so forth.

Here is an example of an "importance" question:

On a 10-point scale with 10 meaning extremely important and 0 meaning not at all important, how important is on-time arrival in choosing an airline to fly? (Check one)

10 __ 9__ 8__ 7__ 6__ 5__ 4__ 3__ 2__ 1 __ 0 __

This now allows you to understand how well you are doing on the more important variables and permits a very useful grid that can guide your next action steps; see Figure 16.1.

	HIGH PERFORMANCE	LOW PERFORMANCE
HIGH IMPORTANCE	These are variables that are both important and on which we do well. *The goal here is to maintain performance.*	These are variables that are currently considered important and on which we do not perform well. *The goal here is to improve performance.*
LOW IMPORTANCE	These are variables that customers do not consider important and on which we do well. *The goal here is either to increase their importance to customers or to de-emphasize our performance (and save $).*	These are variables that customers do not consider important and on which we perform poorly. *The temporary goal here is to do nothing, but keep watching.*

Figure 16.1 Performance vs importance

NET PROMOTER SCORE

There is a widely held belief that by asking customers if they'd recommend a company to a friend, they put their own credibility on the line. They are, therefore, likely to give great thought and consideration to their answer. As a result of this thinking, another dependent variable known as the net promoter score is getting widespread use.

Using the ABC example again, the net promoter question would be:

With 10 meaning you would definitely recommend ABC to a friend and 0 meaning you definitely would not recommend ABC to a friend, how would you rate the airline?

The net promoter score is specifically derived by subtracting the bottom seven scores (termed "detractors", 0–6 in italics in the list below) from the top two scores (termed "promoters", 9 and 10 in bold). In this measurement, the 7 and 8 ratings are considered "passive" customers and are not included in the calculation. Look at the hypothetical table for ABC:

Would recommend ABC to a friend:

Rated	% Giving rating
10	**20**
9	**25**
8	10
7	10
6	5
5	5
4	5
3	5
2	5
1	5
0	5

Here we get a net promoter score of +10 per cent by taking the 45 per cent of customers rating ABC a 10 or 9 and subtracting the 35 per cent who gave it a 6, 5, 4, 3, 2, 1 or 0. The result is the proportion of customers who would "promote" ABC to their friends. The range of possible scores runs from a high of 100 per cent to a low of -100 per cent. Of course, the higher the net promoter score, the better.

Research indicates that leadership companies like Southwest Airlines will have a net promoter score of 60 per cent or higher, so this hypothetical result for ABC would be considered relatively low in comparison.

The key issue with generating only one customer satisfaction score, be it net promoter score or any other dependent variable score, is that used alone, you don't know what actions you should take to improve that score.

DIGGING DEEPER

We thought you might like to see some overall satisfaction scores from several service industries. These are from surveys by the University of Michigan's Ross School of Business and were reported in *The Wall Street Journal* on October 30 2006. With a possible top score of 100, Table 16.1 shows how a number of industries ranked.

The ability to compare your satisfaction results against a norm for your industry is very valuable because it allows you to interpret your sales results in a broader context. This common desire has led research

Table 16.1 Overall satisfaction scores from several service industries

RANK	INDUSTRY	CUSTOMER SATISFACTION SCORE
1	Express Delivery	83
2	Internet Retail	81
3	Internet Search Engines	79
4	Internet Auctions	78
	Property/Casualty Insurance	78
6	Internet Travel	77
	Limited-service Restaurants	77
8	Health/Personal-care Stores	76
	Internet Brokerage	76
	Internet Portals	76
11	Commercial Banking	75
	Department/Discount Stores	75
	Hotels	75
	Life Insurance	75
15	Hospitals	74
	Specialty Retail Stores	74
	Supermarkets	74
18	Internet News/Information	73
19	Energy Utilities	72
20	US Postal Service	71
21	Fixed-line Telephone Service	70
22	Gasoline Stations	69
23	Health Insurance	68
24	Wireless Telephone Service	66
25	Airlines	65
26	Cable/Satellite TV	63
	Newspapers	63

companies like JD Power, for example, to assess satisfaction in several industries such as automobiles, home building and healthcare.

So, one source of satisfaction research is to buy it from a syndicator. Both Pulte and Pasquinelli, who were mentioned earlier, buy the JD Power research, but they also conduct their own to explore internal issues not covered by JD Power. (As we mentioned in Chapter 9, this is always a concern with secondary sources of information.)

17

Sampling

Let us a take a step back for a moment. Polls were as ubiquitous in the 2004 US presidential election as they were in the 2008 election. In 2004 we wrote about one exit survey that reported that the candidate's moral character was the major factor in determining voter choice, as shown in Table 17.1.

We went on to write:

> What nonsense. There isn't a poll or attitude survey in the world that doesn't have an error range associated with each number, that is, the range that exists around each number indicating that, if the study were repeated, the number could vary upward or downward within that range.

The error range, often referred to as the "margin of error," surrounding that 2004 study was +/– 4 per cent. That meant that, if the exit poll had been conducted again, all the numbers could vary either higher or lower by as much as four percentage points. The moral values figure of

Table 17.1   Voter choice issues in 2004

Major issue in determining voter choice	Percentage choosing
Moral values	22
The economy	21
Domestic issues	19
The war in Iraq	18
Other issues	20

22 per cent could go as low as 18 per cent, while the war in Iraq figure could go as high as 22 per cent. In a statistical sense, then, there are five equally important factors that determined voter choice back in 2004, and focusing on only one factor as the prime reason for voter choice is a distortion of the results.

Recall in 2004 that George W Bush narrowly defeated John Kerry. Following the election James E Campbell wrote an article entitled: "Why Bush won the presidential election in 2004." Campbell wrote:

> In the aftermath of the 2004 vote, analysts expressed surprise at responses to the most important issue question: more voters mentioned moral values as the most important issues than mentioned terrorism or Iraq, or the economy. In the exit poll 22 per cent mentioned moral values as their greatest concern and Bush received four out of five of these votes. Some interpreted this as an outpouring of the evangelical vote. Bush won a high percentage of the votes of those who said that they were evangelicals or born-again. The surge in turnout is more accurately interpreted as a broader phenomenon of a mobilized conservative base rallying to the side of a conservative president conducting a war and under siege from the harsh attacks of the opposing party and allied critics.

We will now reemphasize that every poll or survey is subject to a margin of error. Campbell downplays moral values as a prime factor in the election and concludes the war in Iraq was a stronger deciding fact. He's wrong, too. In point of fact, statistically speaking, the five factors above were equally important and any number of interpretations would be equally valid.

In the 2008 presidential race, polling showed the US economy to be the key issue in voter choice with issues such as terrorism and the Iraq war having far less influence on voter choice. Also, many polls had a "nuanced" sample definition that included "likely voters." That is, the polls made their forecasts not just on the basis of registered voters, but whether the voter said he or she was actually going to vote. (See Chapter 15 for the importance of screening the right type of consumer before including them in your survey.)

Table 17.2 shows how close all the polls were in their final predictions. Given the margin of error (+/− 3 or 4 per cent) on these large surveys that had samples of at least 1,000, it turns out all the polls were fairly accurate.

All the final polls in the 2008 election had Obama leading McCain by a difference of 6 to 11 percentage points. In the 2004 election polls had Bush leading Kerry 49 to 47 per cent, or only a 2 per cent difference.

Because most large polls will report a 3 to 4 percentage point margin of error, this means that Bush's 49 per cent could have gone as high as 53 per cent or as low as 45 per cent, and Kerry's 47 per cent could have varied from a high of 51 per cent to a low of 43 per cent – a statistical

Table 17.2 Final poll results*

	Obama %	McCain %	Difference %
Gallup	55	44	+11
Reuters/C-Span/Zogby	54	43	+11
ABC News/*Washington Post*	53	44	+9
NBC News/*Wall Street Journal*	51	43	+8
Fox News	50	43	+7
CNN/Opinion Research	53	46	+7
Pew Research	52	46	+6
Rasmussen Reports	52	46	+6
Actual results	**53**	**46**	**+7**

* Numbers don't add across to 100 per cent as a small percentage of voters indicated they were undecided at the time of the poll or actually voted for a third party candidate.

(Source: "Real clear politics," *Chicago Tribune*, November 6, 2008)

dead heat, too close to predict the winner. And that's exactly why no one could predict, with absolute certainty, who would win the 2004 election.

In the 2008 Obama/McCain race something very interesting occurred. Because he was within the margin of error in some polls, McCain's camp insisted right up to Election Day that he was within striking distance of pulling an upset. Conversely, the Obama camp insisted it had a consistent edge in the polls and would win. We'd guess the Obama camp felt good after looking at the Gallup, Reuters and ABC polls, while the McCain camp perhaps took encouragement from the others.

SAMPLING, ERROR RANGE AND MAKING PREDICTIONS

A poll and a survey are the same thing, only the word "poll" usually refers to a political study. So the theory of sampling as it relates to polls and to survey research studies is the same, and is quite simple.

If you interview a sample of 300 people, you'd want to be sure that their answers would be the same as those of the next 300 you interview, given that the sample was drawn the same way and the questions were the same, and the 300 after that, and so on, until you've interviewed everybody there is to be interviewed. In short, you want your sample to be a confident predictor of attitudes held by the entire population of your target.

Both polls and survey research seek to ensure that a relatively small sample of people will give you the same answers you'd get if you expanded the sample size and interviewed everyone. This is referred to as "projectability."

Start noticing the sample sizes for surveys that are reported in the newspapers or magazines. Many surveys report their results based on sample sizes as small as 400 respondents. National polls like the ones listed in Table 17.2 will rarely exceed 1,000 respondents. This is because the entire basis of sampling theory rests on the inarguable fact that, by interviewing a few well-chosen respondents, it is possible to represent the many that were not chosen to be interviewed – but always within a certain margin of error.

The margin of error is also called the "confidence interval." That is the range around which a number can vary if the study were undertaken exactly the same way a second time, or a third time, or a hundredth time. In point of fact, there is an error range around every number generated in every survey.

You can look at numbers from surveys from many points of view in order to further your political cause or your argument over what marketing decision should be made, but you're only kidding yourself if you follow this path. The error range must always be taken into account and should be used to determine the optimum sample size and considered when analyzing and interpreting data.

Table 17.3 shows the margin of error either higher or lower around given sample sizes at the 95 per cent confidence level.

If you look at a sample size of 150, the margin of error is +/– 8 per cent at the 95 per cent confidence level. That means that, if the survey shows that 60 per cent of the respondents state that they like the taste of your product and 40 per cent say they don't like the taste, there is a statistically reliable difference. With an 8 per cent error range the 60 per cent could go no lower than 52 per cent and the 40 per cent no higher than 48 per cent. Therefore, you can be 95 per cent confident that if you questioned everyone in the universe, you would still find that more people like the taste than dislike the taste.

You should also notice how little the error range decreases as you interview more people. By interviewing 300 respondents instead of 150, the error range only decreases two percentage points, from 8 to 6 per cent. And by interviewing 400 respondents rather than 300, you only pick up one percentage point.

The reason survey research studies are conducted with relatively small numbers of respondents is because there is sometimes no justifi-

Table 17.3   Margin of error

Survey sample size	Margin of error +/– %*
2,000	2
1,500	3
1,000	3
900	3
800	3
700	4
600	4
500	4
400	5
300	6
200	7
150	8
100	10
50	14

*Assumes a 95 per cent confidence level.

cation for spending the extra money to interview more people. The data simply won't be that much more accurate.

However, this thinking applies only to the total sample. If you interview 200 respondents the error of margin is +/– 7 per cent, but if your sample includes 100 men and 100 women and you want to know if there is a difference by gender, the margin of error jumps to 10 per cent.

And if you want to examine younger women vs older women in the same study, the margin of error will be quite high as the 100 women would have to be split into still smaller samples. For these reasons surveys often have large samples as, generally, it's not just the total number of respondents whose opinions are important. Usually, the sub-targets are also important and, therefore, you need an adequate sample size in order to analyze sub-target opinions with adequate statistical reliability.

A word about confidence levels

Unfortunately it is never possible to be 100 per cent confident that data will fall within the sample size error range. If you conduct the study again, there is always a small chance that something strange will occur and that the data will be off by more than the error range. In the real world, being able to read data at a 95 per cent level of confidence, where there is only a 5 per cent chance the data are erroneous, is good enough.

Interestingly, when we began our careers, clients used to insist on a 99 per cent level of confidence, which sometimes required extremely large samples and higher research costs. The standard is now a 95 per cent level of confidence and many clients are satisfied with 90 or even 80 per cent. The reason researchers and marketers have relaxed the way they view confidence levels is that the larger samples and added costs often necessary for achieving 99 per cent levels were not felt to add that much more to the value of the research.

Think about it this way. If you have to make a decision in which large sums of money are on the line, would you rather make that decision knowing there was a 1 per cent or 5 per cent chance of error? To us, the added research cost to achieve a 1 versus 5 per cent chance of error wouldn't change the decision we'd make.

And, of course, if knowing there is only a 1, 5, 10 or even 20 per cent chance that your decision will be wrong isn't good enough odds for you, save your money on survey research.

DETERMINING SAMPLE SIZE

Determining the proper survey sample size for a study revolves around a number of factors. They include the following.

Error range

This is always the biggest shot in the dark. If you are confident that the survey will show big differences in respondent attitude, you could be confident choosing a smaller sample size with a larger error range.

For example, assume that you are doing a survey to determine the most important attributes in choosing which home improvement store to shop at. Table 17.4 shows a list of shopping attribute importance rated for two sample sizes. It shows that, irrespective of the sample size, the same percentage of respondents chose the same attributes as most important.

If you knew going into the study that "convenience" would so dominate the attributes, you could have chosen to go with the 150 sample size. With an 8 per cent error range around the 150 sample, the 80 per cent around "convenience" could go no lower than 72 per cent. And if the 50 per cent around "price" went to 58 percent, "convenience" would still be significantly more important than "price."

However, with a sample size of 150 and an 8 per cent error range you could not have concluded that "one-stop shopping" was significantly

Table 17.4   Attribute importance by sample size

Attribute	Percentage rating as most important with error range indicated	
	150 Sample %	200 Sample %
Convenience	72–80–88	73–80–87
Price	42–50–58	43–50–57
Selection	37–45–53	38–45–52
One-stop shopping	27–35–43	28–35–42
Carries well-known brands	12–20–28	13–20–27

more important than "carries well-known brands." Here, the 35 per cent could be as low as 27 per cent and the 20 per cent as high as 28 per cent, indicating no statistical difference in the number. With a 7 per cent error range around a 200 sample size, though, you would have a statistical difference. Unfortunately, you don't get the luxury of this hindsight when determining your survey's sample size.

Analytical subsets

In the above example, the assumption is that only one target market is important: home improvement store shoppers in general. Here, a sample of 150 would be the minimum you'd want to interview.

If you wanted to determine, however, whether home improvement shoppers who are males have attitudes different from those of females, or younger shoppers have attitudes different from those of older shoppers, your sample size would have to increase to at least 300. Here, you would want to interview 300 respondents: 150 males and 150 females and, within each of these segments, 75 younger respondents and 75 older respondents. In viewing the data with these sample sizes you could determine with a reasonable degree of statistical accuracy whether there are major differences in the attitudes of each target segment.

Cost

It is obvious that the more respondents you interview, the smaller the error range around the numbers that you generate. Also clear is that the bigger the sample, the more costly the study. This reality forces priorities and compromises as there is usually a trade-off between what can be afforded and the optimum sample size.

Theoretical vs practical

There are many books and articles written on how to determine the proper sample size for market research studies. If you are a statistics enthusiast, you can spend hours reading about random stratified sampling as opposed to quota sampling, non-response bias, low response bias, and the dozens of other factors that can play havoc with your study.

When you are through learning all there is to learn about sampling, you'll probably be left shaking your head. What you are likely to conclude is that rigid adherence to scientific sampling principles is impractical in the world of commercial market research. Even if they could be adhered to, you would likely find that the expense of doing so would be prohibitive.

This is not to minimize the importance of understanding good sampling procedures. For the professional researcher, a working knowledge of these influences is essential. The assumption here is that you don't wish to follow a research career or become an expert at sampling, so we will suggest some practical sampling guidelines.

In conducting thousands of surveys, we have established a number of generalities about sample size. They are:

- A minimum sample size of 600 is required for a basic strategy study. This sample will provide flexibility in viewing data across a number of target segments. Rarely will it be necessary for Guerrillas to conduct a study in which the sample size is larger than 1,000. Studies with such large sample sizes are usually undertaken by large companies wishing to understand the attitudes of many different customer and prospect targets.
- A robust sample for most research studies other than a strategy study is 300. Going beyond a sample size of 300 does not generate a lower error range that is worth the added cost.
- Sample sizes of 150 are usually viable for smaller tactical studies such as advertising communications, product, or packaging studies. These are studies in which only two or three alternatives are tested against each other and it is usually not necessary to view the data by more than one target segment.
- Going below a sample of 100 is risky and, if possible, should be avoided. The error range of +/− 10 per cent is considered quite large and will only produce a valid statistical difference when there are wide variations in responses. When there are relatively subtle differences, a sample size of 100 will not provide data that are statistically significant.

Representative sampling

What you are trying to accomplish in any sampling procedure is to be confident that the responses of the people you interview are the same as those of the people you don't interview. That means that you do everything practical to generate a representative sample.

If you send out a mail questionnaire to 10,000 people and 5 per cent respond, you'd have a sample size of 500, which, if looked at in isolation, could be considered a good sample for a survey. However, with only a 5 per cent response rate, you must question whether your 500 sample is representative. Basic to this is the question of whether the attitudes of the 9,500 who did not respond are the same as those of the 500 who did respond. This is the non-response problem discussed in Chapter 14.

With such a small response rate, you are left wondering if those who did respond might have an axe to grind and will tend to be overly negative in their answers. Or it could even be the opposite. Maybe they are particularly positive and will provide overly buoyant responses. They may also be consumers who are atypical demographically and responded because they had nothing better to do.

When conducting telephone surveys, generating a representative sample is also an issue. Say you want to complete 300 telephone interviews, and you have a list of 10,000 phone numbers of people who are likely to qualify for your interview. You will want to ensure that the telephone interviewing service you use has a software program that dials those 10,000 numbers in a random sequence. This ensures that all 10,000 have an equal opportunity of being represented in your ending sample of 300.

Good sampling usually means that every person in your target audience has an equal opportunity of being interviewed. It also mandates that your response rate is high enough to provide confidence that the attitudes of those you don't question are the same as those you do.

ACHIEVING GOOD RESPONSE RATES

Getting a representative sample is largely a function of response rate. If only 5 in 100 people (5 per cent) agree to answer your questionnaire, whether it's over the phone, by mail, or via the internet, you are likely to have a response bias. If, though, 30 or 40 per cent or more agree to be interviewed, you can be far more confident that you have reduced any potential response rate bias.

More people than you might think will give you their opinions if they are approached correctly and there is incentive enough for them to respond.

Approaching respondents

Previously, we discussed how to approach respondents to gain their cooperation to be interviewed. In addition to assuring them that no attempt will be made to sell anything and after identifying the sponsor of the study, intangibles such as interviewer tone and getting to respondents at a convenient time are also important.

Assuming that you are conducting a telephone study, achieving a random sample is an issue to be discussed with your telephone interviewing service. It is important to remember that you can motivate almost anybody to respond to a survey if you offer them the right incentive. Usually, that means money.

SAMPLING GUIDELINES

Here are some guidelines.

Telephone

If your questionnaire is 20 minutes or less, you don't generally need an incentive to keep respondents on the phone. If, though, your questionnaire is in the 20 to 30 minute range, a $5 incentive is usually enough to ensure respondents won't hang up on you. For longer interviews, incentives should increase proportionately: $10 for 35 minutes, $15 for 40 minutes, and so forth is a good rule of thumb.

Remember, though, that the nature of your questioning as well as the type of respondents you are seeking, together with the value they might place on their own time, will influence the amount of the incentive. For consumers who use high-incidence products and services, smaller incentives are generally sufficient as it is less costly to find people to interview. Higher incentives are prudent when contacting consumers who use low-incidence products, as once you find a qualified consumer you don't want to lose them.

Further, when conducting telephone interviews with professionals like lawyers and medical doctors, or owners of companies, purchasing agents or various business executives, incentives will be higher. Start out offering $75 for interviews, but if this proves unsuccessful be ready to spend more. An incentive well in excess $100 is not uncommon when interviewing professionals. For example, physicians will demand $250 for just 10 minutes of their time.

Mail studies

Most studies conducted by mail should have a small incentive included when you mail the questionnaire. We have found that a new $2 bill is great for getting attention and stimulating response. Sometimes you can get by with a $1 bill if the questionnaire is relatively short (two to three pages or four to six sides of questionnaire). Offering an additional incentive to be mailed when the questionnaire is returned will also greatly enhance response. A $5 or $10 bill is common for most studies conducted among consumers.

Again, for professionals, your incentive will have to be higher in order to generate a good sample. We've found that, in most cases, $20 is the highest you would have to promise to get a completed question-naire from consumers. Draws for larger prizes or promises of donations to a charity of choice also work with business-to-business respondents.

For Guerrillas conducting their first mail study, it is prudent to conduct a number of pilot mailings using several incentive variations. Mail 100 questionnaires to one sample enclosing $1 and $5 upon return. Try 100 with $2 enclosed and $5 upon return. If your questionnaire is long, say six pages with questions on 12 sides, try $2 enclosed with the promise of $10 upon return. Testing various incentives first is always wise and will provide you with the information you need when conducting future mail studies.

Internet studies

When conducting internet studies with your own e-mail list, it is only necessary to pay incentives when the questionnaire is completed. Usually the same completion incentives used for mail questionnaires will work for internet questionnaires. Nevertheless, it is wise to find a company that specializes in conducting internet studies to advise you on incentives. What is nice about the internet is that you can test differ-ent incentives almost daily in order to optimize the response.

For some affinity groups like members of organizations, donors, sales reps or distributors, no incentive may be required. The more tightly knit the group, the more passionate the involvement, the less likely an incen-tive will be required. As a broad generalization, consumer goods customers and prospects are not involved enough to avoid offering an incentive. Owners of luxury goods, such as expensive cars, may be, and B2B customers may or may not be depending on how many of them there are.

SOURCES OF SAMPLES

When conducting a survey, there is always the question of where to get your research sample; that is, where to find the respondents whose opinions you seek. There are many sources for acquiring a sample, which in research terms is referred to as the "sampling frame." Let's discuss just a few.

In-house customer lists are a common sampling source. In theory you should have all the information you need to choose a sample: full contact information, including telephone number and perhaps e-mail address, information about purchase behavior, gender and more, depending on the sophistication of your system.

Remember, though, that you'll need to devise a way to select a random and unbiased sample.

Say you have 6,000 current customers who qualify for the research, and you estimate that you'll need a final sample of 200. You further estimate that 10 per cent of those you try to contact will be reachable within a reasonable period of time, and willing to participate. Here's the calculation:

100 per cent / 10 per cent = 10, which means that for every 10 customers you contact you'll get one completed survey.
$10 \times 200 = 2,000$, which is the number of names you'll have to select for the survey.
6,000 / 2,000 = 3, which means that you should select every third name on your customer list to create your sample.

Other in-house lists may also be a good sampling source, for example past customers, prospects, sales reps, distributors, and even vendors.

Years ago the phone book was a reasonable sample source for consumers and some types of businesses. These days, with unlisted numbers being common and many younger consumers only having mobile phones, the phone book under-represents the consumer audience and is rarely useful as a sampling source.

Instead, common practice is to use a technique called *random digit dialing*. When using RDD, you will generate a sequence of telephone numbers that includes all those with land lines, whether listed or unlisted. One company, Survey Sampling International (www.surveysampling.com), is most commonly used by researchers wishing to purchase RDD samples. There are others available that you can investigate by clicking on www.greenbook.org/market-research-firms.cfm/sampling.

Professional directories are often good sources of samples for business targets and many are available on a printed or electronic basis. Examples are trade, professional and voluntary association membership directories, local chapter lists of national associations, faculty directories, and the like.

Trade magazine subscribers are a common and useful sampling source. When using trade magazines, you can be confident subscribers are highly likely to qualify for your study as they clearly have a strong affinity for your industry. Usually, as well, you can select a sample from a trade magazine by title, occupation and geographic location, thus making it easier to reach exactly who you want to interview.

Magazines consider their subscribers a major asset and are careful about providing rights to use these names. While some magazines will provide easy access to their subscribers, many will require that lists go to a reputable third party. They do this in order to restrict access to their subscribers. The third party, in turn, is required to handle the phoning, mailing or e-mailing for your market research study.

Many consumer and trade magazines have research departments that are willing to conduct research for a reasonable fee. If their subscriber list is good for your needs and you choose to purchase the research instead of conducting it on your own, this may be an economical solution.

Note: if you are an advertiser in a consumer or trade magazine that has a research department, you may be able to get your research done for free. Most magazines offer "trade credits" to their advertisers, such as free access to magazine-sponsored trade shows, free "tests" of how your ad performs in their publication and, yes, free market research. They often conduct regular research among their subscribers to support their editorial staff and are generally willing to add a few questions on your behalf if you are a current or potential advertiser.

Quite often research samples are purchased from companies that specialize in providing them to research organizations and marketers. Termed *list brokers*, they can easily be found by going to any search engine and typing in the key words "list broker" or looking in business phone directories under the same heading.

List brokers compete with one another so be sure to contact more than one to get the best price. Some brokers just sell their own proprietary lists while others are resellers of the thousands of available lists. Either type should work for your survey needs if you are careful to define the exact sample specifications you want to the broker.

In addition to providing RDD samples, Survey Sampling International will also provide other samples to your exact specifications. Perhaps your sample calls for younger versus older consumers, higher educated versus lower educated, or even consumers who use certain brands of products or drive certain makes of automobiles. Survey Sampling, list brokers, and other sources such as Experian, Equifax and infoUSA can be a good source of names, addresses and phone numbers for finding the various types of respondents you want for your study.

Most list providers have a minimum fee of $500 and will provide up to 4,000 names and addresses for this cost. There typically is a small up-charge to obtain phone numbers as well. Should you need more than 4,000 names, they'd charge in the vicinity of $125 per thousand names thereafter. If you only needed 2,000 names, you would still pay the minimum – $500. If you needed 5,000 names, you'd pay $625. These costs are presumed to be for one-time use. Purchasing a list for unlimited use, say for a year, costs more.

Again, lists sold by list brokers, magazines and trade associations are considered assets, and the sellers have security systems in place to prevent abuse. Some will "seed" the lists they send you with false names to check on whether you try to contact people more often than you have contracted for. And they sometimes require review of your questionnaire to be sure you are conducting legitimate research and not trying to sell something.

Just as a reminder: if you are using a full-service research supplier for your study, it will build the cost of providing a qualified list into the cost it quotes you, and you would not be billed separately for this expenditure.

18

Organizing data

Surveys require that answers to questions be summarized so that they can be analyzed effectively. The most common means to accomplish this is via a data processing tool called a "cross-tabulation" program (referred to as "cross-tabs").

The cost of tabulating survey data has reached an all-time low, even when conducting telephone studies. In the past, it was necessary for keypunch operators to hand-punch the answer to each and every question asked on each and every questionnaire. Although the labor cost for this process was relatively low, it was, nevertheless, a cost that had to be incurred. And, as we've mentioned before, this process also allowed a small amount of error to creep into the data.

Today, there are still studies that require paper questionnaires and, therefore, manual data entry. In-person, mall intercept, and mail questionnaires are the most common examples. In the latter case, some upfront planning with your supplier will allow your questionnaires to be set up for optical scanning – which can save you both time and money.

However, now, virtually all telephone, internet and IVR data collection services automatically enter data from questionnaires into cross-tabulation software at the moment of the interview, which not only makes completing a study faster, easier and more accurate, but also eliminates the need for any type of data entry whatsoever.

Costs for cross-tabs are dependent on the number of questionnaires as well as the number of questions asked. Long questionnaires with large samples may cost $2,500 to $3,000 or more for data processing, especially if key entry or open-ended coding of questions is necessary. More commonly though, studies are smaller and the data processing expense quite low. And, again, by eliminating manual keypunch entry, you can save upwards of 50 per cent.

CROSS-TAB PLAN

In order to have data tabulated to meet your needs, you should create a cross-tab plan. Creating the tab plan will help you to determine how you want to "cut your data," that is, how you want to see data arrayed for the questions that you've asked. Basically, the tab plan shows the way the data will be organized and presented, and serves as a document for your data-processing company so it can prepare the cross-tabs the way you want.

In determining the tab plan, you will make assumptions regarding segments within the data that might be important to analyze. Obviously, you will tabulate the data in total. If your sample size is 600, you will look at how all 600 respondents answered all the questions. It is beyond the total, however, that your most important findings are likely to be found.

Popcorn study

Let's say that you have conducted an attitude study among 600 respondents on the topic of popcorn. You have the following overall goal:

> To understand the important factors when choosing to purchase one brand of popcorn over another and to determine the extent to which the brands on the market are perceived to deliver on the factors that are important.

Specific research objectives are:

- How do various segments of the market differ on attitudes that are important – heavy versus light popcorn users, large versus small families, etc.?
- Do users of the various brands have different attitudes toward the factors that are important in purchasing their brands?
- Are there differences in attitudes of consumers who use microwave popcorn most often versus consumers who pop from scratch?
- What are the attitudes toward potential new flavors of popcorn? Will new flavors cause greater consumption of popcorn?

Tab plan implications

Your tab plan should reflect the overall study goal and specific objectives. Since the overall goal is to determine brand perceptions, you will want to view how the major brands on the market are perceived. This would suggest organizing or tabulating the data by brand. Assume that the major brands you are most interested in are Orville Redenbacher, Paul Newman and Pop Secret.

Given the specific objective ("How do various segments of the market differ on attitudes that are important – heavy versus light popcorn users, large versus small families, etc.?"), the tab plan implication might be, first, to make an assumption as to a definition of heavy versus light popcorn users. In your questionnaire, you will certainly have asked a question regarding frequency of using popcorn at home.

In developing a tab plan, it is often necessary to first have the company developing your cross-tabs provide you with total counts (which should be free of charge) on certain questions before you make a final decision about the plan. In this case, that is what you should do.

Table 18.1 shows the questions on popcorn consumption that you might have asked and the typical answers you might have received.

A heavy versus light definition could be determined by simply splitting the sample above and below the mean (average). Here the mean is about once a week. So you could decide to organize the data into two groups, with those using popcorn once a week or more often labeled heavy users, and those using once a week or less often, termed light users.

From Table 18.1, the split would generate 228 heavy users (adding together the 3, 5, 10, and 20 per cent and multiplying by the 600 respondents in the study) and 372 light users (adding together all the rest).

Table 18.1 Popcorn consumption example

How often do you pop and eat popcorn at home?	%
Every day	3
Four to six times per week	5
One to three times per week	10
About once per week	20
Once every two weeks	25
Once every three to four weeks	20
Once a month	10
Less often than once per month	7

Mean = once every 6.60 days

Another way is just to make a judgment based on the frequency of responses. You could decide to combine some groups. You could take the three times a week and more respondents (18 per cent in total), giving you 108 respondents, which is a good base of respondents to analyze. You could combine the once a week and once every two weeks (45 per cent) to generate 270 respondents. The remaining 37 per cent would give you 222 respondents.

This approach would give you three different user definitions:

1. Heavy users = 108
2. Regular users = 270
3. Light users = 222

If you want to view the data by size of family, income or other breaks, for example, you would go through the same process.

These are important judgments that you must make in determining how you wish to organize and view your data. In these instances, there is rarely a right and wrong approach. Decisions are usually based on common sense and the actions you might take if your analysis shows major differences between groups.

Another specific objective is to determine if there are differences in attitudes of consumers who use microwave popcorn most often as opposed to consumers who pop from scratch. Here the tab plan implication is that you should organize the data by microwave users versus pop-from-scratch users.

The question is how to do this. Since many families do both, perhaps you ask several questions in your questionnaire regarding usage. You might have asked:

What do you pop at home most often – microwave popcorn or pop-from-scratch popcorn?

You could have asked:

How often do you pop and eat microwave popcorn at home?

Every day	____
Four to six times per week	____
Two to three times per week	____
About once per week	____
Once every two weeks	____
Once every three to four weeks	____
Less often than once per month	____

How often do you pop and eat pop-from-scratch popcorn at home?

Every day	_____
Four to six times per week	_____
Two to three times per week	_____
About once per week	_____
Once every two weeks	_____
Once every three to four weeks	_____
Less often than once per month	_____

If you used this more complex series of questions in determining microwave versus pop-from-scratch usage, the data could be organized more precisely and the analysis would be more insightful.

BANNER POINTS AND STUB

When you complete your tab plan, you or your supplier will prepare the data to those specifications. The final result will be a printout of all the questions in your questionnaire organized and arrayed by all the ways you wish to view the data. In relation to this, you should be aware of the terms "banner points" and "stub."

"Banner points" refer to the number of variables arrayed across the top – total, heavy, regular and light popcorn users, men, women, etc. Typically you can choose about 20 such breakouts, banner points, or data cuts per page in your tabulated report. "Stub" refers to the questions that were asked.

Look at a typical printout, as shown in Table 18.2. Down the left side of the printout page is the stub or the question that was asked. Across the top of the page is the banner or the way the data are organized.

When you complete your tab plan, you may have specified up to 20 banner points that you want on your printout. If you wish to organize the data beyond 20 banner points, you'll simply request that a second banner be developed. Once you have set up your first banner, the cost of a second banner is quite nominal.

For example, we've done a monthly customer satisfaction study for a multi-market homebuilder. We analyze its data by key demographics, levels of satisfaction, and cost of the home. We also analyze the data by each of the 10 cities in which it builds, and we compare month-to-month results. This required three complete tabulations of all the data, which we've illustrated at the end of the chapter.

You will also have indicated how you want your stub to appear. In the printout example in Table 18.2, notice the question stub and you will see what are referred to as "nets." A net refers to the sum or total of two

Table 18.2 Typical tabulation printout of survey data

XYZ retail copy, print and delivery study

Q. amount would use XYZ if they did the following allow you to check the status of your job online

		Users				In home user					Business user			
			Business			Amount spent on copying			Household size		Amount spent on copying			
	TOTAL (A)	In home (B)	1-5 (C)	6-19 (D)	Total (E)	$50 to $99 (F)	$100 to $299 (G)	$300+ (H)	2 or Less (I)	3+ (J)	$299 or Less (K)	$300 to $999 (L)	$1,000 to $2,999 (M)	$3,000+ (N)
TOTAL	475	175	150	150	300	84	47	40	77	82	76	84	43	42
Net: Top 2 Box	218 45.9%	68 38.9%	81 54.0% B	69 46.0%	150 50.0% B	30 35.7%	17 36.2%	19 47.5%	23 29.9%	39 47.6% I	45 59.2%	40 47.6%	21 48.8%	19 45.2%
3 – For all my copying and printing jobs	107 22.5%	39 22.3%	43 28.7% D	25 16.7%	68 22.7%	16 19.0%	11 23.4%	12 30.0%	13 16.9%	24 29.3% i	21 27.6%	18 21.4%	11 25.6%	11 26.2%
2 – For most of my jobs	111 23.4%	29 16.6%	38 25.3% b	44 29.3% B	82 27.3% B	14 16.7%	6 12.8%	7 17.5%	10 13.0%	15 18.3%	24 31.6%	22 26.2%	19 23.3%	8 19.0%
1 – For just an occasional job	143 30.1%	55 31.4%	39 26.0%	49 32.7%	88 29.3%	27 32.1%	18 38.3%	10 25.0%	25 32.5%	27 32.9%	20 26.3%	30 35.7%	14 32.6%	11 26.2%
0 – For none of my copying and printing jobs	90 18.9%	32 18.3%	27 18.0%	31 20.7%	58 19.3%	19 22.6% G	3 6.4%	8 20.0% g	18 23.4% J	9 11.0%	10 13.2%	14 16.7%	8 18.6%	11 26.2% k
Net: Bottom 2 Box	233 49.1%	87 49.7%	66 44.0%	80 53.3%	146 48.7%	46 54.8%	21 44.7%	18 45.0%	43 55.8%	36 43.9%	30 39.5%	44 52.4%	22 51.2%	22 52.4%
Don't know	24 5.1%	20 11.4% CDE	3 2.0%	1 0.7%	4 1.3%	8 9.5%	9 19.1%	3 7.5%	11 14.3%	7 8.5%	1 1.3%	0 –	0 –	1 2.4%
Mean	1.52	1.48	1.66	1.42	1.54	1.36	1.66	1.62	1.27	1.72	1.75	1.52	1.56	1.46
Std Devn	1.06	1.08	1.09	1.00	1.05	1.08	0.99	1.16	1.07	1.05	1.01	1.01	1.08	1.16

NOTE: Significance Testing done at the following levels: Upper case letters = 95 percent, lower case letters = 90 percent
Groups/pairs tested: B/C/D/E, F/G/H, I/J, K/L/M/N

or more answers to a given question. In this example, four responses are given.

The net here is simply a sum. The Net Top 2 Box sums those answering "3" and "2" and the Net Bottom 2 Box adds together those answering "1" or "0." Showing the net score in the stub saves time in analyzing the data, since a quick glance indicates the percentage of respondents having generally positive attitudes on the question as opposed to those having generally neutral or negative attitudes. The analyst doesn't have to add the two together.

TAB PLAN EXAMPLE

Below is an example of how to write a tab plan indicating how you want the cross-tabs arrayed. It calls for 19 banner points and features the number of the question in the questionnaire from which each banner point is derived. It also highlights the base number of respondents for some of the banner points. The question number and the base number of respondents are for the tab provider's benefit, making it easier to set up the correct banner specifications.

Further, it provides instructions for desired significance tests. Note that statistical tests will be provided at the 95 and 90 per cent confidence levels:

1. Total (Base = 325).
2. 1 to 19 company employees (Q.14).
3. 20 to 49 company employees (Q.14).
4. 50 to 99 company employees (Q.14).
5. 100 or more company employees (Q.14).
6. Company revenue less than $500,000 (Q.16).
7. Company revenue $500,000 to $1 million (Q.16).
8. Company revenue $1 million to $10 million (Q.16).
9. Company revenue $10 million plus (Q.16).
10. Most often use source for printing and copying services (Q.11a Base = 68).
11. Use "other" sources most often for printing and copying (Q.11a Base = 222).
12. Have used Alpha for printing and copying in the past (Q.12a Base = 88).
13. Have not used Alpha for printing in past (Q.12a Base = 169).
14. Company receives special printing and copying discounts from Alpha (Q.13c).
15. Company does not receive special printing discounts from Alpha (Q.13c).

16. Company industry – professional (includes accounting, banking, education, health care, law services, real estate).
17. Company industry – industrial (includes construction, manufacturing, transportation).
18. Receive special bonus promotions from Alpha (Q.13d).
19. Receive special bonus promotions from other companies (Q.13d).

T-tests of significance at 95 and 90 per cent: compare columns 2 through 5, 6 through 9, 10 vs 11, 12 vs 13, 14 vs 15, 16 vs 17, 18 vs 19.

Creating a tab plan yourself is always helpful in thinking through how you want to analyze the data. However, it is not essential because any market research data-processing supplier will, for little if any cost, help you determine how to set up cross-tabs and create your tab plan.

Here is another example of how we set up the three cross-tab banners for a homebuilder client. In this case we didn't use the question numbers in the plan, which is quite acceptable for most companies you might use to develop your cross-tabs.

Tab 1: The demographic banner

1. Total
2. Top 3 box (10, 9, 8) overall satisfaction score
3. Bottom 3 Box (1, 2, 3) overall satisfaction score
4. Male
5. Female
6. Less than college education
7. College education
8. More than college education
9. Under age 35
10. Age 35–54
11. Age 55+
12. House selling price under $150,000
13. House selling price $150,000 or higher

T-tests at 95 and 90 per cent: 2 vs 3, 4 vs 5, 6–8, 9–11, 12 vs 13.

Tab 2: The monthly banner

1. Total
2. Jan.
3. Feb.
4. March
5. April

6. May
7. June
8. July
9. Aug.
10. Sept.
11. Oct.
12. Nov.
13. Dec.

T-tests at 95 and 90 per cent: 2 vs 3, 3 vs 4, 4 vs 5, etc. Each month is compared to the next for month-to-month changes.

Tab 3: The market banner

1. Total
2. Market 1
3. Market 2
4. Market 3
5. Market 4
6. Market 5
7. Market 6
8. Market 7
9. Market 8
10. Market 9
11. Market 10

T-tests at 95 and 90 per cent: compare the result of each market to the total (average) and to every other market.

19

Statistical techniques

We are not statisticians nor are most people working as professional marketing researchers. Nevertheless, we do have a working knowledge of various techniques and a general understanding of when it is appropriate to use them. You should too – and they are set out in the following sections.

SIGNIFICANCE TESTS

The majority of research studies do not require the use of sophisticated statistical techniques to analyze the data. In fact, simply tabulating the data and looking at the responses is often enough to give you clear answers. Nevertheless, data in surveys should always be subjected to tests of statistical significance.

A significance test, which is typically a t-test and sometimes a chi-square test, tells you whether there is a difference between two or more numbers. The numbers could be percentages (for example, 60 vs 40 per cent) or averages, termed "means," (for example, 5.5 vs 4.5) that appear in a cross-tab. This is a simple, inexpensive test that you should make sure is applied to all your studies using cross-tabulations.

Look at Table 19.1. If you asked 200 beer drinkers whether they would try a new lemon-flavored beer, the error range would be +/– 7 per cent. With 60 per cent saying yes and 40 per cent saying no, a t-test indicates that we can be 95 per cent confident in concluding that more beer drinkers like the idea than don't like it. Please note that we compared the two numbers labeled A.

With a sample size of 100 heavy beer drinkers and 100 light beer drinkers, the error range around this smaller sample size would be +/–

Table 19.1 Attitude toward lemon-flavored beer

Question:
"Would you try a new beer if it contained a touch of lemon in the flavor?"

	Total	Heavy Drinkers	Light Drinkers
Number of interviews:	200	100	100
Yes	60%A	55%B	65%B
No	40%A	45%	35%

10 per cent. Here a t-test indicates that you cannot be 95 per cent confident that there is no difference between the answers given by heavy beer drinkers and those given by light beer drinkers. That is, heavy and light beer drinkers like the idea of a lemon-flavored beer to the same degree, even though the 55 per cent as against 65 per cent figures alone might lead you to conclude otherwise. Here, we compared the two numbers labeled B.

Here's a reminder about what achieving a 95 per cent confidence level signifies. It means if the study were repeated with the sample drawn the same way and with the same questionnaire used, there is a 95 per cent chance the above numbers would not vary more than the statistical error range. Stated another way, there is only a 5 per cent chance that you would reach a different conclusion on the appeal of a lemon-flavored beer if the study were repeated.

Statistical significance is a function of *both* the size of the samples being compared and the size of the difference that is found. Really large differences can be statistically significant with small samples, but smaller differences will require bigger samples to draw statistically significant conclusions.

There is also a distinction between what might be termed "managerial meaningfulness" and statistical significance. Just because there is a statistically significant difference between two numbers does not mean that it will impact a decision you need to make. It only means the difference is real and not a result of a random fluke. In surveys with very large samples, nearly everything is statistically significant, but the only differences that matter relate to the goals and specific objectives of the research.

A good example of "managerial meaningfulness" is when there is a clear pattern in the data, but the level of statistical significance is not reached.

Take a look at Table 19.2, which is taken from an actual customer satisfaction study for a home builder. Data that evaluate the perform-

Table 19.2 Evaluation of sales representatives (mean score on 10-point scale)

| | Market 1 | | Market 2 | |
	Year 1	Year 2	Year 1	Year 2
Professional appearance	9.01	8.42	8.20	8.60
Integrity	8.83	7.68	6.91	8.15
Ability to answer questions	8.90	7.85	6.29	8.17
Knowledge of home features	9.00	8.12	7.00	8.25
Knowledge of competitors' features	8.47	7.13	5.88	7.22
Knowledge of community attributes	8.75	7.77	6.27	7.98
Knowledge of financing options	8.75	8.24	7.06	8.09
Timely response to questions	8.87	7.92	6.91	7.98
Understood needs	8.88	8.02	6.47	8.21
Established uniqueness of home	8.71	7.73	6.21	7.73

ance of the company's sales representatives are presented for two markets and for two consecutive years.

The samples from both markets were too small for year-to-year changes to reach statistical significance, but that doesn't prevent certain conclusions from being drawn. Just looking at the mean scores you can see that most are close to 7.00 or higher in both years. The ratings in the 9.00 and 8.00 range are on a 10-point scale so we might conclude that the sales teams in both markets are doing well.

Additionally, in Market 1 the ratings declined on all 10 attributes between Year 1 and Year 2. And in Market 2 the ratings improved on all 10 attributes between Year 1 and Year 2. While no changes reached statistical significance, these patterns are managerially meaningful and it is reasonable to think that the sales force may be slipping in Market 1 and improving in Market 2.

In this case, management would be wise to look further at why Market 1 is trending down in the various ratings while Market 2 is trending up.

In market research studies, the rule of thumb is to use a 95 or 90 per cent confidence level when conducting tests of significance and making decisions. Nevertheless, it is sometimes reasonable to make conclusions and decisions using even lower levels of confidence. Please be aware that, for no additional cost, you can order tabulations that will test your data at 99, 95, 90, or 85 per cent confidence levels.

Table 19.3 shows another example of significance testing. In this case, there is a 20 percentage point difference between the answers given by

Table 19.3   Attitude toward lemon-flavored beer – no statistical difference

Question:
"Would you try a new beer if it contained a touch of lemon in the flavor?"

	Total	**Heavy Drinkers**	**Light Drinkers**
Number of interviews:	200	100	100
Yes	60%A	50%C	70%C
No	40%A	50%	30%

heavy as opposed to light beer drinkers. With the same error range of +/− 10 per cent, the t-test would tell you that you cannot be 95 per cent confident that the difference is statistically significant. You could not conclude that light beer drinkers are, in fact, more likely to try a new lemon-flavored beer than are heavy beer drinkers and would be a better target for the new product than would heavy beer drinkers. Here we compared the two numbers labeled C.

Table 19.4 provides yet another example of what happens when you increase the sample size. It shows exactly the same results as were found in Table 19.3, only this time 300 total interviews were conducted instead of 200, with 150 each among heavy and light beer drinkers instead of 100. With the larger samples of 150, the error range would be +/− 8 per cent and the t-test now shows that there is a statistical difference. We compared the two numbers labeled D.

Table 19.4   Attitude toward lemon-flavored beer – increased sample size

Question:
"Would you try a new beer if it contained a touch of lemon in the flavor?"

	Total	**Heavy Drinkers**	**Light Drinkers**
Number of interviews:	300	150	150
Yes	60%	50%D	70%D
No	40%	50%	30%

A WORD ABOUT DETERMINING SAMPLE SIZES

As discussed earlier, cost is always a factor in determining how many respondents you can interview. Nevertheless, there is a point at which choosing to go with a sample size that is too small is as wasteful as going overboard with a sample size that is too large.

In the lemon-flavored beer example, the 70 per cent vs 50 per cent split with 100 respondents per target proved too small for there to be a significant difference. With a sample size of 150 per target, there *was* a statistical difference. We again stress the point that statistical significance is a function of both the sample sizes and the size of the difference between the two measures being compared.

Now, if you only knew the results before you did your studies, you would then be able to know the minimum sample size you would need for statistically reliable results and could spend as little as possible getting actionable data. Since you cannot know the results in advance, use Table 19.5 as a partial guide.

With a sample of 25, no matter how big or small the difference between the answers, the error ranges are relatively large: +/– 19.6 per cent, +/– 16.6 per cent and +/– 8.5 per cent. And with a sample of 2,500, no matter the size of the difference, the error ranges are small: +/– 1.9 per cent, +/– 1.6 per cent and +/– less than 1.0 per cent. Again, as the sample sizes increase, the error ranges decrease.

Look at how the differences between the answers impact the error range. With a sample of 100 when both answers are close to 50 per cent, the error range is +/– 10 per cent, as we saw in the beer example. As the difference between results gets larger, i.e. when one answer is about 75

Table 19.5 Guide to determining sample size at the 95 per cent confidence level

Sample size	Error range if both answers are near 50% +/–%	Error range if answers are about 75% or 25% +/–%	Error range if answers are near 90% or 10% +/–%
25	19.6	16.6	8.5
50	13.9	11.6	6.2
75	11.3	9.4	4.9
100	10.0	8.2	4.2
150	8.0	6.6	3.5
250	6.2	5.1	2.7
500	4.4	3.7	1.9
1,000	3.1	2.5	1.2
2,000	2.2	1.8	<1.0
2,500	1.9	1.6	<1.0

per cent or 25 per cent, the error range on a sample size of 100 becomes smaller: +/– 8.2 per cent. And when the differences between the two results are stark, i.e. with an answer near 90 per cent or 10 per cent, the error range shrinks to +/– 4.2 per cent.

You can use this table to pick a sample size at the 95 per cent confidence level by looking at the error range and then trying to "guesstimate" the likely difference you think you'll find. Note that the most conservative answer, both near 50 per cent, always requires the largest sample. Alternatively, you can first calculate how large a sample you can afford and then see the error range you're going to have to live with.

Always, it is inexpensive and good practice to have your survey data subjected to t-testing. It is the only way to know if one set of percentages or means is truly different from another.

REGRESSION ANALYSIS

Let's take the case of a museum that conducted a customer survey and achieved a high mean rating of 7.92 on a 9-point "overall satisfaction" question. We can term this question a "dependent variable," one whose behaviour is thought to be influenced by other variables in the same study. The same study also questioned customers on 39 different attributes about the museum, which can be described as "independent" variables.

A regression analysis is a statistical tool that was used to relate overall satisfaction (the dependent variable) with scores on the 39 attributes (independent variables). The goal here was to determine the particular attributes that were most influential in causing the high satisfaction score.

The regression is really an equation which predicts something called an R^2 (R-squared) score – which weighs the importance of each of the independent variables. The higher the R^2 score, the better the statistical model.

The museum attributes produced an R^2 accounting for 60 per cent of the variance in the overall satisfaction score – which we consider a good model. It showed that of the 39 variables, *only 8* strongly influenced the overall rating. The table opposite shows mean scores the most important attributes received.

This regression suggests that to increase visitor satisfaction the museum should communicate that it is a place to learn and discover. Right now it only gets a 6.08 on the 9-point scale so there is room for improvement. It should also maintain or increase its performance with respect to providing useful information, being a place you must see, being intellectually stimulating, and offering useful internal signage. If it does these things, it will likely maintain the very highly rated feeling

Table 19.6 Regression results

Variables that Entered the Regression Model (Decreasing order of importance)	Overall Rating (9-point scale)
Attitude "I was delighted with my visit to the museum"	8.5
Performance in "providing useful information"	7.35
Attitude "I am likely to recommend the museum to a friend/family"	8.59
Performance as "a place you must see"	7.35
Performance in being "intellectually stimulating"	7.49
Expectation that the museum was a "place to learn and discover"	6.08
Performance in "providing good signs to find the exhibits"	7.15
Attitude "I had mixed feelings about visiting the museum" (negative)	4.05

of delight among those visiting the museum and further reduce the relatively low proportion of those with mixed feelings.

This is a very simple explanation of a more complex statistical procedure. What is important to remember about regression analysis is that it can help explain the actions you should take to achieve the customer behaviour you desire – in this case, increased visitor satisfaction. Remember, just because customers might feel strongly about certain attributes of a business, product or museum, it doesn't necessarily mean those attributes are important to motivating customer to purchase or visitors to visit more often. As is evident in the case of the museum, only 8 of the 39 variables had strong influence on visitor satisfaction, and of these, some needed more improvement than others.

TURF ANALYSIS

TURF stands for "total unduplicated reach and frequency." TURF analysis was originally devised for use in analyzing advertising media campaigns to answer the question of what combination of media options delivers the largest audience of unique individuals.

Take three different TV shows as an example – show 1, show 2 and show 3. Determining the unduplicated audience is more complicated than just adding up the number of people who watch each show. That's because some viewers watch all three shows (1, 2 and 3) and some watch two shows (1 and 2, or 2 and 3, or 1 and 3) and some just watch a single show (1, or 2, or 3).

The TURF algorithm eliminates the viewers who are duplicated in the audience. Hence we get a new total of how many unduplicated audience members are reached when advertising on these shows. You can see where the name came from.

This thinking has been expanded to apply elsewhere. A directly analogous example would be to perform a TURF analysis to maximize the total number of consumers who will buy at least one item in a product line while minimizing overlap across all items.

This statistical model can be used to answer questions like:

- Where should we place ads to reach the widest possible audience?
- What potential market share will we gain if we add a new product to the product line we currently sell?
- Will new customers be gained if we add a new flavor, color, scent, or formula to the line of products we currently sell?
- What combination of messages should be communicated in our advertising, promotion, or other selling literature to motivate the greatest number of consumers to take the actions we want?

Table 19.7 shows a practical example of how a TURF analysis works. Assume you have 10 possible advertising messages you could communicate to prospects that would motivate them to visit your retail store. The messages are shown in the table along with the percentage of people who indicated each message is important in causing them to shop.

As you see, there are five different messages that motivate 50 per cent or more of prospects. A first inclination might be to give strong emphasis to these top five messages in a series of marketing communications programs.

A TURF analysis, however, will determine the unduplicated number of respondents who will be motivated to visit the store, given various combinations of messages. This matters because, for example, it might turn out that "lowest price," "money-back guarantee" and "discounts for frequent purchasing" appeal to the same people. Table 19.8 illustrates this.

As Table 19.8 shows, the "lowest price" message will reach 35 per cent of prospects and motivate a store visit. "Lowest price" and "fast service" combined will motivate a total of 49 per cent. "Lowest price," "fast service," and "knowledgeable salespeople" will motivate 59 per cent.

While "widest selection" was the second most important when considered alone in Table 19.7, it only adds 7 per cent more reach when combined with "lowest price," "fast service" and "knowledgeable salespeople." And "convenient parking" wasn't in the top five in Table 19.7, but it adds 6 per cent in the TURF analysis. Further, "money back guarantee," third most important in Table 19.7, wasn't in Table 19.8 at all.

Table 19.7 Rating of messages that motivate a visit to a retail store

Prospects indicating message is important

Message		%
1.	Lowest price	65
2.	Widest selection	60
3.	Money-back guarantee	55
4.	Knowledgeable salespeople	50
5.	Fast service	50
6.	Well-known brands	45
7.	Discounts for frequent purchasing	35
8.	Open 18 hours a day, seven days a week	30
9.	Convenient parking	25
10.	Play area for children	15

Table 19.8 Top five messages to reach the largest unduplicated audience

Unduplicated reach

Message		%
1.	Lowest price	35
2.	Fast service	49
3.	Knowledgeable salespeople	59
4.	Widest selection	66
5.	Convenient parking	72

In total these five specific messages, when used in this combination, will reach 72 per cent of prospects with a particular message that would motivate a store visit. The point is that you reach a very different conclusion about what to communicate by using the TURF analysis than you would have by just looking at the importance ratings.

A TURF analysis should be part of every Guerrilla's research tool kit. It will help in optimizing the extent to which new products, new product formulations, line extensions and so forth add incremental business, rather than just switch current customers from one variation to another.

FACTOR ANALYSIS

Factor analysis is usually a good tool to use when there are a large number of variables, such as attitudes toward products or services a company offers, or perceptions of companies or brands. In such cases the many attributes or attitudes that are rated can be combined, based on the similarity of responses given by respondents. The result is to reduce the number of variables to a smaller set of what are termed "factors."

Take a look in Table 19.9 at the long list of attributes that were used in a customer satisfaction study for a museum. You will note that, after the factor analysis, they have been divided into three columns based on the similarity of the respondents' responses to the attributes.

Table 19.9 Factor analysis grouping of various attitudes related to visiting a museum

	Factor 1: The Museum Experience	Factor 2: Operational Efficiency	Factor 3: Aids in Understanding
entertaining and fun	.826		
being a place to learn and discover	.812		
great place to bring children	.797		
exhibits enjoyable to revisit	.780		
exhibits that appeal to adults	.774		
place to enjoy family and friends	.773		
creates good memories		.758	
you can explore for a long time		.755	
intellectually stimulating	.755		
hands on activities	.750		
good food in the café		.823	
service oriented staff in the café		.807	
staff good in the snack bar		.762	
signs adequate to find restaurants		.745	
food good in the snack bar		.725	
clean restrooms		.714	
staff good in the gift store		.705	
helps understand your own culture			.745
helps understand different cultures			.624
helps understand the environment			.519

Column 1 contains 10 variables that relate to different aspects of being at the museum. We named this factor "the museum experience."

The middle column includes seven variables that relate to operational aspects of the museum, such as signage, rest rooms, food, easy to use website, and so on. We termed this the "operational efficiency" factor.

The third column just includes three variables, all of which feature the word "understand" so calling this factor "aids in understanding" was obvious.

In discussing the findings consider how much easier it is to talk about three underlying "factors" rather than 20 separate variables. Factor analysis is a powerful and useful statistical tool; what's more, you can use the factors in a regression analysis, where doing so simplifies the task of analyzing the data.

CLUSTER ANALYSIS

Cluster analysis is similar to factor analysis in that it works to combine a large number of items into smaller homogeneous groups that are called "clusters."

In this case respondents are sorted into clusters, so that the degree of association is strong between respondents in one cluster and weak when compared to respondents of different clusters. In other words, it is based on the degree to which respondents in each cluster hold the same attitudes and opinions, engage in the same behaviors, or have similar demographics.

Below are three groups of respondents and the characteristics that cluster together to describe each. As with factor analysis, once the statistical program forms the clusters, the research analyst gives each a name that describes it. The following are examples:

Cluster 1: Good-Time Joes
love parties
celebrate whenever possible
enjoy being the center of attention
love to tell stories
age under 25

Cluster 2: Involved Observers
enjoy movies and plays
would rather listen to stories others tell
enjoy historical novels
take joy in the accomplishments of others
gender: female

Cluster 3: Wallflowers
hate crowds
don't go out unless invited
find it hard to make new friends
income <$50,000
like to watch soap operas on TV

Cluster analysis is a technique for better understanding how respondents differ in terms of attitudes, behaviors and demographics. By knowing lifestyles such as the ones described above, marketers can determine the kinds of appeals that are most likely to motivate each cluster grouping.

In this example, once the Good-Time Joes, Involved Observers and Wallflowers clusters are identified, they could become part of a cross-tab banner. This would allow a determination of whether differences exist in how the clusters answered the other questions in your survey. Having insight into the lifestyles of respondents and the clusters to which they belong gives marketers a unique opportunity to target specific lifestyles when creating marketing and advertising programs or when developing new products or services.

OTHER STATISTICAL TECHNIQUES

Most Guerrillas analyzing research data will find it unnecessary to go beyond basic cross-tabs (as described in Chapter 18) or the few more common statistical techniques previously described. Nevertheless, here are some other useful techniques worth mentioning.

Conjoint analysis

Conjoint analysis is often called "trade-off analysis" and is a statistical tool that allows researchers to discover the relative importance that is placed on product features – including price – when they are presented together or jointly.

In an automotive study, for example, respondents might be asked to compare various combinations of features such as safety, price, luxury, mileage and so on. In addition, each of these features would be available at several levels. For example, different combinations might include: "15 miles city/20 highway – car cost is $20,000," "20 miles city/25 highway – car cost is $25,000," "25 miles city/30 highway – car cost is $30,000" and so forth.

In a conjoint analysis, respondents are shown possible combinations of features and prices in pairs and forced to select the one preferred option for each pair. They are forced to make trade-offs. In the above example, if "20 miles city/25 highway – car cost is $25,000" is the strongest of the three options, the manufacturer might focus on this ratio in developing new models.

When this is analyzed for all the features and all the price levels, the market's underlying preferences for what it will pay to receive which specific features is revealed.

Conjoint analysis is also a popular technique to solve product development challenges and is one of the best ways to do pricing research.

Multidimensional scaling and perceptual mapping

Multidimensional scaling and perceptual mapping refer to a set of statistical procedures that create spacial representations of data that reveal relationships between companies, brands, products, or services based on how consumers perceive them.

Actual pictorial maps are generated that show how respondents perceive products or companies in terms of their similarities or differences. Perceptual maps are used as a planning tool when conducting sophisticated market segmentation and strategy studies. They also allow marketers to track company or product changes in perceptions from year to year.

Multidimensional scaling requires specific questions to assess what respondents consider ideal, to measure similarities between options, and to determine which options are preferred. This tool cannot be used as an analytical afterthought and must be planned upfront when considering the study goal and specific objectives.

KEEP YOUR WITS ABOUT YOU

Let's recall reporting on the youth vote in the 2004 US Presidential election. Analysts said all the money spent to get out the youth vote, 18- to 29-year old voters, essentially did nothing. They pointed out that 17 per cent of the voters who participated in the 2000 election were 18 to 29, which is exactly the same figure as in the 2004 election.

In fact, more 18- to 29-year olds voted in 2004 than ever before because more people voted in 2004 than in any previous election. The 17 per cent share of almost 120 million voters was an astounding 21 million voters. This can be contrasted with 17 per cent of the approximately 95 million voters in 2000, or 16.1 million in the 18- to 29 year old range. So almost 5 million more voted in 2004 than in 2000, a whopping 30 per cent increase.

In your market research studies don't make this type of mistake. Remember that numbers are only useful in the context of how the questions are asked, how the answers are interpreted, and the statistical reliability that can be attributed to those answers.

20

Telling the story: analyzing survey results

The topic of data analysis is extremely broad because analytic effort depends on the types of studies and their goals. Complex background studies can be analyzed from many points of view and over long periods. They often take a great deal of digging to reveal the information that is of ultimate use. Smaller tactical studies may require little more than a glance at the cross-tabs to know the action that is indicated. We like to say:

> A good analysis tells a story, a consistent, coherent story. Several questions taken together should point to the same conclusions. We don't believe in silver bullets, one statistic that by itself determines what must be done.

However, just as writing an effective questionnaire is a never-ending learning process, analyzing research data requires a perspective that only experience can bring.

Contained in the data of every study is the story. It may be one that jumps out or one that has to be teased out. There may be consistency in the answers from one question to the next that leads to clear and obvious conclusions. Or the information generated from question to question might take you in circles, leaving you perplexed and confused as to the meaning of the data. When this happens, it might mean you didn't capture all of the topic's complexity in your research and it sometimes points to the need for additional clarifying research in the future. It may also mean you haven't spent enough time with the data to see the big picture.

If you are totally new to market research and have yet to work with a set of cross-tabs and what it is telling you, you will be faced with a steep, but not insurmountable, learning curve.

We like to use an air traffic controller analogy. Air traffic controllers look at a computer screen that represents their portion of the sky. The information displayed identifies the planes, their directional heading, their speed and their height. Further, it's dynamic – everything is moving. To do their job they have to discern a pattern amidst the many points of information and then they need to maintain it during their entire shift.

Looking at a data set is similar. You have to study the data until a pattern emerges. There are many pages of data, sometimes hundreds. At first it makes no sense, but slowly a pattern emerges and then – you've got it. And happily, the more often you work with data, the less time it takes to see the essential patterns.

Be warned: it is impossible to analyze data 10 minutes at a time, going from this task to another and back again. It takes an extended period of concentration without interruption. We've found that the best approach is to set aside a couple of hours, clear your mind, find a quiet room, and have at it.

For us, we encounter a thick set of cross-tabs with a sense of excitement. The data set is a reflection of the time spent developing the research goal and objectives, writing the questionnaire, collecting the interviews, and developing the tab plan and cross-tabs. Finally, it's time to see the payoff.

We're good at devouring data and can leaf through cross-tabs quickly and spot interesting numbers. Differences between targets pop out quickly. Sometimes questions we thought would produce interesting information produce little that is valuable. Other times questions that weren't expected to provide a clear direction happily do and form the basis for exciting strategies and precise action plans.

When first analyzing data, we sit quietly with cross-tabs and read the tables. We look at each question and how all the respondents answered. We scan across every table to see if the t-tests identify certain targets answering the question differently.

With a pencil, we circle interesting, surprising, or puzzling numbers. Often, it doesn't take long before there's a sense of the data, and a clear story starts to emerge. Other times, the data are bland and uninspiring. The pattern is unclear and the direction vague and we know it will be a struggle before the story emerges.

If you are new to analyzing data we suggest letting the story emerge slowly, over several days if possible. Follow our suggestion to read each table and circle key numbers. With patience, persistence, determination, and curiosity, you will uncover the story being told by the data – one that holds together and provides direction that you can be confident in following.

THE ZEN OF DATA

In and of themselves data have very little meaning. Data exist to be analyzed and interpreted so they can be converted into actionable information.

If you describe a new product you feel has potential in a survey, and 25 per cent of the respondents indicate they would buy it, would you think that's good or bad? If 50 per cent of your customers rated your customer service as excellent, would you be happy or unhappy? If 75 per cent say they'd purchase from you again, would you take that to the bank?

The question you must constantly be asking yourself when analyzing data is, "compared to what?"

If you had previous research indicating that when you achieve a 25 per cent intention-to-buy rating on a survey, it will translate into a successful product, then 25 per cent is good. If your 50 per cent customer service rating compares to a 75 per cent rating for your major competitor, then you would be unhappy. And, if your 75 per cent repurchase intent score was 90 per cent six months ago, you'd probably have a big problem on your hands.

USING CONTROLS AND COMPARISONS TO ANALYZE SURVEY RESULTS

So, when you analyze survey results you can do so from many different perspectives. These include:

1. Using a control.
2. Making comparisons to previous research.
3. Making comparisons to industry norms.
4. Making comparisons to actual purchase behavior.
5. Comparing one target to another.
6. Comparing alternatives to each other.

Let's take a look at each.

1. Using a control

A control can be any useful comparison you can make. In choosing a control, though, there should be the assumption that, in matching or bettering the control, you will have a winner. For example, it could be:

● Your ratings on a new product or new service compared to the ratings on the same product or service that a competitor might have successfully introduced. This might be the actual product you've developed compared to a competitive product already on the market. It could also be a simple concept statement that describes the benefits of your product compared to the benefits of an existing product.

- Your ratings compared to the ratings for the market leader and/or other competition. Comparisons can be made across any dimension including products or services sold, company image, attitudes, perceptions, or previous experiences.

- Your ratings compared to rating goals you have set for yourself and are intent on achieving.

When you are using a control as comparison, the goal is at least to meet, and preferably exceed, the scores achieved by your control. If you are developing a new peanut butter, you will presumably want a product that tastes at least as good as a leading control brand. If you test your peanut butter product against the control, and it doesn't meet or exceed acceptance ratings achieved by the control, you should probably reformulate your product.

If you have an idea for a new fitness center, your competition might be a nationwide fitness chain or a local gym. You could write a one- or two-paragraph "concept" statement that describes the benefits of joining your fitness center and a similar statement for the nationwide fitness chain, or the local gym, or both. Here, you'd have two controls – both competitors. If more consumers in your target failed to rate interest in joining your fitness center higher than interest in joining at least one of the two control competitors, you should probably rethink your benefits.

Making comparisons to a successful control is one of the most powerful uses of research and presents one of the easiest techniques for analyzing data.

If your objective is to be at least on a par with a successful competitor, the data will quickly reveal whether you should move forward. If your objective is to be twice as good as your competitor, the data will tell you if you are there or if you have more work to do.

We've done taste-testing for a beer client, where the objective was for its beer to taste at least as good as the leader. Here our client's beer achieved ratings that were comparable to an already successful brand and its subsequent product reformulation attracted many new customers.

We've also conducted research for a manufacturer of a cough suppressant whose new product was a gelcap that had to be crushed in the mouth to release a concentrated cough syrup. This was a totally new idea – a cough syrup that could be taken without a measuring spoon, thus eliminating the mess and hassle while adding the ability to take cough medicine anywhere.

The research focused primarily on the taste and mouth feel of the gelcap and its contents, but the client could never figure out an appropriate control. It conducted several iterations of research and reformulated the product a number of times, but finally abandoned the project. Lacking a successful control, there was no economical way to determine if the product would be a success. "After all," the marketing director said, "maybe the next test would produce even better results than the last."

2. *Making comparisons to previous research*

Another potent control is comparing the results from previous research studies. If you are conducting an image and attitude study, an awareness study, or a customer satisfaction study, you would start with a benchmark study that determines current existing levels. Follow-up studies conducted at regular intervals are then compared to the benchmark control and progress judged.

Also, previous research levels achieved when introducing new advertising or marketing approaches or new products or services should serve you well, assuming you know how those programs and products performed in the marketplace. If you know that scores achieved in surveys indicate actual market success or failure, you will have created very powerful control measurements.

Companies that conduct a great deal of research have a strong advantage when considering go/no-go decisions. The scores achieved on previous research can be used as reliable predictors of success. It would be questionable, for example, for HP to introduce a new generation of computer printers unless the scores that research testers gave the new printers were better than scores that HP received among customers when its current line was tested.

3. *Making comparisons to industry norms*

Many market research companies make normative data available to their clients. Research companies that specialize in testing advertising are particularly good in this regard. If you've developed advertising for a new soft drink, for example, you could test your ad or commercial with copy-testing companies, and they can tell you how your ad scored versus all the other soft drink ads they've tested.

Other research companies have normative data regarding the scores (also called "hurdle rates") that a new product should achieve before it has a chance of success.

Associations are also a good source of normative data. The Direct Marketing Association (DMA), for example, occasionally conducts studies among consumers buying direct and provides aggregate satisfaction data in regard to the companies from which they purchase. If you are an internet marketer, there are services available that will provide satisfaction scores for people coming to your site as against going to other sites. You can go to any search engine and type in "attitude research" followed by your industry (e.g. "attitude research home remodeling") and you'll find a wealth of information that just might yield extremely valuable normative data.

When you use normative data, you must make sure that you word your questions exactly the same as they are worded in the normative data surveys. Further, the respondents you interview would have to be exactly comparable to those interviewed in the normative research. That's the only way to usefully compare the data you get from your targets with pre-existing norms.

4. Making comparisons to actual purchase behavior

If you have a database of customers, you have built-in controls for certain types of studies. Perhaps you are trying to determine what changes should be made to motivate certain customer groups to purchase more often. Your control group might be chosen from two customer groups with similar profiles. The difference will be that one group is behaving exactly the way you want, while the other is not. By comparing the attitudes of the two groups, you'll see the areas that need improvement or attention for the lagging group.

5. Comparing one target to another

By far the most frequent comparisons you'll do in analyzing a dataset will be those in which you compare the responses of one group of respondents to those of another group in the same study.

In defining the objectives of your study and determining the targets for interviewing, you'll already have made assumptions. Perhaps you'll have determined the control target against which other targets should be compared. If so, your control is obvious and becomes one of your banner points.

In some studies, though, a control might not be obvious. If the purpose of the research is to identify the best targets, you could make some assumptions about a control after you view the initial cross-tab data. This is particularly true when you are conducting background studies aimed at helping you determine strategic direction.

In larger-sample strategic/background studies (600 sample size or more), you'll undoubtedly generate data that allow you to develop various customer or prospect profiles. You could profile customers who you feel are your better customers, your competitors' better customers, or prospects you think have potential to be converted into your customers. It's quite easy to combine various characteristics identified in the questionnaire to form groups of respondents who will then make up one or more controls.

Once the characteristics of a control target are determined, you give it a name and make it a banner point in your tabs. Then you are comparing the attitudes of your control group(s) to those of the other groups in your banner. By making such comparisons, the issues important to a wide number of targets will become evident.

6. Comparing alternatives to each other

There are times when you might find it hard to determine a control. Perhaps your product or service is so unique that comparisons are difficult or meaningless and you are inclined to move ahead without conducting any research.

In cases in which you think control comparisons won't work, consider creating several alternative approaches or benefits for positioning your product or service. Write two or three concepts that stress different selling approaches and test them against each other. If interest in all the positions you test appears similarly weak and indicates a lack of enthusiasm, the data may be telling you the idea is inherently weak. On the other hand, if the data for one position are much stronger than for the other positions, you'll know where your best chance of success lies.

Remember, when looking at data without the benefit of a control, findings you consider encouraging might really portend disaster. And results that look discouraging might really indicate a blockbuster success. Without some kind of control, you just can't know.

BEYOND THE FIRST BLUSH

Determining control comparisons is job number one. Then it will be time to look at the data in detail.

Sometimes you can get lucky, and the story is told in your cross-tabs. Additional research analysis or special statistical procedures aren't required to determine the actions you should take. If the data clearly point the direction and you are in a position to take the appropriate action, you have a successful study and can confidently move forward.

Often you will have to work with the cross-tabs and dig at the data. This means taking data from the cross-tabs and creating customized tables. Researchers call it "pulling the data."

The job in pulling data is to array the numbers in the cross-tabs from a different perspective. To do so, researchers usually take a pencil and paper and handwrite new tables. The sections below show examples of how data can be pulled and arrayed.

Analyzing string questions

Analyzing string questions is an important challenge when interpreting survey data. Table 20.1 illustrates a typical string question that was asked on a study about catalogs. The question was, "When buying from clothing catalogs, how important or unimportant is each of the following statements?"

In looking at Table 20.1, you could make a number of observations. You might look only at the "Total" column and conclude that customer service, lowest prices, high-quality brands, and familiar brands are far less important than the other factors.

In comparing frequent and infrequent buyers, though, you see startling differences. To frequent buyers, great customer service, high-quality brands, and brands that you are aware of are significantly more important than to infrequent buyers. For infrequent buyers, easy to order, easy returns, satisfaction guarantee, free shipping, great value, and lowest prices are of greater significance than to frequent buyers.

Table 20.1 Example of arraying factors rated as extremely important

	Buy frequently from clothing catalogs %	Buy infrequently from clothing catalogs %	Total %
Percentage rating the statement as extremely important:			
Makes it easy to order	58*	50	55
Allows you to return your order for any reason whatsoever	56*	41	48
Has a 100% satisfaction guarantee policy	49	43	45
Provides free shipping	48	42	45
Gives you great value for your money	45*	30	32
Has great customer service	34	43*	32
Has the lowest prices	31	11	22
Has high-quality brands	30	40*	36
Has brands you are aware of	27	39*	33

* Indicates a statistically significant difference at the 95 per cent confidence level between frequent and infrequent buyers.

Of course, the manner in which you interpret the data is dependent on your marketing goals. If you want to appeal equally to both groups, you would look at the totals and conclude that the best way of doing it is to focus on easy ordering, easy returns, and 100 per cent satisfaction.

If, though, you are trying to convince infrequent buyers to buy more frequently you would likely focus more on value, prices, satisfaction, and ease of ordering. To reinforce frequent buyers, you would be likely to remind them about great customer service and the ability to find familiar, high-quality brands.

Importance vs agreement

Once important elements are identified, the question often becomes how well you and/or your competitors are delivering on those elements. Take the catalog statements that are important compared to how catalog company Bob and catalog company Gerry are performing on each element. Table 20.2 shows the elements that are extremely important and whether respondents agree strongly that the Bob and Gerry catalogs are delivering them.

Table 20.2 Comparison of extremely important factors when rating catalogs

	Rated as extremely important	Agree strongly with the statement when rating the:	
	Total %	Bob Catalog %	Gerry Catalog %
Makes it easy to order	58	70*	60
Allows you to return your order for any reason whatsoever	56	43*	35
100% satisfaction guarantee	49	40*	35
Provides free shipping	48	35	53*
Gives you great value for your money	45	45	60*
Has great customer service	34	50*	40
Has the lowest prices	31	25	55*
Has high-quality brands	30	45*	25
Has brands you are aware of	27	40*	20

* Indicates a statistical difference at the 95 per cent confidence level between the starred number and the adjacent number in the same row (e.g. 70 per cent on "Makes it easy to order" is significantly different from 60 per cent).

The findings from Table 20.2 are that, on allowing returns for any reason and having a 100 per cent satisfaction guarantee policy, both catalogs are performing at low levels on what the market indicates is extremely important, and both should focus attention on improving in these areas.

On ease of ordering and having great customer service, both catalogs are performing well on variables the market says are less important. Therefore, improvement in these areas should not be a priority for either.

Nevertheless, the Bob catalog is at a competitive advantage when it comes to ease of ordering, returns, 100 per cent satisfaction guaranteed, great customer service, having high-quality brands, and having familiar brands. The Gerry catalog would have to improve in these areas if it wants to be more competitive with the Bob catalog.

Finally, the Gerry catalog is at a competitive advantage when it comes to giving great value for money, having the lowest prices, and providing free shipping. The Bob catalog would have to improve in these areas if it wants to be more competitive with the Gerry catalog.

Gap analysis

Another form of analysis is gap analysis. A gap score indicates the extent to which a company is performing better or worse than demanded by customers.

Here, the gap score is simply the difference between the level of performance customers expect from an "ideal" catalog, and the extent to which they agree it is being delivered by you and/or competitors. Table 20.3 highlights how gap scores are derived.

Note that, on "Makes it easy to order," the gap score is +8. This is simply the difference between what is felt to be important for an ideal catalog to deliver, subtracted from the score the Bob catalog achieved. This indicates that the Bob catalog is performing better than is actually necessary to meet the expectations of the marketplace for this characteristic. And on the other plus scores, the Bob catalog is also exceeding expectations.

The –11 score on "Allows you to return your order for any reason whatsoever" and the other minus scores indicate that the Bob catalog is not meeting the expectations of the marketplace. The Bob catalog might consider diverting funds from promoting its brands, where it is over-performing, to creating a more liberal return policy, where it is under-performing.

Gap analysis is a strong tool for understanding where the company should put emphasis. In theory, a company should achieve a 0 score on all factors, which would indicate that it is delivering exactly what the marketplace expects – no more and no less. In reality, though, companies will always over-perform in some areas and under-perform in others.

Table 20.3   Gap scores for the Bob catalog

	Agreement for an ideal catalog	Agree with the statement when rating the Bob catalog	Gap %
Makes it easy to order	62	70	+ 8
Allows you to return your order for any reason whatsoever	54	43	− 11
100% satisfaction guarantee	44	40	− 4
Provides free shipping	43	35	− 8
Great value for your money	42	45	+ 3
Has great customer service	50	50	0
Has the lowest prices	45	25	− 20
Has high-quality brands	45	45	0
Has brands you are aware of	35	45	+ 10

In fact, by over-performing, companies often arrive at unique positions in the marketplace. Nordstrom has developed a unique position in the market by over-performing when it comes to customer service. Porsche is likely to be perceived as over-performing on automobile performance. And while Walmart probably under-performs on carrying the highest-quality products, it over-performs on providing low prices – which has become its core position and a strong reason for its success.

In all, gap analysis paints a clear picture of a company's position in the marketplace relative to what might be considered ideal. In doing so, it provides guidance for improving weak areas that are hindering growth, or setting benchmarks for areas where over-performing might be the best course for developing or maintaining a unique position.

The dependent variable

The vast majority of studies should include a dependent variable. A dependent variable is a key question about a company, product, or service, the answer to which is thought to be provided by answers from the rest of the questionnaire. Recall the discussion of regression analysis in Chapter 19.

Here are two questions you could use as dependent variables. The first question relates to future purchase intention, while the second relates to overall attitude:

In the future, how likely are you to buy [insert name of company/product/service]?

Definitely will buy   ____
Probably will buy   ____
Might or might not buy   ____
Probably will not buy   ____
Definitely will not buy   ____

Overall, how would you rate [insert name of company/product/service]?

Way above average   ____
Above average   ____
Average   ____
Below average   ____
Way below average   ____

A dependent variable can also relate to other company or product goals. If you are striving to achieve a high-quality image or the best customer service, the dependent variable question could be:

> When it comes to high quality, how would you rate [insert company/product/service]? A "10" rating would mean that you rate it the highest quality, a "1" rating would mean the lowest quality, or you could rate it anywhere between 10 and 1.

> When it comes to customer service, how would you rate [insert company/service]? A "10" rating would mean you rate its customer service the highest, a "1" rating would mean you rate it the lowest, or you could rate it anywhere between 10 and 1.

Perhaps your dependent variable is frequency of purchase. For example:

> Think about the next 10 times you purchase [insert product type]. How many of those times would you purchase [insert product name]?

The dependent variable is important in measuring what your overall market effort is trying to influence. If your goal is to get more people to buy, you want to understand the key factors that you should address to achieve more purchasers. If your goal is to convince people that you have the best customer service, you want to know the precise actions that will affect a stronger perception of your customer service.

There are several ways to use the dependent variable. Table 20.4 shows the attitudes of respondents toward several factors on the basis of purchase intent. Notice how the data are split out by respondents indicating that they will likely purchase in the future compared to those who are unlikely to purchase.

By using the dependent variable in this manner, it is easy to see that those who are likely to purchase more strongly agree that the Bob catalog has great customer service and carries unique products. Those less likely to purchase agree strongly that the company has low prices, but not great customer service.

Ultimately, the goal would be to convince the less likely to buy customer to become more likely to buy. From Table 20.4 it is reasonable to conclude the Bob catalog would need to convince customers who are negatively inclined to purchase that the company has great customer service and unique products.

The same would be true when using other dependent variables. If people who think you have a great company or will give you a larger percentage of their purchases hold certain strong attitudes, you'd conclude that those are the attitudes you'd want everyone to hold.

Therefore, in determining your dependent variable, think about the action or opinion you are trying to achieve. You can set up banner points that compare the positive attitudes you have achieved for some customer groups to the negative attitudes you would like to change for other groups. Then you can look at the areas that have to be improved to move the negative customers into the same mindset as the positive customers.

Table 20.4 Respondents' rating of the Bob catalog

Respondents who said they would

	definitely/probably purchase %	probably not/ definitely not purchase %
Agree strongly the Bob catalog:		
Carries unique products	50	20
Has easy ordering	20	25
Has low prices	30	50
Has great customer service	60	10

GOING BEYOND CROSS-TABS

Chapter 19 on statistical techniques discussed a number of techniques you can use to provide additional insight into your data. Deciding whether to go beyond the cross-tabs is usually driven by how comfortable you are with the story that emerges from the cross-tabs, the time you have to dig deeper into the data and your willingness to employ a statistician.

If your analysis leaves you questioning something, discuss with a statistician what you think you've learnt and why you're still struggling. We've found that a relatively small sum of money spent on statistics can shift a blurry picture towards clarity and set you off on the best course of action. In such instances, consider whether a regression analysis might clarify what's important or whether a TURF analysis or some other type of statistical analysis might help you set clear priorities.

Many statistical applications need to be anticipated at the beginning of the study and may require specific questions to be asked in specific ways, as well as require a larger sample size than would otherwise be necessary. If your study is particularly strategic in nature, we suggest you show your questionnaire to a research statistician before you collect data. Most statisticians you might use later on won't charge you to review your questionnaire – and they might suggest valuable questions that add a new dimension to how you analyze the data.

Analytic satisfaction

When should you be satisfied that you have mined your study for all it's worth?

Some analysts will spend very little time with data, and the story will come to them. They have a knack for quickly seeing where the results point and the actions that they should take. In such cases, "over and out."

Other analysts sweat the data. They have a personal curiosity and tenacity for digging beyond the obvious. They are naturally inquisitive and not content with the first answers that emerge. They like the challenge of turning seemingly insignificant data into creative findings. By taking their time to do so, they produce unique action plans that wouldn't otherwise have surfaced.

Analytic satisfaction, though, depends on the scope of your study and your tolerance for complex stories.

Here's some advice: the first few times that you analyze research data, review your conclusions with a research professional. The analytic learning curve is steep – so steep, in fact, that attempting to analyze anything but the simplest of research efforts without input from a professional would likely be unwise. Retaining an experienced researcher during your initial analytic efforts is prudent. Without doing so, your best learning is likely to remain hidden in the data.

WRITING THE REPORT

If you work for a company for which it is important to write a research report, and you have no experience in this regard, we'll make a few suggestions. Use old reports others have written as a guide or bring in a research professional for a couple of hours of consultation on how to write a report.

Market research reports can be highly detailed or relatively simple summaries of the information. The nature of your study and the reasons for even writing a report are important in determining its scope. If you are a research supplier or work in the research department of a company, you would probably write a report that is detailed enough so that strangers could get a complete picture of the project. If you are writing for a small audience you interact with frequently, going over-board on detail is probably unnecessary.

Here is the most important advice we can offer:

Rule 1: Consider the needs of the audience to whom you are reporting and presenting the research.
Rule 2: See Rule 1.

We have seen research that cost $250,000 and took six months to produce, totally ignored because of a failure to obey Rule 1. This was a study done on the US restaurant industry. This comprehensive analysis was intended to provide the client with the intellectual fuel to manage its business for at least five years.

The presentation was held in the Board Room and the most senior executives of the company and its ad agency were present. The research supplier began with an arcane discussion of the statistical analyses that were performed. After 10 minutes of seething, the Chairman of the Board demanded the supplier leave and declared the presentation was over. Not only were the results never shared, but no one was ever allowed to even refer to the study from that day forward. See Rule 1.

Always consider who will see your written report or presentation. If it's just you, all that might be necessary are some simple notes. If, though, it's others in your company who need to buy into the findings, or if it's your bank, your Board, your investors and partners, your vendors, sub-contractors or members of your industry, you must consider their perspectives.

Each of these audiences has a different set of needs and might require a different level of detail. A top-line overview using simple graphs and charts followed by a brief summary of findings might work perfectly for the Board. However, a detailed examination that shows the exact wording of each question, a discussion of how the interviewing took place, tables, graphs, charts and detailed findings might be necessary if your are trying to convince your bank to lend you a million dollars.

Therefore, to ensure you are getting the most from your research, it's not unusual to develop several versions of a report or presentation with each targeted to the idiosyncrasies of your audience.

Below is a general outline that could be followed when writing a research report for a survey when the audience is interested in full details:

1. *Title page.* This is a simple title describing the study and the month and year it is being issued.
2. *Study goal and specific objectives.* This is usually a bullet-point page that outlines the overall goal and the specific objectives of your study.
3. *Study methodology.* This is a description of how data were collected, the number of interviews that were conducted, a description of the target respondents, and where and when the study took place.
4. *Management summary.* A two- to four-page text description of the key findings will suffice for the management summary. Findings written in brief bullet points usually work best; often, key charts and graphs might be used as well.
5. *Recommendations.* Recommendations should be separate from the management summary. The recommendations and actions that you as the analyst feel come from the data can be quite different from other perspectives. This section should put forth what you feel the data imply.
6. *Detailed findings.* This section should consist of research tables, charts and graphs that highlight the key data that emerged from the analysis. At the top of each table or chart should be a one- to three-sentence description of the points that the table makes.
7. *Demographics.* The demographics of respondents in the survey can be depicted in tables or charts and should appear toward the end of the report.
8. *Appendix.* The appendix consists of the questionnaire used for the study plus other documents that might be important for a better understanding of how the study was conducted.

In writing a focus group report, points 1 through 5 above can be followed. The writing of the detailed findings section (point 6) of a focus group report is somewhat like writing a book. It consists of a text discussion of what was learnt in the study.

Because of an increasing data overload and time pressures, many audiences prefer the use of PowerPoint and bulleted reports and presentations instead of a more detailed document.

Below is a detailed findings section of an actual focus group report illustrating how information might be organized:

- Sub-section A. Needs and wants for the ideal clothing catalog.
- Sub-section B. What distinguishes one catalog from another.
- Sub-section C. Attitudes toward catalog customer service.
- Sub-section D. Major areas where catalogs can improve:
  - speed and efficiency of service;
  - assortment and choice;
  - personalization;
  - having a caring attitude;
  - price;
  - providing information.

In each of the above sub-sections, up to five pages of text were written elaborating on the topic. Actual quotes from respondents are typically used to make a point or illustrate an attitude. The detailed findings section of a focus group report can be very short and to the point, or a lengthy treatise on the attitudes, perceptions, and ideas that emerged. This depends on the audience being served. Rule 1.

There is no need to add a demographic section (point 7 above) in a focus group report, but a description of the targets is necessary. The Discussion Guide and Screeners should be part of an appendix.

21

Putting results into action

By now, you should have a good idea of the importance of marketing research. Hopefully you are clear on how to plan a study, execute it, and analyze the results. However, for many of you the battle has just begun.

If you are the sole research action-taker, consider yourself lucky. If the research isn't used to its fullest, you have no one to blame but yourself. However, if you have anyone else to convince of the virtues of your study, you are likely to face challenges.

There are many research reports that are tactical in nature in which results point to a clear course of action. There is little to communicate or mull over. You read the results, and the action steps jump from the page. You move ahead, confident of the direction you're taking.

Other studies are strategic in nature or have company-changing implications. Such studies are usually open to interpretation and differing points of view. Alternative action steps might be costly or strongly compete for company resources that could also be used elsewhere.

Studies with far-reaching implications are usually a challenge to digest and implement, and the status of the people in your company who are charged with putting the data into action will play a pivotal role. It is wise, therefore, to process meaty studies in a collaborative manner – where considering alternatives should be done from various viewpoints and where obtaining team "buy-in" is important before moving ahead.

If you are the boss, people are likely to pay more attention when you communicate the results. And you can always choose to dictate the direction you want to follow. On the other hand, if you need the support of others, this approach is probably unwise.

Unequivocally, the worst thing you can do with your research report is to circulate it and hope people will be moved to action.

Communicating research results can be categorized two ways. First, if you want to waste your effort:

- circulate the report and hope others get something out of it;
- circulate the report and wait for feedback;
- circulate the report with your recommendations for action and wait for action to happen;
- write a short summary of the findings with your recommendation and hope this will motivate action by others;
- do the above without setting dates for discussion or feedback;
- let the report sit until you feel it's the right time to show it to others.

Alternatively, if you want to increase the likelihood of action being taken:

- consider the report as the beginning of a process to change course, take new actions, or examine new opportunities;
- consider the report as a stimulus to brainstorming;
- consider the report as a starting point for discussion of previous strategies and potential new ones;
- consider the report as having company-wide impact that, if used correctly, will benefit everyone.

Although we wrote this is in a previous chapter, we'll elaborate upon it here. In order to optimize the use of the research by you, others in your company, and/or by outside consultants or vendors, try the approaches detailed in the following sections.

COMMUNICATING RESULTS AND ACTIONS

Circulate the report with a subsequent presentation date

Don't ever fail to gather your team together and present the results of the research.

Understand it's one thing to circulate a research report and quite another to motivate people to read it before a presentation. There is no doubt that if the report is studied prior to being presented, it will amplify involvement and set the stage for taking actions.

Further, if you followed our suggestions in Chapter 2 and developed potential actions you could take once the research was completed, now is the time to revisit that early thinking. You can do this by following our proposed action sheet below.

Create a proposed action sheet

Here is a five-point action sheet you should circulate with the report. Check with everybody the day before the presentation to make sure their action sheets are complete. If not, reschedule the presentation.

The five-point action sheet should appear as follows. We suggest each person receiving the report also receive at least five copies of this form. On each sheet they should write down a key research finding they identify and action ideas that support the finding.

Research action sheet

1. Research finding:

2. Write down one action idea you might take a result of the finding:

3. Write down a second action idea you might take as a result of the finding:

4. Write down a third action idea you might take as a result of the finding:

5. If different from the above, write down the action ideas originally considered when planning this research:

Use the presentation to kick off action

Many times we've seen research presentations end with people nodding or agreeing that the results were "interesting," "surprising," "nothing really new," and so forth. If this happens to you, you have just wasted your money. It is likely that nothing more will happen – at least, nothing of consequence.

To avoid this pitfall, immediately following the presentation or the next day at the latest, and with everyone present, go over their action sheets. Write the ideas on an easel. Brainstorm new ideas as you go.

Have each person rank all the action ideas and post the scores. Use a simple three-point categorizing system as follows:

1. Let's get started on that one.
2. Ideas with merit, but in need of greater thought. Revisit in two weeks.
3. Longer-term good ideas. Revisit in three months.

At the end of the meeting, you should have lists in each of these three areas. Then assign responsibility for each action to a specific individual. Each agreed upon action should have a date for completion.

CHAMPION THE PROCESS

As with anything worth accomplishing, a champion is critical. Someone must own the process and the responsibility for taking action(s).

Completing the above steps is a great start but, if responsibility for action is in several hands, follow-through is essential. It is usually productive for the person who originally championed the research to stay with the process even after the research is complete.

The best-laid action plans will get bogged down unless someone is their champion. Further, the best action plans have a way of morphing into something that wasn't suggested by the research in the first place. At realistic intervals, the study champion should meet personally with the people assigned to take action on the various tasks. The relevant research findings and actions should be reviewed with that person to determine whether he or she is still on target and moving forward.

If actions are bogged down or not being taken, the champion should be able to press those responsible and to assist them in meeting their deadlines.

REVIEW THE RESEARCH THREE MONTHS LATER

It's worth the time for everyone to reconvene and view the same research presentation again, in retrospect. Review the actions that have been taken and the results. If all the meeting accomplishes is to reinforce that actions have been or are being taken, there will be satisfaction that the research has made an important contribution. Importantly, time has a way of altering perspective.

Revisiting the results will suggest new or better approaches for implementing actions that have not been taken. Time will also bring to light ideas not previously conceptualized. Most importantly, those involved will have learnt that research is a dynamic tool and an important part of the company's culture and a driver of its momentum.

PERIODICALLY REVIEW THE RESEARCH

A study is always timely until a new study replaces it. Just because six months or a year passes doesn't mean your study is irrelevant. When unforeseen company problems and challenges surface, revisit the research. You'll be amazed at the new insights that pop off the pages of old reports.

LAND MINES

Getting research utilized to its fullest not only requires a process, a champion, and follow-up, but also the knowledge to avoid land mines. Chief among those is the not-invented-here syndrome.

There will always be someone who is the group skeptic – the person who, for whatever reason, enjoys taking the role of devil's advocate. We can hear them now:

Why didn't you interview more people?
Well, our customer service people tell us different.
Please explain again exactly how you conducted that regression analysis.

There are people who just don't want to acknowledge research as objective or unbiased and will be threatened or intimidated by the changes that might be indicated by your study.

Status quo people will just kill research – if you let them.

Another land mine is: "What you're suggesting will take too long a time." Well, that's total nonsense. If everything were an easy fix, you'd already be doing it. If you conduct research in the first place, you undoubtedly have problems to fix. You have an itch in your business that needs scratching. What a shame to go through the whole process only to be discouraged from changing because of the time you think it takes.

Keep in mind that the rate of change is always magnified while you are doing it.

Then there is the response, "We're already doing that." This land mine is the ultimate in protecting turf and resisting improvements. Our thought on such a remark is, "Doing what?" We assure you that you might be doing something, but it's probably not getting the emphasis that the research is suggesting.

If the research findings question what you're doing, you can be pretty sure that you could be doing it a lot better.

Yet another great land mine is the attitude, "What's in it for me?" This is often covert and not easily discernible. If the data suggest change and you have people justifying the status quo, you have a big problem. What is discouraging about this attitude is that you can conduct research until you're completely broke, and no amount of cajoling or even fear of being fired will motivate such self-centered employees to work on improving the situation.

TRY THE BONUS SYSTEM

In working for hundreds of companies, we've known a few who used research results to determine staff bonuses. In one case the sales team were rewarded based on improvements in customer satisfaction scores. How interesting! They were being rewarded not just for selling, but for selling the right solution for the customer and for then being sure the entire company lived up to customer expectations.

In another case, customer service personnel knew they'd be rewarded based on customer feedback about their performance. The results the company received were amazing.

It never ceases to amaze why companies are so resistant to tying employee bonuses to research results.

Research can be used as an incentive for improving almost any company function. Tracking studies that provide attitude measurements of company image, product satisfaction, incidence of purchase by new customers or repurchase by existing customers, increasing average spending by customers, customer satisfaction, and many others are great motivators for your staff when a bonus is at stake.

Conduct a benchmark tracking study. Take measurements across the company functions that touch customers and prospects. Set up a company bonus pool that can be paid out partially or completely. Set tracking study levels that must be improved in order for bonuses to be paid.

Present the benchmark results to key company managers, tell them how much money is at stake for their departments, and give them the tracking study levels that must be achieved. Then, importantly, let them and their staff have the autonomy to do as they see fit to improve the levels, within given cost parameters of course.

Conduct another study in six to 12 months and start paying the bonuses where they are deserved. You can also watch happily as the departments that don't achieve bonuses redouble their efforts during the next period – and as your company's bottom line improves.

A CULTURE FOR CHANGE

Ultimately research can be effective only if a company's culture allows it to be. Good research will mostly certainly uncover many areas where change is needed. Unfortunately, management at many companies often give lip service to the importance of research, but become invisible when it comes to supporting research results.

Happily, as a Guerrilla, your very nature is to embrace change suggested by research rather than feel content with the status quo.

We came across an article published in 2006 by the American Productive and Quality Center. While it was talking about the rules of innovation, the philosophy applies directly to the rules for research. We took the liberty of substituting the word "research" for the word "innovation." Here are the Center's rules:

- For research to thrive, it needs to be embedded in the organization's value system and culture.
- A culture of collaboration is an essential element in achieving research success.
- Rewards for using research effectively are often part of the organization's overall reward and recognition program.
- For the organizational culture to embrace research, it should be seen not as an addition to work, but as part of how an organization works.
- The not-invented-here syndrome has been removed from the equation when using research.

Every company, established or start-up, small or large, has a culture. Some companies have top-down cultures and others bottom-up. Some are dictatorial in the way they approach problems and others are collaborative when seeking growth and opportunity. Whatever your company culture, if you conduct marketing research you will likely be faced with making important decisions that affect the future of your company.

Back in 2000, Dr Carol Kinsey Gorman, president of Kinsey Consulting Services, advised, "One of the biggest mistakes a company can make is to manage transformation with the same strategies used for incremental change." She went on to write:

> Incremental change – is linear, predictable, logical, and based on a progressive acceleration of past performance. Transformation is a redefinition of who we are and what we do. It's often unpredictable (responding to unforeseen circumstance, challenges and opportunities), illogical (demanding people and organizations change when they are the most successful). And most importantly, in a transformative change, our past success is not a valid indicator of future success. In fact, our past success may be our greatest obstacle.

Marketing research is science and art. It is the process of asking the question: "What do I think I should know to grow my business?" and then acting on the answers you get. Marketing research almost never generates a single silver bullet as the answer, but clear direction almost always lays embedded in the answers.

Hopefully, you are striving for incremental improvement every day and you let research guide you. At the same time, we trust you are always looking for transformative change, for ultimately that's what's needed to endure in today's mega-competitive marketplace. If you are open to it, and the culture of your company embraces it, marketing research will help you find the answers.

A FINAL WORD

Researching the marketplace never stops. Just by having an open mind, you will be bombarded in the media by new research, facts, and information that will help you grow your business. You don't even have to try that hard.

However, you and your business will be better served if you take a proactive approach. The internet is an ever-expanding sea of information. Use it often. Ask it questions about your business. Go to the library. Talk to friends and relatives. Do everything that is free and that your time allows.

As your business grows, however, you will reach a level of sophistication where continued growth will be dependent on the answers only primary research can provide.

We hope that you are encouraged to budget money every year for marketing research. You'll find that it stimulates creativity and generates inspiration to explore new options. You will vastly improve the manner in which you think about your business and you most certainly will make smarter choices.

22

The future of marketing research

We view Guerrillas as nimble and eager to embrace new thinking. Being flexible by nature, and hopefully less bureaucratic by design, it's far easier for Guerrillas to be early adopters than it is for large companies. As the marketing research profession moves into the next decade and new approaches become state of the art, we are confident Guerrillas will be eager participants.

For Guerrillas, exploring the untried, being among the first to understand what works and to prosper as a result is indeed their very nature.

There is no question that the way companies market themselves and their products is changing. The classic model of marketing is broken and no new broadly accepted alternative has arisen to fix it. In a sense, marketers are driving blind and historical wisdom is no longer fully applicable.

We can feel famous economist Joseph Schumpeter's "creative winds of destruction" blowing right in our faces. Want evidence? Just look at how digital convergence – the unification of cable, broadcast TV and radio, computers, the internet and telephony – changes everything it touches.

In media alone, DVRs alter TV viewing patterns; the explosion of cable channels deeply segments TV viewership; XM/Sirius is stirring up the radio market; new, ubiquitous and ever changing information sources driven by both the internet and GPS are shifting media behavior; and reading habits have so changed that newspapers are dying. Vastly populated social networks are now key drivers in creating new trends, and quickly changing communications platforms allow us to be instantly in touch with everyone, no matter where we and they are.

Alvin Toffler wrote *Future Shock* in 1970 and diagnosed an uncomfortable personal disorientation caused by "too much change in too short a period of time." That was nearly 40 years ago; he wasn't even close. And, perhaps most important, this year and next, is unprecedented economic upheaval and the impact it will have on the way we conduct business and consume.

The truth is this future is the perfect world for Guerrillas and for their use of marketing research.

As companies and their marketing leaders seek to understand and address these challenges, so must marketing research. The future is at our doorstep. Continuing to conduct business as usual will one day become unusually bad business.

One of the goals of *MORE Guerrilla Marketing Research* was to expand, enhance and update the tried and true research approaches written about three years ago. We also sought to further educate Guerrillas as to the importance of research in growing their business and getting the most for their research dollar.

By now we hope you'll agree this book provides a practical and pragmatic foundation for Guerrillas who want to use marketing research as a tool to make more money. Still, let's take a look at some new research approaches on the horizon that perhaps we'll be writing about a few years from now – in *EVEN MORE Guerrilla Marketing Research*.

THE CHALLENGE

We're fond of saying, "Like it or not, the world keeps spinning." We've already pointed out the radical changes impacting marketing in general and media in particular. Consider these thoughtful opinions about how marketing research needs to change:

> Without transforming our capabilities into approaches that are more in touch with the lifestyles of the consumer we seek to understand, the consumer-research industry as we know it today will be on life support by 2012. (Kim Dedeker, V-P External Capabilities Leadership, Global Consumer and Market Knowledge for P&G, *Advertising Age*, September 15 2008)

> I don't know if we are going to have a choice but to move away from survey research. We continue to torture consumers with boring and antiquated research methods. (Donna Goldfarb, V-P Consumer and Market Insight for Unilever, *Advertising Age*, September 15 2008)

> Conventional research which tries to understand the consumer through direct questioning – such as why they buy a specific brand – has limited

effect. We are trying to generate insights in order to generate a more emotional and powerful understanding of consumer behavior. Our approach: 1. assumes much information is hidden, 2. uses different information sources, 3. entails much higher personal involvement with the consumer to win empathy, 4. involves the real world environment, 5. tries to become the consumer. (Diego Kerner, Managing Partner, The Brand Gym, *Brand Strategy,* March 2008)

And way back in 2000, David Taylor wrote:

In my experience, the problem lies in mistaking findings from consumer research for consumer insights. They are entirely different. We define insight as a penetrating, discerning understanding that unlocks an opportunity. We suggest developing insight teams and running insight drills such as:

- How could the brand/category do more to help improve people's lives?
- What does it feel like when the product really delivers, or fails?
- What do people really value in a category and what would they not miss?
- What conflicting needs do people have?
- What bigger market is the brand really competing in from the consumer viewpoint? What could the brand do more to better meet these "higher" order needs?
- How is the product used in reality? What other products are used instead of the brand, where the brand could do a better job?
    (David Taylor, Group Director of Brand Strategy for Added Value,
    The Strategic Marketing Consultancy, *Brand Strategy,* March 2000)

Further, Doug User, PhD, a senior VP with Widmeyer Research & Polling, speaks about how consumer fragmentation makes it harder to find and understand target audiences:

Traditional methodologies were designed for a different culture than today. Traditional methods have become less reliable and raise issues of data quality. We need new metrics and methods: video blogs, online portals, emotional measurement, data harvesting, analysis of comments in online forums, and private online communities.

Mary Ann Packo, the CEO of Millward Brown, one of the largest marketing research firms in the world, sums up the challenges affecting the future of market research this way:

For marketers, the challenge is building brands in a fast changing world; for consumers, the challenge is deciding between so many options and choices; for researchers, the challenge is – given all this – how to connect marketers and consumers.

C Frederick John, a senior executive with MasterCard, feels that time and financial pressure are reducing the quality of the data that researchers collect. He is particularly concerned that consumers who belong to internet research panels may become professional respondents and, while demographically representative, are not attitudinally representative of the target population.

Indeed, many research practitioners are concerned that when conducting telephone and internet research the sample of consumers that is generated is becoming less and less representative than in the past. Because federal law prohibits the automatic dialing of cell phones, many telephone surveys exclude cell phone users. Not to mention the fact that consumer concerns about privacy issues and telemarketing calls cause almost a third of the population to simply hang up even when confronted by a legitimate interviewer conducting a telephone survey where confidentiality is assured.

Several of those we interviewed before writing this book, including Ty Albert, a Managing Director of Guideline Research, agreed that in the future "triangulation" will be required in the way we collect data. They feel that short bits of data gathered from several sources, employing scientific sampling models, will come together to provide insights. And they argue that the industry needs more creative ways of engaging respondents in providing data and less 35-minute telephone surveys on attitudes and usage.

Is there any good news? The answer is "Yes," and that's because marketers and researchers alike are finally acknowledging what they don't know and are beginning to embrace new thinking and technologies.

PREDICTIONS

As we conclude *MORE Guerrilla Marketing Research*, we'll take our look at the future. Our prognostications are drawn from a variety of sources as well as from our combined 75 years toiling in the research trenches and watching the industry evolve. However, as anyone trying to predict the future must, we do so with a sense of humility.

Here are our predictions.

1. Combining data mines and attitude research will become more widespread

A data mine can be thought of as the accumulation of information into one large database that extends back in time. Here we are referring to a combination of proprietary database a company develops on its own, databases that might be accessed from outside sources, and custom-designed marketing research surveys.

Proprietary databases can consist of almost any information a company captures and generally include the following:

- Customer transaction and historical data:
  - purchases of specific items;
  - frequency of purchases;
  - at what prices;
  - from what channel(s);
  - on what exact days;
  - at what exact times;
  - given what exact promotion;
  - given a customer credit rating;
  - returns;
  - customer satisfaction scores.
- Company operational data:
  - margins;
  - inventory;
  - region, territory, zone;
  - distributor.
- Data about the timing, nature and success rates of marketing activities.

Public domain databases that can be accessed include thousands of corporate, government, and media options. Data from corporate 10K financial filings are also available and can be accessed. Companies like Dun & Bradstreet and Experian provide company and consumer information that can be economically purchased and become part of your data mine.

In addition there is critical information derived from marketing research surveys about whatever a business wants to know about its own brands, competitive brands and the needs and wants of customers and prospects.

We're finally learning how to more effectively combine consumer attitudes as gathered in surveys with actual consumer behavior as gathered from proprietary and public access databases. The advent of new software along with newer more sophisticated statistical scoring models is providing new approaches for analyzing data and for better predicting the specific type of marketing programs, and advertising communication, that will be effective in motivating consumers to try new brands or remain loyal to their current brands.

In the future, marketers will be reluctant to look at survey data alone when trying to determine the strongest messages to various targets. They'll be able to target highly specific, highly individualized audiences with particular messages that are nuanced and that speak directly to how each target feels and behaves. In this vision of the future the majority of strategic attitude studies will not be deemed useful unless consumer attitudes as generated in surveys are combined with all elements of a data mine – and recommendations for marketing actions are made from this viewpoint.

Guerrillas should start planning now by either building or fine-tuning their data mines. Many companies and consultants are willing and able to help you develop this powerful tool. And you'll be surprised how quickly your investment will pay off.

2. Monitoring digital conversation will be a common form of research

The term "digital customer conversations" defines the current phenomenon occurring in billions of blogs, chat rooms, e-mails, phone calls, text messaging, and social networks where customers are talking about products, services and companies. These digital conversations contain millions of real-time, unfiltered attitudes, behaviors, and intentions.

A report released in 2008 by PricewaterhouseCoopers, LLP predicted that:

digital conversations will be commonly accessed in order to better understand customers. Those conversations can be translated into actionable knowledge that will transform business and help drive competitive advantage.

The same report notes that:

the explosion of consumer conversation has changed how people communicate about products and services. Consumers now have the ability and freedom to rapidly self-organize across geographical borders in order to express constantly evolving needs. Consumers have the power to demand what they want and they now expect rapid responses to their immediate desires.

Marketers who continually monitor these digital conversations will be among the first to spot trends and uncover new and ever-changing marketplace needs.

3. Social networks will open new channels for data collection

Facebook, MySpace, LinkedIn, Twitter and hundreds more have attracted millions of people to social networking. And the affinity people have with the social networks they frequent are presenting exploitable research revenue streams for these companies.

For example, Facebook Polling is a new way to find out quick answers to simple questions. Users log in, type a simple question, specify a geographic location and a sample size, pay as little as $50 (for 100 interviews) and the results start flowing in. With Facebook Polling, a first research step could be to spend $200–$300 asking a series of questions over a couple of days, refining the scope of the problem, and even answering some queries on the way.

LinkedIn recently announced the survey route looks particularly promising because of the network's ability to sort its database into samples according to areas of expertise, experience, seniority and geography. It is now testing the degree to which it can send surveys to members without alienating them, as well as determining the fees it might command from marketers wishing to access its members.

In the near term, using social networks for research will undoubtedly raise questions among research purists about sample representativeness, respondent anonymity and research sponsor security. It will also raise the hackles of some social network members who will feel such a use is a violation of their trust.

For Guerrillas, the relatively low prices and fast results will provide a good opportunity to determine if social network research provides value.

4. Web 2.0 research sites will develop

The phrase Web 2.0 was coined by O'Reilly Media in 2004 to describe how people were starting to contribute their own content, rather than simply downloading what was already there. Obvious examples are Wikipedia, MySpace and Twitter.

Research vendors, or even companies themselves, will find ways to motivate consumers to come to Web 2.0 sites and write in comments about the companies and brands they have used, why they are satisfied or dissatisfied with them, and what the companies could do to command greater customer loyalty.

5. Mobile research panels will evolve

Online has surpassed the telephone as the most popular data-gathering method and this will soon cause the industry to run out of fresh internet research participants. So large is the demand for online research that the major providers of access to respondents are finding it more and more difficult to obtain useful samples. This is driving up costs by increasing the size of respondent incentives and by requiring more effort to ensure data quality.

The establishment of panels of mobile users offers a new approaching for collecting research information.

Today, cell phone panels have already been set up by several companies – essentially the same ones that offer online panels. You can expect more on the way. And they are operating differently than typical phone panels.

Members are not called on the phone to participate; instead they receive a text message informing them that a survey is underway. The questions are posed as text messages and the answers are sent back as messages. Obviously, cell screens are small so the questions cannot be long, nor can the number of possible answers. And the entire survey must be of short duration as well.

Currently the industry is feeling its way a bit and there is lots of experimentation. We'll participate by conjuring a future in which members of cell panels take pictures and send them back. Imagine the insights you could glean by having hundreds of consumers uploading pictures of products in use, pantry shelves, the TV show they are watching right now, the food they are eating, or anything else that relates to your business.

For the right situation, cell phone panels will become still another tool in our data-gathering arsenal.

6. Pop-up research

Any company that attracts thousands of visitors a week to its website has a potentially valuable research tool – and one that is probably being underused. In the next few years, companies will be infinitely more attuned to using their own websites as research tools.

As with social networks, there are questions of validity and representativeness in conducting surveys with your own website visitors. However, of the thousands who might visit a website daily, weekly or even monthly, some are satisfied customers, some dissatisfied, some are prospects who buy from competitors, and some prospects just scoping out products in order to determine if they are relevant to their lives. Whoever they happen to be, they are a source of information to the company.

There are all sorts of ways to question website visitors. Simple one-reply or question pop-up surveys can yield valuable tactical information and robust responses.

Offers of cash or other incentives to complete a longer company questionnaire by clicking on a link are easy to highlight and provide quick access for website visitors to offer their opinions. Various incentives can also be tested as to their effectiveness in generating telephone numbers for follow-up personal interviews or assessing willingness to complete an online questionnaire at a point in the future.

Guerrillas should certainly take advantage of their website traffic by turning visitors into a quick, economical, information tool for growing their businesses.

7. *Proprietary online research networks will become popular*

Akin to pop-up research, companies will realize the benefit of developing their own online research networks. As reported by Inside Research, a firm that tracks marketing research spending online, networks are already in use and were projected to reach $69 million in research revenue in 2008.

Online research networks consist of consumers who have similar characteristics and are recruited from company databases to join "like and kind" people. For example, an "I Love My Dog" group was created by Del Monte. Its 400 members were handpicked to join the private network, which the company uses to help create products and test marketing campaigns.

The Wall Street Journal online notes that:

> These private networks are part of companies' efforts to figure out how to use the web to assess and shape the way consumers think about their products. They are often cheaper and more effective than phone surveys or traditional focus groups because companies can draw on the participants in a much broader and deeper way than they could in an offline setting.

8. *Customer emotions and feelings will take center stage*

It will be more important than ever for brands to connect emotionally with customers. Because lasting impressions and loyalties are cemented by sentiments, emotions and feelings, tomorrow's marketing wars will be fought more for consumers' hearts than for their minds.

Customers are tuning out old sales pitches that yell, "My products are better, cheaper, more convenient, offer greater variety or will do this or do that" and connecting with them on this level is become increasingly difficult. As a result, companies will shift their emphasis from stressing the rational benefits of using their brands to more emotional ones.

Marketing researchers will have to move quickly to better uncover the kinds of consumer emotions that more strongly connect consumers to individual brands. And, they will have to find better survey approaches for testing a multitude of emotions to determine the one that best captures the consumer's heart and should be adopted by the brand they are studying.

9. *Physiometric measures are finally adopted*

In Chapter 12 on emotions we discussed how the early attempts to use physiological responses such as galvanic skin response, eye pupilometrics, changes in voice pitch, etc. were eventually abandoned, in part because of difficulties in interpreting results.

The search for such autonomic behavioral responses to marketing stimuli has not stopped, however, because, if you recall, they by-pass asking customers rational questions. This means the techniques provide answers to questions about emotions or underlying motivations that may not be known to the customers themselves. And they provide answers where respondents may not accurately remember what they were thinking when they made a purchase decision. Importantly, they also provide answers to difficult questions about which respondents may choose to hedge or stretch the truth.

What's new is the advanced technology that's being applied to measure such things as skin conductance, micro-body movement, tiny muscle movements in the face, heart rate, respiration and electroencephalography (EEG), the measurement of electrical voltages from the brain.

There are about a dozen companies operating in this high-tech market research space, each with a different approach, and they have gained significant traction among large users of market research. The most successful so far is NeuroFocus, which measures marketing stimuli on three key variables: attention-getting value, emotional engagement, and extent of being remembered. This advanced technology is being applied to assess virtually all marketing communications including TV, print, radio, outdoor advertising, internet banners and text, interactive content, and packaging.

Right now these tools are quite expensive to employ and should still be considered experimental. Guerrillas can expect the price to fall rapidly; this is an area to watch.

10. Marketing researchers will change

We offer these points of view about the researcher of the future.

David Smith, Chairman of Incepta Marketing Intelligence, said:

> I'm looking forward to working with researchers who are able to synthesize not just the data of their own surveys, but also that of a variety of sources. This could be anything from hard data and other databases, to anecdotal information. This is a skill that requires the ability to generalize from a great deal of information. You call it "reading between the lines." Subjective skills, but ultimately based on very hard research data. Not easy to learn.

Marketing Professor Neeraj Arora, executive director of the AC Nielsen Center for Marketing Research at the UW-Madison School of Business, says:

Marketing research used to be a backroom function, but nowadays the distinctions are blurring between marketing researchers and brand managers. Marketing researchers must have the business savvy of a brand manager, the analytical mind of a researcher. They need to be creative, take risks and spot market trends and pass this information onto CEOs.

According to Monika Wingate, the director of the Nielsen Center:

> There is an increasing expectation on the part of management for researchers to uncover breakthrough insights. The marketing researcher's role is becoming less about measurement and evaluation and more about providing strategic guidance for businesses. The role of marketing researchers is ascending in importance throughout the corporate world. Growing numbers of companies are embracing the value of marketing research in reducing risk through data-driven decision making, identifying new market opportunities and ultimately increasing profitability.

We'll summarize by suggesting that the marketing research professional of tomorrow will most assuredly have different skills. No longer confined to the backroom, they will have to be part psychologist, part sociologist, part interrogator and part keen observer of society. They will have to view information as logically as in the past but far more creatively.

They will need the ability to synthesize large quantities of information from many sources and to boil things down to a few pivotal insights. They will have to command respect from all they serve, be compelling in their approach, dare to carry a large stick and not be fearful of venturing into the unknown.

Finally, even armed with all these new skills, they will have to be marketing people first and research people second, because research will always be a tool to help make better marketing decisions.

11. Guerrilla marketers will adopt marketing research as a primary tool

In the *Harvard Business Review,* January 2006, Thomas Davenport wrote, "Some companies have built their very businesses on their ability to collect, analyze and act on data." Davenport elaborates:

> It's virtually impossible to differentiate yourself from competitors based on products alone. Your rivals sell offerings similar to yours. And thanks to cheap offshore labor, you're hard-pressed to beat overseas competitors on product cost.

So what should Guerrillas do? Become, in Davenport's words, an "analytics competitor," and win on the basis of better information, superior understanding and deeper knowledge.

The Davenport article names the following leadership companies that beat their competition using the very tools we have been discussing throughout this book, as well as data mining: Amazon, Capital One, Boston Red Sox, Dell, E & J Gallo, Harrah's, Marriott International, New England Patriots, Oakland A's, Owens & Minor (hospital supplies), Procter & Gamble, Progressive (insurance), UPS, and Walmart.

You won't be surprised to find we applaud the Davenport philosophy and these terrific companies. They have succeeded because they know more about their customers' needs, more about what produces loyalty, more about pricing, more about product development and more about effective advertising and promotion than their many competitors.

They are rigorous users of primary marketing research. They have built databases and mined them for their riches. They have conducted marketing experiments and tests. Most importantly, the hallmark of their cultures is that they never stop doing these things. As it is said, "knowledge is power."

We like the plaque that retired CEO of Sarah Lee Bakery Group, Barry Beracha, kept on his desk:

In God we trust. All others bring data.

So in closing, we foresee a future where Guerrillas pick up a copy of this book and begin to run their businesses based on knowledge, not intuition. They'll do it because marketing research works – and because it's the quickest and surest way to make more money.

Glossary of terms

brainstorming   One of several specific techniques for developing new ideas, this method asks attendees to suspend negative judgment and build on ideas proposed by others.

brand personality   The personality of the brand, as if it were a living person, as defined by customers.

break-even   In the marketing research context a break-even analysis is a calculation of how many additional product units will need to be sold to cover the cost of the research. This simple tool is a powerful aid in determining whether a specific research project is worth doing.

cluster analysis   Cluster analysis is a statistical routine that sorts survey respondents into groups, such that the degree of association is strong between respondents *within* one cluster and the differences are as large as possible *between* clusters. Cluster analysis is often used to identify lifestyle segments among customers.

confidence interval (or margin of error or error range)   *See* error range.

confidence level   A statistical measure of the degree of certainty, i.e. 95 per cent, that the same results would occur if the study were conducted again in the identical fashion.

conjoint analysis   Conjoint analysis is often called "trade-off analysis" and is a statistical tool that allows researchers to discover the relative importance that is placed on product features, including price, when they are presented together or jointly.

cost per interview   (CPI) The cost of a research study can be viewed in cost-per-interview terms. By taking the total cost of the research (e.g. $20,000) and dividing by the number of interviews (e.g. 200), the CPI is derived (e.g. $100). The CPI allows companies pricing research from competing suppliers to determine which supplier is providing the most competitive price. CPI comparisons should be assessed from various points of view (e.g. the services the suppliers will provide, their experience and expertise, and their ability to provide research results when needed) in determining which supplier to use.

creative consumers   Specially recruited respondents who tend to be more verbal, expressive, and able to speculate about issues and ideas. They are often more aggressive and opinionated about issues than less creative consumers. They are particularly helpful when developing new ideas or products.

customer satisfaction   The degree to which customers are satisfied with a product or service they have used is considered a key element in motivating customer loyalty. In order to understand whether customers are satisfied they must be formally surveyed *after* they have purchased and used a company's product or service.

dependent variable   A key measure in research generally consisting of one or two questions that measure level of overall satisfaction with a product or service, overall attitude toward a company or brand, or levels of purchase behavior. Scores achieved on a dependent variable question are influenced by other marketing elements that are also measured and may include attitudes toward customer service, convenience and product quality.

discussion guide   A dynamic outline listing the areas a moderator will address in a qualitative study. Areas of questioning in a guide often change to better address issues emerging during the discussion.

dyad   A form of qualitative research in which two respondents are interviewed at the same time. Typical dyads are spousal pairs or parent and child pairs.

error range (or confidence interval or margin of error)   In survey research there is always a statistical boundary around the findings. This is the range between which the data could be expected to vary if the research were reproduced or conducted repeatedly. The larger the sample of target respondents, the smaller the error range.

exploratory research   An umbrella term indicating that the research is limited in nature. It is often conducted when issues are unclear or when the marketer wants to keep up with market conditions and/or wants to better determine the need for larger-scale research.

factor analysis   Factor analysis is usually a good tool to use when there are a large number of variables, such as attitudes toward products or perceptions of brands. In such cases the many rated attributes or attitudes can be combined, based on the similarity of responses given by respondents. The result is to reduce the number of variables to a smaller set of what are termed "factors."

field service   A marketing research company whose prime business is recruiting respondents for qualitative research or administering questionnaires for quantitative studies. Field services do not generally offer strong consultative services and are best used as data-collection sources when a knowledgeable researcher provides clear direction to them.

focus group   A gathering of 8–12 people, who have the desired qualifications in common, e.g. demographics or product usage. This group is led through a discussion of the topic at issue by a skilled moderator. Focus groups allow language and issues to be observed and theories generated. They can help in determining the research objectives to be addressed in follow-up research efforts. Focus groups do not determine if an issue is true for one person or a million people. The focus group is the most prominent form of qualitative research.

full-service supplier   A marketing research company that can conduct a research study from beginning to end, and is generally consultative in nature. Full-service suppliers are often looked to for help in determining research objectives, questionnaire development, collecting and processing data, using special statistical procedures when analyzing data, preparing a report and recommendations on the findings, and the presentation of results.

guerrilla   In popular business parlance a Guerrilla is a company or entrepreneur who applies unconventional and creative methods in a disciplined fashion to achieve marketing goals. Typically, this has come to mean a small company that lacks a big marketing budget. More broadly though, Guerrillas can be any size provided they maintain their maverick mindset. Southwest Airlines (sales $10 billion+) could still be considered a Guerrilla.

interviewer- and self-administered questionnaires   Interviewer-administered questionnaires employ a trained person to ask the questions of the respondent. Self-administered questionnaires are filled out by the respondent. There are different considerations when constructing an interviewer-administered questionnaire vs one that is self-administered.

margin of error (or confidence interval or error range)   *See* error range.

one-on-one interview   A form of qualitative research in which one respondent is interviewed at a time.

overall research goal   A one- or two-sentence statement that captures the essence of the learning that is expected from the research.

primary research   Research that you pay for and that requires interviewing or observing customers or prospects. Primary research is custom-designed and seeks to develop information that will help a company achieve its marketing goals and objectives.

probing   When an interviewer follows up on a respondent's answer to produce a deeper level of understanding, he or she is probing. Probing is most frequently used when conducting qualitative research, but is also used in quantitative research when open-ended questions are asked.

projectable research   Research that is conducted with a sample size large enough for the results to be indicative of how the target population in general would answer the same questions.

qualiquant   A combination of qualitative and quantitative techniques in the same study.

qualitative research   An umbrella term for small-sample research that is not projectable to the audience from which the sample was drawn. Non-projectable research is used to generate opinions and hypotheses about customer and prospect attitudes. It encompasses a variety of research techniques including focus groups, one-on-one interviews, dyads, triads and brainstorming sessions.

quantitative research   An umbrella term for large-sample survey research that is projectable. Results can be generalized to large-population targets. Telephone, internet, mail, and mall intercept are the common data-collection techniques used when gathering quantitative data. Quantitative research is often used to validate hypotheses developed via qualitative research.

questionnaire   The script used when collecting data for a quantitative survey. Interviewers must not vary from asking the questions exactly as written and in the order written. A questionnaire is not a dynamic tool.

regression analysis   Regression analysis seeks to determine what variables are important in determining the responses obtained to a dependent variable question.

representative sample   A sample resulting from a representative sampling procedure (the manner in which potential respondents are selected). Having a representative sample means the responses of the people interviewed can be assumed to be the same as the responses of the people not interviewed.

research action plan   Broad term for the actions the marketer might take as a result of having conducted marketing research.

research control   In many research studies it is necessary to compare one set of data to another set, called the control. A control might be the results from an earlier study, or industry norms, or result from a study where the market's reaction is known. Usually the results must meet or exceed the control in order to make a decision to go forward.

research objectives   Objectives clarify the goal(s) of a market research study. Research objectives are often derived from previously agreed marketing objectives. Clear research objectives are essential for determining the most action-oriented questions to ask when creating questionnaires or discussion guides.

research plan   The research plan describes *all* the research that needs to be undertaken over a period of time, usually one year. The act of preparing a research plan will clarify thinking about the goal and objectives of the research and the actions that might be taken with the results.

research professional   Broad term for a person who has specific experience working in the marketing research industry. The length of time a person has worked in the research industry coupled with expertise in a wide array of research techniques generally determines the level to which he or she can claim to be a professional researcher.

respondent   The customer, prospect, user or influencer from whom answers are sought when conducting primary research.

screener   The name for the questionnaire used to recruit people with specific characteristics to attend focus groups. Respondents are "screened" to see if they qualify and to eliminate those who do not.

secondary research   Refers to research gathered by others to satisfy *their* needs, but which is readily available in the public domain for free or at a price significantly lower than it would cost if funding primary research to address similar questions. Good examples are government offerings like the Census of the Population, reports from trade associations, articles in print media, annual surveys conducted by trade publications, etc.

significance test   A test to determine whether there is a statistically reliable difference between two or more numbers. The numbers could be percentages (for example, 60 per cent vs 40 per cent) or averages, termed "means" (for example, 5.5 vs 4.5).

strategic research   A type of study that assists in determining the most promising courses of action a company or brand should follow to optimize sales and/or profits.

tab plan   The plan for arraying answers from survey questionnaires. In creating a tab plan the researcher is compelled to determine how the data will be analyzed.

tactical research   Research that is limited in nature and that assists in determining how best to achieve the overarching strategic direction. It helps determine the important smaller elements that will be effective for achieving the overarching strategic direction.

target respondents   Customers, prospects or influencers who have particular characteristics and are interviewed in either qualitative or quantitative research.

triad   A form of qualitative research in which three respondents are interviewed at the same time. Triads are used when it is deemed beneficial to interview respondents in smaller groups rather than in larger focus groups. The nature of the subject as well as research cost concerns can make triads a preferred qualitative approach.

TURF analysis   TURF stands for "total unduplicated reach and frequency." TURF analysis was originally devised for use in analyzing advertising media campaigns to answer the question of what combination of media options delivers the largest audience of unique individuals, when it is known that the audience is variously exposed to more than one of those media options. The same technique can be used to analyze line extensions and other marketing options.

Index

American Association of Public
Opinion Research (AAPOR)
247
Absolut 92
AC Neilsen Center for Marketing
Research 334–35
actualizing research results 92
a culture for change 322–23
action sheets 319
avoiding landmines 321
bonus system 321–22
championing the process 320
circulating the report 318
presenting results 319
reviewing research 320
advertising execution studies
41–42
Adamy, J 24
Advertising Age 113, 326
Air Wick 55
Albert, Tye 328
Alberto-Culver 6
Amazon 92, 336
American Management Association
118

American Marketing Association 73,
78, 247
American Productive and Quality
Center 322
analyzing results
analyzing string questions 306–07
comparing alternatives 305
comparing targets 304–05
the dependent variable 309–11
GAP analysis 308–09
importance vs agreement 307
making comparisons to purchase
behavior 304
telling the story 299–300
using a control 301–03
using normative data 303–04
using previous research 303
writing the report 313–15
Anheuser-Busch 179
APC Research 204
Apex Company 128
Apple 55, 75, 114, 178, 179, 182
iPhone 45
iPod, iPod Nano 92, 111
Arnold, Jon 17

Arora Neera   334
asking questions
   insuring questions are actionable
      27–28
   getting at the right issues   18
   getting input from others   26
   going beyond the obvious   24
   knowing what questions to ask
      49–50

brainstorming   117
   conducting a brainstorming session
      116–17
   other ideation processes   117–20
   rules of   116–17
   what to do with results   120
Bail, D   24
Bank of America   37
Barron's   113
BBDO   118
Bear Sterns   38
Best Buy   37
Blackberry   92
BMW   23
Boston Red Sox   336
Brand Gym   327
Brand Strategy   327
Brand Trust   177
Brand Week   113
Budweiser   179, 182
   Bud Light Lime   45
Business Week   113
budgeting research
   how to   61–63
   determining a meaningful budget
      63–66
   marketing research ROI   67–71
buying research / research suppliers
   being a good client   88–89
   costing a project   77–80
   focus group costs   80–83
   judging supplier credentials   73–76
   pricing a telephone survey   83–87
   saving money on focus groups
      81–83
   saving money on surveys   85–87
   understanding supplier pricing   77

Cabela's   57–58
Cadillac   182
Calvin Klein   46
Campbell, James E   262
Capital One   336
CASRO   78, 88, 198, 201, 247
Caterpillar   181, 185, 186
Chicago Bears   6
Chicago Tribune   263
Citibank   37, 175
Coca-Cola, Classic, Coke, New   7, 88,
      175, 182, 230, 249
creative consumers   165–67
collecting data
   determining the best approach   197
communication studies   41
Costco   92
Creative Education Foundation (CEF)
      118
Crest   174
customer attitudes   5
   listening to customers   6–8
   do customers lie   9
   customer needs, wants, wishes,
      desires   23
   understanding opportunities   27
customer behavior   11
   attitudes vs behavior   50–51
   getting customer to buy more   57
   taking customers from competition
      58
   increasing the size of the market
      59
customers
   listening to them   6–9
   do they tell you the truth   9–11
   say one thing, do another   11–12
customer satisfaction research   42,
      190
   definition   253–54
   frequency of measurement   251–52
   importance of   250
   measuring customer satisfaction
      254–57
   net promoter score   258–59
   performance variables   257–58
   tracking customer satisfaction   56

Davenport, Thomas 335–36
de Bono, Edward 118, 119, 165
DEC 55
Dedeker, Kim 326
defining target respondents 17,
 104–06
Del Monte 333
determining the best research
 approach 52
developing a research plan
 what is a research plan 99
 developing a research plan 100
 how much research is enough
 91–92, 97
 setting goals and objectives
 101–04
 determining research targets
 104–06
 how to get started 37–39
 examples of objective setting
 19–21
Dichter, Dr. Ernst 182
Disney, Walt 6
DM (Direct Marketing) 113
Dr Pepper 182
Dun & Bradstreet 329
DuPont 55

E&J Gallo 336
EFAMRO 79
Einstein, Albert 119
Elkman, Dr Paul 174
Ellison, S 24
emotions
 brand personality 180–86
 evoking emotions in marketing
 174–75
 list of emotion responses 173–74
emotives 175
entrepreneurial ego 9, 95
Equifax 273
ESOMAR (European Society for
 Marketing and Opinion
 Research) 247
Experian 273, 329
exploratory research 27–28, 30
Exxon 37

Facebook 92, 330–31
Fannie Mae 38
Febreze Scentstories 45
Financial Times 113
Forbes 113
Fortune 113
Freddie Mac 38
Frito-Lay 249
focus groups
 being and effective moderator
 141–55
 decision making and focus groups
 123–27
 defined 121–23
 discussion guides 128–31
 focus groups facilities 133–34
 focus group facility costs 135–36
 group exercises 155–56
 group homework 157–58
 how much do groups cost 80–83
 how to save money on groups
 81–83
 "qualiquant" 164
 recalling respondents 158
 screening respondents 136–41
 setting up groups 131–36
 types of qualitative research
 159–60
 using creative respondents 165–67
focus group moderating
 awareness of where you're going
 143–44
 be relaxed 142–43
 changing topics 151–53
 call respondents by name 146–47
 following the discussion guide
 153–55
 listening 147–49
 moderator reversal 148–49
 paraphrasing 147
 probing 149–51
 recapping 148
 suspend ego 141–42
 warm up 144–46
 writing down respondent comments
 148
fugging 247

future of marketing research
  data mining and attitude research
      328–30
  emotions and feelings   333
  mobile research panels   331–32
  monitoring digital conversation
      330
  on line research networks   333
  physiometric measures   333–34
  pop-up research   332
  social networks   330–31
  the challenge   326–28
  web   2.0 331
Future Shock   326

Gallup Organization   77
Gates, Bill   6
General Motors   75
Gillette   55
Glade   55
Goldfarb, Donna   326
Google   92
Gorman, Dr Carol Kinsey   323
Greenfield On-Line / Ciao   16, 198
Guideline Research   328

Halas, George   6
Harrah's   336
Harley Davidson   336
Harvard Business Review   335
Harvard University   182
Home Depot   37, 38, 178, 179
Hooter's   182

Impulse Survey of Focus Facilities
    134
Incepta Marketing Intelligence   334
Info USA   273
Insight On-Line   163
Intel   6
internet studies   197–201
in-person interviewing   207
Investors's Daily   113
ISO   79

J Arnold & Associates   17
J D Powers and Associates   77, 260

Jain, Dipak   123
Jet Blue   251
John, C Frederick   328

Katz, Art   174, 177
Kellogg Graduate School of
    Management   123
Kellogg   33
Kerner, Diego   327
KFC   6
Kinsey Consulting Services   323
K-Mart   6
Kotnelnikovy, Vadim   175
Kraft   37, 44, 61, 75, 88, 180, 249

Lavin, Leonard   6
learning something new   12
Lehman Bros.   38
Levinson, Jay Conrad   173, 174, 179
LinkedIn   330, 331
Lowe's   38

marketing navigation   164
Marketing News   113
Marlboro   182
marketing research
  appropriate for all types of
      businesses   15–16
  defined   2–3
  how much to do   95–98
  insights   14–15
  marketing research myths   17–18
  shelf life   92–93
  maximizing return   93–94
  what you need to know   13–14
mail survey   204–06
Marriott International   336
Martineau, Pierre   182
MasterCard   328
McDonald's   42, 44, 179
Mercedes Benz   175
Michalko, Michael   118
Mickey Mouse   6
Microsoft   6, 75, 114, 180
Micro-Switch   6
Millward Brown   327
Moore, Gordon   6

Mr Clean AutoDry Car Wash   24
MySpace   330

name studies   42
National Family Opinion (NFO)   77
Neiman-Marcus   175
Nestle   249
NeuroFocus   334
New England Patriots   336
new product research   44–45
New York Times   113
Nicor   37
Northwestern University   123
Noyce, Robert   6

one-on-one interviews   40
O'Reilly Media   31
Oakland A's   336
Oldsmobile   6, 180
organizing data   275
  banner points and stub   279, 281
  cross tabs plan   276–79
  nets   279, 281
Osborn, Alex   118
Owens & Minor   336

packaging studies   42
Packo, Mary Ann   327
panel studies   208
Pasquinelli Homes   252
Pew Research   197
premium, promotion studies   190
Proctor & Gamble (P&G)   24, 37,
    44–45, 61, 75, 88, 249, 326, 336
pricing studies   43
product testing   43
progressive insurance   336
PT Cruiser   23
Pulte Home Builders   252

questionnaires   213
  aided questioning   231–3
  demographic phase   246
  gaining respondents cooperation
    215–16
  identifying the sponsor   230–31
  main body   220–45

open end, closed end questioning
    222–23
  question phrasing, how to   233–45
  questionnaire flow   245
  questioning scales   223–29
  sample questions   239–45
  screening/qualifying target
    respondents   217–20
  self-administered questionnaires
    235–38
  series questioning   221
  setting respondent quotas   219–20
  stand alone questioning   220
  string   221–22
  thank you phase   247
  unaided questioning   231–33

research objectives
  attitudes vs behavior   50–51
  determining the best research
    approach   52–54
  exploratory research   30–31
  increasing the size of the market
    59
  investing in marketing research   29
  knowing what question to ask
    49–50
  making research objectives
    actionable   27–29
  meeting customer expectation
    55–56
  more business from current
    customers   57–58
  refining goals and objectives
    26–27, 30
  product-market matrix   48
  strategic vs tactical research   54–55
  setting objectives   19–22
  taking on the competition   58
  turning questions into goals and
    objectives   24–26
  understanding needs   23–24
  understanding opportunities   47
Reis, Jack   173
Rolex   23, 175
Roper Company   77
Ross School of Business   259–60

sampling   261
    determining sample sizes   266–69,
        288–90
    error range / margin of error
        262–66
    response rates   269–70
    representative sampling   269
    theoretical vs practical sampling
        268
    sampling guidelines   270–71
    sources of samples   272–74
    statistical confidence   265–66
Sanders, Harland   6
screening studies   43
secondary research
    assessing the value   110–11
    attractiveness of   111–12
    defined   109
    sources of secondary information
        112–14
segmentation studies   41
serious creativity   165
service merchandise   5–6, 55
shopping center interviewing
    207–08
Siemens   55, 78
Silverman, George   164
Socrates   49
Sperry-Rand   55
Spiegel   6
Staples   37
Starbucks   92, 96
statistics, statistical techniques   285
    cluster analysis   295–96
    confidence levels   286
    conjoint analysis   296–97
    factor analysis   294–95
    multi-dimension scaling / perceptual
        mapping   297
    regression analysis   290–91
    significance tests   285–88
    t-tests   285
    turf analysis   291–8
strategic research   35–38
sugging   247
surveys
    comparative costs   210

how much do surveys cost   77–79,
    83–84
in person surveys   208
internet surveys   197–201
mail surveys   204–06
panels   208
saving money on surveys   85–87
telephone surveys   201–04
telephone survey costs   203–04
Survey Sample International   272–73
Synovate   77

Taylor, David   327
Ten3 Business e-Coach   175
telephone interviewing   201–03
telephone interviewing costs   203–04
Toffler, Dr Alvin   326
Travis, Daryl   177
tracking studies   42
Twitter   330
tactical research   35–38
test market research   43–44
telephone studies   201–04
tracking customer satisfaction   43,
    56, 251–52
tracking studies   42, 190
types of research
    observation studies   40
    qualitative research   39–41
        dyads   40
        focus groups   39
        in-depth personal interview   40
        mini focus groups   39
        triads   40
    quantitative studies   41
        advertising awareness and
            tracking   42, 190
        advertising
            execution / communication
            41–42, 190
        benchmarking   41
        communication   41
        customer satisfaction   43, 189
        name   42, 190
        new product development
            44–45, 190
        packaging   42–43, 190

pricing   43, 190
premium, promotion studies
    190
product testing   43
"quick and dirty"   45–46
screening   43, 190
segmentation   41
test market research   43–44
tracking studies   42, 190

Ultrasonic Dog Barking Deterrent
    45
Unilever   326
UPS   336
US Census of Business   111

US Census of the Population   111,
    207
User, Doug, PhD   327

Van Oech, Roger   118

Wall St Journal   24, 113, 175, 252, 259,
    260, 333
Walmart   175–76, 336
Way of the Guerrilla, The   173
Widmeyer Research & Polling   327
Wikipedia   114
Wingate, Monika   335

Zyman, Sergio   7